A vegetarian cookbo

"What a beautiful book! It deserves to be a bestseller in its field."
—*Swami Kriyananda*, *direct disciple of Paramhansa Yogananda, founder of Ananda*

"Never before have dietary spiritual principles been explained so clearly. You will gain a deep understanding of the importance of a natural diet and its contribution to your physical, mental and spiritual wellbeing, so badly needed in this age.

I cannot recommend this cookbook highly enough. Read, enjoy, start cooking and feel the benefit in your life. Thank you Mahiya for this outstanding contribution to Yogic cuisine." —*Tony Sananda O'Connell*, *vegetarian chef and trainer, Co Clare, Ireland*

"What a marvellous book! Mahiya explains how, by changing your diet and the way you eat, you can improve your physical, mental, emotional and spiritual health. I especially like the way Mahiya presents this information. She invites you into her kitchen; she makes various offerings, and you can choose what sounds right for you; you can take small steps or bigger steps, as you feel inspired. The unwritten message seems to be 'Don't just take my word for it, but test it out for yourself.'

For many years, I have been passionate about our potential as human beings. This book can help you move towards your own highest potential – towards living more vibrantly and more joyfully."
—*Stan Giles*, *nutritionist, kinesiologist, yoga and meditation teacher, Cornwall, UK*

"There is a plethora of books on the market on the subject of diet and healthy eating, but what makes this book shine brightly is that it not only takes the physical aspects of diet into account, but the mind and the spiritual aspects as well.

This book will appeal to all those who are spiritually aware, practising yoga and meditation, as well as those who want to awaken their consciousness to a higher level.

If there is only one book you need on diet and healthy eating, that also gives a spiritual perspective, without doubt, *A Taste of Joy* is that book!" —*Stephen Sturgess*, *kriya yoga meditation teacher, author of* The Yoga Book, The Book of Chakras, *and many others, London, UK*

"My husband Piero and I have been vegetarians for more than 20 years and we proclaim, through direct experience, that your wonderful *Ananda* food has never been matched by any other place, either national or international, that we have visited."
—*Daniela di Savino*, *Journalist,* Lux Terrae, *Rome, Italy*

"This book brought a smile to my face as soon as I started to read it. It is full of energy and life and made me want to run straight out and buy all the yummy scrummy goodies that are so great for our health and wellbeing!

This is the only book I know that has all the information that I find helpful in one place. If you need advice about the benefits of sprouts, raw food, cleansing diets, juicing or the benefits of alkaline foods, to name but a few, you will find it all here in this clear and beautifully presented book.

I would recommend this book to anyone, whether they are vegetarian or not, on a spiritual path or not; it is the sort of book that will open a doorway into a whole new world. I am convinced it has the power to transform lives."

–*Nalini Deane*, *holistic health and wellbeing practitioner, meditation teacher, Sussex, UK*

"Your book has changed my life, for the better obviously! I bought it because I liked the title. I was looking for a book on food and diet that was different from the usual ones that have diets that are either sad, difficult to follow or superficial.

Your book has taught me to love what I eat; to love to cook for others; to balance ingredients; to see food from a more spiritual perspective; and to live Yoga in the kitchen, at the market, and at the table." –*Paola Converso*, *yoga teacher, Turin, Italy*

"*A Taste of Joy* is the best book on vegetarianism that I have ever read. It should be used as a text book in universities because, apart from sharing excellent recipes that are practical and easy to make, it explains in a serious, and at the same time simple, way what a good diet is and how to balance all of the nutrients needed for the human body etc. The most moving thing that one feels when reading this book is the powerful presence of Master Paramhansa Yogananda, expressed in a sweet and clear way by Mahiya."–*Vinaya Serra*, *food and health sales representative, Rome, Italy*

"Browsing through this book is like "browsing" your taste buds with a hot and fragrant croissant in a Parisian cafe, eyes closed, filled with amazement and gratitude for the sweet and warm aromas that embrace your heart on an early autumn morning. This is the sensation one has with every page turned – a gift of Joy. A gift, for every word, every recipe, known or unknown: worlds revealed to the taste buds and heart, an unfailing experience of True Joy! Thank you, Mahiya!"

–*Cecilia Sharma*, *teacher and expert in Indian cooking, Delhi, India*

"This book has been so useful to me because it doesn't just talk about food, but about everything that is linked to food, like fasting, cleansing and the properties of food: things that I have since learned to practise and insert in my life with "Joy".

–*Deborah Prendin*, *interior designer and feng shui consultant, Pordenone, Italy*

A Taste of Joy

Published by Yogaland, 1 Lilley Mead, Redhill RH1 2NY
www.yogaland.co.uk

Originally published in italian under the title *Il gusto della Gioia*

ISBN: 978-0-9956889-2-6

A Taste

of

Joy

150 Vegetarian Recipes for
a Happy and Healthy Life

Mahiya Zoé Matthews

With photographs by Andrea Roach

Dedicated to Paramhansa Yogananda,

whose teachings fill my life with joy and whose words of wisdom
provide the primary ingredient for this book.

Index

RECITES

Author's Note

My sole intention in writing this book has been to help you, the reader, understand that a more natural diet, which also includes fasting and other purification practices, can improve your health and help you to live life with more energy, enthusiasm and joy.

The information given in this book is the fruit of my research and studies in the field of diet. The core of the information given comes from the teachings of the great Indian master, Paramhansa Yogananda and subsequently, from books, articles and accredited internet sites.

The words of Paramhansa Yogananda quoted in this book come from numerous unpublished articles and lessons, written in the period between 1926 and 1940 inclusive, as well as from the 1924 edition of his book *Scientific Healing Affirmations*. All quotes by Paramhansa Yogananda are indicated by the symbol **P.Y.**, as are quotes by his disciple Swami Kriyananda indicated by the symbol **S.K.**. In the bibliography you will find specific information on Yogananda's works, as well as all other sources used.

The advice given in this book is obviously general and may not be suitable for everyone. If you know you have a specific medical condition, I strongly encourage you to consult your doctor before following any of the advice given.

I also encourage you to consider the information that I have provided, not so much as the final word, but rather as a starting point for personal verification, further analysis and, above all, for an enthusiastic journey towards ever-more radiant health!

In friendship,
Mahiya Zoé Matthews

Introduction

A Taste of Joy is for anyone who wants to experience more joy in their lives. However we may search for it, isn't joy, in the end, what we are all really looking for? Whatever our culture or religion may be, not one of us is looking for suffering. This book is based on the teachings of the great Indian master, Paramhansa Yogananda (see page 420), who came from India to the West to show others how to find this joy; a joy that is not dependent on outward circumstances but that comes from within.

Perhaps you are saying to yourself, "It's all very well talking about joy, but what's it got to do with food?" Let's begin by defining what joy is. Joy, contrary to the messages that we are bombarded with every day, cannot be found by working your way to the top of the business ladder, becoming rich, having more possessions, designer clothes, good looks and others' admiration and approval. Neither can it be achieved by having the perfect relationship, the perfect children or the perfect house. All of these things, it's true, can satisfy you for a while, but how long does this feeling of satisfaction last? It's not long before we become restless and unsatisfied and we are off in search of fulfilment again. This is because true joy is a state of *inner* happiness. The soul, which is your true Self, is made of joy and needs nothing outside of itself to make it happy. It simply *is* joy.

The ancient teachings of India say that everything that surrounds you - whether it be buildings, colours, people, music, art – influence you, or more specifically your mind, in different ways. The food you eat also influences you. Some foods help to calm your mind and uplift your consciousness in order to "taste" and experience the true joy of your soul; some foods agitate your mind and make it restless, causing you to look everywhere but inside of yourself for happiness; and some foods bring your mind down into a state of negativity and inertia, where happiness seems some unreachable goal. Knowing which foods have which effect on your mind can be an important tool for accessing joy and bringing about changes on all levels of your life. Part Two of the book, "Feeding the Soul", is therefore dedicated to these little-known spiritual aspects of food.

To talk *only* about the spiritual aspects of food, however, would be incomplete, as true teachings address all levels of our existence. Yogananda himself, though a great spiritual master, wrote and lectured extensively on the importance of food for the health of the body. For this reason, the book begins by addressing the more common aspects of diet. In Part One of the book, "Back to Basics", you will learn: how to balance your diet in the correct way; the importance of eating alkaline foods; the role of different nutrients for your health and well-being; how to get enough protein with a vegetarian/vegan diet and many, many other things. This section also looks at the energetic, or biodynamic, properties of food (another little known area). It explains the principle of *Life Energy* and how to select foods that can boost your immunity to disease.

Part Three of the book, "The Next Level", discusses topics such as fasting and special diets. Although these subjects might seem too large a step at the beginning, they are important aspects of health and wellbeing, and you may like to come back to them once you have changed a few of your general eating habits.

Part Four of the book, "Table Talk", contains stories from members of the Ananda community near Assisi, Italy, in which they share their personal experiences with food and diet for your inspiration, encouragement and enjoyment.

"Well," I hear you say, "that's quite enough about the theory… what about the *recipes*?" *A Taste of Joy* contains an entire section (over half the book) dedicated to recipes, in which all of the Ananda kitchen's secrets are revealed! You'll find everything you need to put theory into practice (such as detailed information on how to grow sprouts and basic cooking techniques for legumes and grains), as well as 150 vegetarian recipes, all of which are suitable for those who, through choice or because of food intolerance, have adopted a vegan diet (see the index on pg 377). The recipes in this section are the result of the creativity and experience of many Ananda cooks, past and present. They are recipes that have been tried and tested on guests and community members, recipes that have won Ananda a reputation for being a spiritual yoga retreat where the food is delicious.

The tale of how I myself became a cook is related at the beginning of the recipe section. I think my experience is enough to give hope and encouragement to anyone!

I have tried to write this book in a way that makes it easy for you to bring about practical changes in your diet. For this reason, at the end of every recipe you'll find the symbol " ", which refers back to information you read in the first part of the book and indicates a particular benefit of the recipe for the body, mind or soul.

So, all that remains to be said is enjoy the book! I hope *A Taste of Joy* inspires your life as much as it has inspired mine.

PART ONE

Back to Basics

What is a
Balanced Diet?

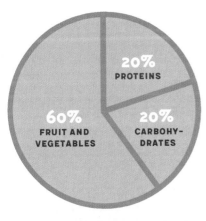

Paramhansa Yogananda recommends a diet based on the following proportions:*

- 60% Fruit and vegetables
- 20% Carbohydrates
- 20% Proteins

If you maintain this formula as your dietary ideal, you can see that the food you eat should consist mostly of fruit and vegetables, with smaller proportions of proteins and carbohydrates. Eating mostly fruit and vegetables does not mean that you must starve to death or stop eating a plate of pasta for lunch. It just means, for example, *balancing* that plate of pasta with a large fresh salad, eating a fruit and nut smoothie for breakfast instead of a slice of bread and jam or having a light dinner of soup, fruit or cooked vegetables instead of heavy starches.

The reasons why Yogananda recommends a diet based on lots of fruit and vegetables and a limited amount of carbohydrates and protein will become apparent in the following chapters. For now, let's look at some ideas for how to incorporate more fruit and vegetables into your diet.

---

*Although fruit and vegetables are usually classified as carbohydrates, note that Yogananda has allocated them a category of their own in order to underline their extreme importance in diet. Throughout this book, therefore, any reference to carbohydrates as a category excludes fruit and vegetables, and refers to pasta, rice, bread, potatoes, sugar, sweeteners etc. (For more information see the chapter "Carbohydrates and Gravity"). The Proteins category includes legumes, tofu, dairy, nuts, seeds, eggs etc. (See chapter "The Protein Myth").

13

Fruit and Vegetable Juices

One of the best ways to begin is by drinking fresh fruit and vegetable juices. The juice is extracted from the fruit or vegetable by means of a *juicer* or *juice extractor* that, in a matter of seconds, separates the juice from the fibrous part. A glass of juice contains the nourishment of more fruit or vegetables than you would eat at one sitting in their solid form (a small glass of carrot juice, for example, contains about 4 or 5 carrots). Fresh juices are therefore, an easy way to help maintain your 60% fruit and vegetable target. Green vegetable juices (from celery, chard, parsley, spinach, etc.), as well as carrot juice, are considered the healthiest.

> "GREAT BENEFIT MAY BE OBTAINED *by*
> *taking health cocktails made of fresh vegetable juices...*
> *Carrot juice, celery juice, radish juice, and*
> *cucumber juice are some of those most commonly used.*
> *Have a health cocktail at least once a day."* **P.Y.**

Fruit and vegetable juices are a concentrated source of easy-to-assimilate nutrition: the body assimilates an astonishing 95% of the nutrition contained in the juice in only 20-25 minutes.

Fresh fruit and vegetable juices are detoxifying and regenerating for your body cells. This is demonstrated by an experiment conducted by Dr. Alexis Carrel (Nobel Prize winner for medicine in 1912) in which he managed to keep a selection of cells alive for 30 years by keeping them in vegetable juice! At the end of the experiment, the cells were still perfectly active and healthy. Dr. Carrel stated that the experiment could have continued for a further 100 years, or even 1000 years, without the cells showing any sign of degeneration or ageing.[*]

You'll find a whole chapter dedicated to delicious fruit and vegetable juice combinations in the recipe section. Instructions and guidelines for how to make juices are given at the beginning of the chapter.

Smoothies

Smoothies are made by blending fruit together with a liquid, such as soya milk, fruit juice, water or yoghurt. Nuts, spices and sweeteners can also be added. Sweet fruit and acidic fruit, however, with the exception of apples and lemons, should never be combined together. A whole chapter is dedicated to smoothies in the recipe section.

[*] Gala D.R.; Gala, Dhiren; Gala, Sanjay. *Nature Cure for Common Diseases.* Navneet Publications (India) Limited, pg 62

Salads

Including fresh salads in your diet is also a good way to increase the amount of fruit and vegetables you eat. There are many delicious ways to combine raw ingredients together, as well as many different dressings, that will make your salad appealing. You can look for ideas and inspiration in the "Salads" chapter of the recipe section.

Vegetable Soups

Having a vegetable soup for dinner is a great way to boost your daily intake of vegetables. The beauty of soups is that they are so versatile: depending on the season and your mood, you can make your soup thick or thin, substantial or light, hot or cold, chunky or blended, etc. An array of spice combinations can be used to give the same vegetable different flavours. Although it is ideal to make vegetables the main ingredient of your soups, legumes, pasta or whole grains can be added when you want something a little more substantial. A whole chapter is dedicated to soups in the recipe section. In this chapter you will find soups that are ideal for every season.

The Daily Diet

In order to help maintain this dietary balance, Yogananda suggests including some, or all, of the following foods in your daily diet. These foods, he says, contain all of the elements needed for the proper maintenance of your body. The quantities given can be increased or decreased in accordance with your individual needs.

Some years ago this list was sent off to a major American health publication to be analysed. The report came back that this was the most nutritionally complete diet they had ever encountered!

- ½ apple
- 1 lime
- ¼ grapefruit
- 1 orange
- 6 leaves raw spinach
- 1 small piece fresh pineapple
- 6 figs, dates or prunes
- 1 handful raisins
- 1 baked, half-grilled or steamed vegetable with its juice

- 1 tsp honey
- 1 lemon
- 1 raw carrot, including part of green top
- ¼ heart lettuce
- 1 tsp olive oil
- 1 glass milk
- 1 Tbsp cottage cheese
- 1 Tbsp clabber*
- 1 glass orange juice with 1 Tbsp finely ground nuts.

* Milk which has been allowed to stand in a warm place, preferably in an earthen vessel, for a day or longer, until it has soured or curdled. (Yoghurt would also suffice).

Helpful Hints

❖ Buy a fruit and vegetable juicer; it's one of the best investments for your health you could ever make.

❖ Drink a glass of carrot or green juice every day. Add a touch of lemon or ginger for a little 'kick.'

❖ Drink smoothies for breakfast. Blend in some nuts and dried fruit and you'll feel satisfied for hours.

❖ Build your lunch around the salad plate: start with a large green salad, adding some juicy cherry tomatoes or maybe some olives.

Then think about what to eat with your salad: a little pasta, rice or tofu perhaps but make the salad the main part of your meal.

❖ Eat vegetable soups and/or cooked vegetables for your evening meal.

The Chef Recommends...

❖ Fennel-Carrot Mix / **197**

❖ Zangy Zesty Apple / **198**

❖ Dried Fruit Smoothie / **204**

❖ Cabbage and Pineapple Salad / **211**

❖ Curried Squash Soup / **234**

CHAPTER 2

The Secret of an Alkaline Body

"IN ORDER TO KEEP THE BODY in an alkaline condition, at least eighty per cent of our diet should be chosen from the foods which have an alkaline reaction." **P.Y.**

Your body was made to be alkaline. It is only in an inner alkaline environment that your cells and organs function properly, and you can enjoy good health and vital strength. Acids in your body are a natural by-product of cell activity. Things like stress, environmental factors and the food you eat also produce them. When the amount of acids in your body is kept to a minimum, your organism is able to neutralise them, making them harmless. As soon as the amount of acids reaches a certain limit, your body is no longer able to neutralise them, and it enters into a state of 'acidosis'. This acidic state weakens all your bodily systems and gives rise to an internal environment that is conducive to disease. Acidosis, in fact, is considered by some experts to be the cause of 90% of all illnesses.

Most enzymes, for example, only function in an alkaline environment. When your body is in an acidic state, the catalysis activity of enzymes is inevitably modified or even inhibited. Enzymes are the workers in your bodily factory and facilitate most of its metabolic processes. They help fight ageing, lower cholesterol, clean your colon, break down fats, strengthen your immune system, improve mental capacity, eliminate carbon dioxide from your lungs, digest foods, purify your blood and rid your body of waste products, etc. The inhibition of enzymes has an effect on many aspects of your health.

The corrosive effect of acids damages your body's tissues and organs, as well as cellular activity. This leads to the progression of most degenerative diseases, including cardiovascular and heart disease, high blood pressure, high cholesterol, kidney stones, urinary incontinence, arthritis, osteoporosis, cancer, diabetes and obesity.

Other imbalances caused by acidosis are: chronic tiredness, insomnia, nervous tension, headaches, constipation, digestive problems, heartburn and frequent colds, just to mention a few.

Acid and Alkaline Foods

As hinted at above, the food you eat is one of the main determining factors of the acidity or alkalinity of your body. Every food, depending on the reaction that it has, is classified as either acidic or alkaline. This classification refers to the *ash value* of a food, meaning the type of residue that remains after the food is digested and processed. In order to maintain the proper acid-alkaline balance, 80% of the foods you eat should have an alkaline reaction.

Fruit and vegetables are all alkaline, some of them, such as lemons, extremely so. Therefore, returning to the proportions given earlier, as recommended by Yogananda, making fruit and vegetables 60% of your diet is fundamental for an alkaline body. Some of the other foods that have an alkaline reaction are: algae, sprouts, potatoes, lentils, almonds, cashew nuts, herbs, herbal teas, soya beans and soya products.

As a general rule, carbohydrates (pasta, bread, rice, cous cous etc) are acidic.

This is one of the main reasons why Yogananda recommends limiting carbohydrates to only 20% of your overall diet. Whole grains, such as millet, spelt, oats and quinoa are only slightly acidic, whereas refined grains (white bread, white rice, white pasta) are significantly more acidic. It is best, therefore, to try and eat wholegrain options as much as possible and limit or eliminate refined grains. Sprouted grains (sprouted spelt, sprouted wheat, sprouted oats etc) become alkaline in the sprouting process.

Most animal sources of proteins (meat, fish, eggs, cheese) are highly acidic, although raw, un-boiled milk and plain yoghurt are considered by some as alkaline. Most legumes are acidic, although soya beans and lentils are both alkalinising. Most nuts are acidic, although almonds, chestnuts, Brazil nuts, cashew nuts and fresh coconut are usually considered alkaline. Seeds are considered alkaline by some and acidic by others. Again, because most proteins are acidifying, proteins should ideally be limited to only 20% of your diet. *N.B. All sprouted legumes, nuts and seeds become alkaline in the sprouting process.*

Chemical and processed foods are all highly acidic: the less natural a food, the more acidic it is.

> "THROUGH EATING AN ABUNDANCE *of alkaline foods, either in bulk, reducing them to juices, or through the process of sun-drying and powdering, we can go far toward arresting physical decay and restoring a condition of youth to prematurely aging body cells…"* **P.Y.**

If your diet contains an insufficient amount of alkaline foods, the pressure falls on your body's regulating system to neutralise the overload of acids (a system known as 'buffering'). In this emergency system, minerals, such as sodium, magnesium, potassium and calcium, which are highly alkaline, are taken from your vital organs and bones, and used to re-establish a state of alkalinity. Please note that these minerals are not being taken from a plentiful storehouse but from parts of your body! Over the years, your body can suffer severe and prolonged damage: osteoporosis, for example, is one of the consequences of the continuous removal of calcium from your bones due to repeated buffering.

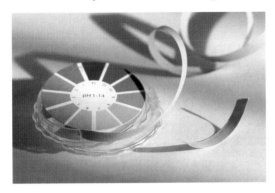

How Do You Know if Your Body Is Acidic?

The system used to measure acidity and alkalinity is called the pH: p = potential and H = hydrogen. The pH scale goes from 0 to 14. Zero indicates complete and absolute acidity and 14 indicates complete and absolute alkalinity. A pH of 7 is neither acidic nor alkaline and is therefore neutral. One of the ways to have an indication of whether your body is acidic or alkaline is to measure the pH of your urine several times every day over the course of a week (the pH of urine indicates the level of sufficiency of the body's alkaline reserves). Small pieces of card, especially designed to measure the pH of your urine, can be bought from any chemist or ordered from the internet. For more precise results, use pH cards that measure decimals instead of rounding up or down to the nearest whole number. The test should be done at the following times: upon waking (i.e. with the first urine of the day), before lunch and before dinner. It is very important to take the test *before* meals, after your last meal has been fully digested, as food and drink temporarily vary your pH reading significantly. Do not snack between meals while doing the test. Hold the card under the flow of your urine for a second or two and then remove it; the card will have changed colour. A key will be given on the packaging indicating the pH to which each colour corresponds. Before lunch and dinner, what you are ideally looking for is a urinary pH between 7 and 7.5. The first urine of the day is usually more acidic than the urine before lunch and dinner. This is because our bodies naturally detoxify during the night. An ideal pH for the first urine of the day would be between 6 and 7.

If the readings first thing in the morning show an average of less than 6 over the course of a week, and the readings before lunch and dinner an average of less than 7, your urinary pH, and therefore your body, has some acidity, and you would benefit from making changes in your diet and lifestyle. If the cards indicate an average of less than 5, your body is highly acidic, and it would be wise to consult your doctor.

Increasing Alkalinity

The first thing to realise is that no result is ever negative. If you use that result as an incentive to make adjustments to your diet and lifestyle, that is positive.

As you will notice above, both diet *and* lifestyle are mentioned. Food is the main subject of this book, and therefore diet will be the main emphasis here. However, it's important to understand that there are several other factors which can affect your pH, either positively or negatively. Stress is one of the most significant acidifiers of the body. Even with a 100% alkaline diet, you may still be getting acidic results if you are experiencing stress or negative emotions. Bad sleeping patterns, exhaustion, radiation from computers and phones, and a sedentary lifestyle also play significant roles in creating or maintaining acidity in the body. On the other hand, regular exercise, laughter and cheerfulness, as well as activities that create deep relaxation of the body and mind (yoga, shiatsu, massage, Tai Chi, meditation), have a very alkalinising effect on the body.

In terms of food, one of the first things you can do is increase the amount of fruit and vegetables in your diet until you reach the recommended 60% target. Buy yourself a juicer and make a habit of having at least one juice a day, or two when possible. If you're not at home, you can make a large amount of juice in the morning, put it in a thermos and take it to work. Green leafy vegetables and herbs, such as spinach, chard and parsley, are very alkalinising and should be added to your fresh juices whenever possible. Having smoothies or fruit salads for breakfast is another good habit to establish. In the winter months you can even heat your smoothies to just under 40 degrees. Lemon is extremely alkalinising, and a great way to start each day is with a cup of hot water and lemon juice. A squeeze of lemon juice can also be added to your water throughout the day. Algae, such as spirulina and chlorella are extremely alkalinising and can be taken in the form of tablets or powder dissolved in water.

Apart from studying the list of alkaline and acidic foods and including more alkaline foods in your diet, respect for your digestive system is also important. Try not overeat, not to mix too many foods together and to eat calmly and slowly. Do not eat late at night and keep evening meals light in general (Yogananda said to eat like a prince at breakfast, a king at lunch and a pauper at dinner).

Clearing the body of old and stored up toxins is also an important step towards alkalinising the body. Regular, short fasts, as well as the occasional longer fast, are excellent for this, as are colon cleanses, liver cleanses and kidney cleanses etc.

You may not see your pH results change overnight. Years of bad habits need time to resolve themselves. Be patient and be persistent, and you will see that your pH gradually becomes more alkaline over time.

Alkaline Foods

- ❖ All fresh and dried fruit *(not tinned)*
- ❖ All vegetables, potatoes and roots
- ❖ Sprouts *(including sprouted grains and legumes)*
- ❖ Algae
- ❖ Soya beans and soya products *(tofu, soya yoghurt, tempeh, etc.)*
- ❖ Lentils
- ❖ Some nuts *(almonds, Brazil nuts, chestnuts, cashew nuts, coconut)*
- ❖ Extra virgin olive oil *(cold pressed)*
- ❖ Herbs and infusions
- ❖ Mineral and spring water

Acidic Foods

- ❖ Meat
- ❖ Fish
- ❖ Eggs
- ❖ Most dairy *(raw milk and yoghurt are considered by some to be alkaline)*
- ❖ Grains *(wholegrains are more alkaline than refined grains)*
- ❖ Most legumes *(soya beans and lentils are alkaline)*
- ❖ Some nuts *(hazelnuts, walnuts, pecan nuts, peanuts, pine nuts, pistachio nuts)*
- ❖ Most seeds *(sunflower and squash seeds are sometimes considered alkaline)*
- ❖ Chocolate
- ❖ Caffeine
- ❖ Alcohol
- ❖ Sugar and all products that contain sugar
- ❖ Fizzy drinks, including fizzy water
- ❖ Refined, processed and chemical-laden foods
- ❖ Margarine
- ❖ Chlorinated tap water

In Part Four of the book, "Table Talk", Sahaja relates her experience of the benefits she felt when changing over to a primarily alkaline diet. See: "An Alkaline Miracle".

Helpful Hints

❖ Think alkaline! Have you had your fruit juice today?

❖ Snack attack: instead of reaching for acidic potato chips train yourself to munch on a handful of alkaline raisins or figs.

❖ Be creative with fruit: prepare yourself delicious fruit salads and dress with a little soya yoghurt.

❖ Include highly alkaline green vegetables and algae in your diet.

❖ Try substituting caffeinated drinks with herbal teas.

❖ Measure your pH over the course of a week at least once a month: it's a good incentive to keep going!

The Chef Recommends...

❖ Celery Cleanse / **197**

❖ Simple Potato Salad / **215**

❖ Miso-Tofu Soup / **236**

❖ Iranian Spinach / **344**

❖ Ginger Tea / **373**

CHAPTER 3

Mother Nature's Garden

"AN ALL-WISE CREATOR *has provided herbs, fruits,
berries and vegetables with a specific purpose, and we
who are striving for a definite goal of development of the
Spiritual Being must not overlook even so apparently
a lowly first step (but none the less important)
as to get our physical house in order."* **P.Y.**

Mother Nature provides you with everything that you need. In Her garden grow an abundance of foods that, as well as being a delight for your taste buds and eyes, contain everything you need to keep your body and mind strong, healthy and in a state of well-being.

When talking about natural, wholesome foods, such as fruit, vegetables, nuts, seeds, grains and legumes, it is common to hear words such as *minerals, vitamins, enzymes, antioxidants, carotenoids, flavanoids, essential fatty acids and chlorophyll,* to name a few. All of these are natural nutrients, contained within the foods themselves. These nutrients play an important part in maintaining the radiant health of both your body and your mind. Each nutrient has not just one but usually many specific and important tasks to carry out. The exact role of each nutrient is complicated and detailed, but a general overview is given below.

Foods that contain an abundance of vitamins, minerals and other life-giving nutrients are called *'protective foods'*. It is essential to eat *protective foods* every day, remembering that it best to eat mostly fruit and vegetables and a lesser amount of proteins and carbohydrates. In general, a balanced and varied diet of natural and wholesome foods will provide you with enough nutrients to live a healthy and energetic life.

Minerals

Minerals are essential for the proper functioning of your body. They regulate and control the normal functioning of your tissues, muscles and organs. Your body cannot produce minerals, so they must be obtained through food. There are about 20 minerals considered essential for maintaining good health, some of the most familiar being iron, calcium, iodine, fluorine, silicon, sodium, potassium, magnesium and manganese. One of the most common mineral deficiencies among vegetarians is iron. Therefore, it's useful to know that Vitamin C is important for the absorption of non-heme iron (the iron found in plant foods). Adding a source of Vitamin C to a meal containing non-heme iron can increase absorption of the iron by up to six times. Calcium, on the other hand, is thought to reduce the absorption of iron. Foods which have a high content of calcium should be eaten at a distance of several hours.

"PROPER DIET IS VERY IMPORTANT *in building vitality. Each one of the billions of cells within the human body is a tiny mouth taking nourishment."* **P.Y.**

Vitamins

Vitamins are organic substances, absolutely essential for the health and proper growth of your body. There are many well-identified vitamins: A, B complex (which consists of 8 B vitamins, including thiamine, riboflavin, niacin, biotin and folic acid), C, D, E and K are the most well-known. Most vitamins can be classified as either fat-soluble or water-soluble. Fat-soluble vitamins (A, D, E and K) can be stored in your body's fat, so although they should be eaten regularly, do not necessarily need to be eaten every day. Water-soluble vitamins (B and C) cannot be stored in your body and should therefore be eaten frequently, preferably every day. Every vitamin has a distinct mission to perform, which cannot be supplied by any other.

"VITAMINS ARE THE BRAINS OF THE FOOD YOU EAT. *They direct the digestion and absorption of food while the food builds the different tissues. No matter what you eat, never forget to include vitamins in your menu."* **P.Y.**

N.B.: Exact data about some of the best food sources for vitamins and minerals can be found in charts in the appendix. If you know you have a deficiency in a certain vitamin, use the charts; if not, including a variety of the listed foods in your diet (for each mineral and vitamin) will ensure you receive the recommended dietary allowances.

Enzymes

Enzymes are specialised proteins at the heart of all your body's activities. Since the human body is actually a series of thousands of enzymatic reactions happening at every moment, without enzymes, there would be no life as we know it!

Although your body is capable of producing enzymes, it can only produce a limited amount (the older you get, the less it is able to produce). Eating foods that already contain enzymes allows the digestion of that particular food to take place without your pancreas having to produce digestive enzymes. This leaves your body free to produce more metabolic enzymes, necessary to keep you in good health.

The best sources of food enzymes are raw fruit and vegetables, raw seeds, raw nuts, un-pasteurised dairy products and sprouts. Fresh, raw, organic foods contain enough enzymes to digest themselves. Cooked, processed and refined foods contain few or no enzymes.

Antioxidants

Antioxidants play an essential role in the prevention of many serious diseases. Vitamins C and E, selenium (a mineral), carotenoids (see below) as well as flavonoids (see below) are all antioxidants. Antioxidants combat harmful particles called free radicals. Free radicals can cause damage to cell walls, certain cell structures and genetic material within the cells. In the worst-case scenario and over a long period of time, such damage can become irreversible and lead to diseases such as cancer. Antioxidants interact safely with free radicals and stop the reactive process before any harm is done to your body.

It is important to eat a high percentage of foods that contain Vitamins C and E, selenium, flavonoids and carotenoids. This can easily be achieved by eating a large amount of fruit, vegetables, nuts, seeds and healthy oils.

Carotenoids

Carotenoids are a colourful group of plant pigments that exert antioxidant activity. These compounds are largely responsible for the red, yellow and orange colour of fruit and vegetables and are also found in many dark green vegetables. The brighter the colour, the more concentrated the amount of carotenoids.

Some of the foods that contain carotenoids are: peppers, carrots, squash, tomatoes, broccoli, green beans, green peas, Brussels sprouts, cabbage, kale, spinach, lettuce, avocados, corn, apricots, cantaloupe, watermelons, honeydew melons, yellow grapefruits, pink grapefruits, lemons, oranges, limes, papayas, raspberries, strawberries, bananas, peaches, mangos, prunes and kiwis.

Flavonoids

Flavonoids are also principally known for their powerful antioxidant properties. However, they also play many other important roles in your body: they improve memory and concentration, prevent blood clots, lower blood pressure, reduce inflammation and bolster the immune system. Flavonoids are present in almost all fruit and vegetables. Broccoli, onions and apples, moreover, are known to be three of the best sources.

Essential Fatty Acids

The fatty acids so frequently talked about in the news these days can be saturated or unsaturated. The unsaturated fats can be divided into monounsaturated fats and polyunsaturated fats. These have been nominated as 'good fats' because they are necessary fats that the human body cannot produce and must therefore be obtained through diet.

There are two families of polyunsaturated essential fatty acids: Omega-3 and Omega-6. Most people consume too many Omega-6 fatty acids and not enough Omega-3s. The ideal intake ratio of Omega-6 to Omega-3 fatty acids should be between 1:1 and 4:1—between one and four Omega-6 to one Omega-3. Most Western diets can be up to 25:1 in favour of Omega-6, which is not good for health.

The best vegetarian sources of Omega-3 essential fatty acids are linseeds* and walnuts. Linseed oil has the highest Omega-3 content of all plant foods: two tablespoons per day of linseed oil provide the recommended daily adult portion. Other good vegetarian sources are: hempseed oil, hempseeds, pumpkin seeds, Brazil nuts, sesame seeds, avocados, some dark leafy green vegetables, canola oil, soyabean oil and wheat germ oil.

Some of the best vegetarian sources of Omega-6 essential fatty acids are: linseed oil, linseeds, hempseed oil, hempseeds, grapeseed oil, pumpkin seeds, pine nuts, pistachio nuts, sunflower seeds (raw), olive oil, olives, borage oil, evening primrose oil, black currant seed oil and chestnut oil.

N.B.: High heat, light and oxygen destroy essential fatty acids, so when consuming foods for their essential fatty acid content, avoid heated and refined forms. For example, raw nuts are a better source than roasted nuts, and cold-pressed oils a better source than refined oils.

* Linseeds contain cianidrico acid, which can cause disturbances in the body if consumed for months in a row. Every three months, therefore, it's best to take a one-month break, in which you consume linseed oil instead of the seeds.

Chlorophyll

Chlorophyll is one of the most important substances found in plants and green vegetables. The greener the vegetable, the more chlorophyll it contains. Chlorophyll works by allowing plants and green vegetables to absorb light from the sun. That light is then converted into usable energy. This process is called photosynthesis. Plants and green vegetables are, therefore, concentrated forms of solar energy.

"WITH SPRING WE ASSOCIATE *the fresh leaves of dandelion, young grass, the budding tree, bush, and vine foliage. From this it is not difficult to see the powerful inter-relation between green and Life itself."* **P.Y.**

The health benefits of chlorophyll are astounding. One of the most amazing discoveries has been that chlorophyll's chemical structure is nearly identical to that of haemoglobin, the protein found within your red blood cells that is responsible for transporting oxygen to your body cells. The only difference is that haemoglobin contains an atom of iron at its centre, whereas chlorophyll contains an atom of magnesium at its centre. Dr. Yoshihide Hagiwara, a Japanese scientist, presented her theory in the 1970s that, because of this nearly identical molecular structure, the human body is actually able to transform chlorophyll into haemoglobin. Many experiments conducted since Dr. Hagiwara's research support her theory, demonstrating that chlorophyll enriches and vitalises the blood and can help against anaemia.

"GREEN IS THE MOST OUTSTANDING PIGMENT *on Mother Nature's palette of exterior decorating. In the science of food values, that coloring is known as chlorophyll, the green substance of plant life which, when taken into the body, becomes the hemoglobin of the blood."* **P.Y.**

Some of the other roles that chlorophyll plays in maintaining good health are: purifying the blood; dissolving wounds formed in the lungs due to smoke and air pollution; eliminating the effect of carbon dioxide; protecting against radiation, x-rays, emanations from computers and radioactive pollution; killing germs; raising energy levels and eliminating bad breath (try experimenting yourself by eating a clove of raw garlic and then a sprig of green parsley!). A lot of research is now being focused on the role that chlorophyll plays in the prevention and treatment of cancer.

Spinach is one of the most concentrated sources of chlorophyll, containing about 300-600 milligrams in every 30 grams. Anything green, however, contains chlorophyll: chard, turnip greens, broccoli, algae, green Romaine lettuce, Brussels sprouts, green cabbage, celery, asparagus, green peppers, green beans, green peas, leeks, green olives, parsley, sprouts with green leaves (for example, alfalfa and red clover sprouts) and baby greens.

Dietary Fibre

Although dietary fibre is not a 'nutrient', it is nevertheless an important component of a healthy diet. Dietary fibre is derived from the edible parts of plants that are not broken down by human digestive enzymes. The fact that fibre passes through your body without being absorbed is the main reason why it is so important.

Dietary fibre exists in two forms: soluble and insoluble. Soluble fibres are thought to help lower cholesterol levels and protect against heart disease. Certain types of soluble fibre are referred to as fermentable fibres. Fermentable fibres help maintain healthy populations of friendly bacteria. These bacteria play an important role in your immune system by preventing disease-causing bacteria from surviving in your intestinal tract.

Insoluble fibres help maintain bowel regularity by increasing the bulk of your faeces and decreasing the transit time of faecal matter through your intestines.

Sources of dietary fibre are very common among the protective foods. Most fruit and vegetables, all whole grains, all legumes, as well as sesame seeds and miso, contain fibre.

Vitamin and Mineral Robbers

The twofold nature of this world works like a law: wherever there is good, there is an equal but opposite force that tries its best to extinguish that good. Nature, through foods containing vitamins, minerals and other nutrients, provides you with all that you need to remain in vibrant health. There are, however, many substances (mostly man-made substances) that, when taken internally, diminish, destroy and interfere with those life-giving nutrients. Below are listed a few examples, although many more exist. In general, most medicines and drugs, unless natural, are likely to interfere in some way with your nutrient supply. Stress, whether emotional or physical, can also destroy many nutrients, including niacin, folic acid and Vitamin C.

Air pollutants destroy Vitamin A.

Alcohol consumes reserves of thiamine, riboflavin, niacin, pyridoxine, folic acid, calcium, iron, zinc, magnesium, selenium, Vitamins B12, A, C and D.

Antibiotics destroy intestinal flora which produces B vitamins and Vitamin K.

Antihistamines destroy Vitamin C.

Aspirin can triple the rate of excretion of Vitamin C, thiamine, folic acid and iron, in addition to decreasing the absorption of glucose, amino acids, folic acid, Vitamin K, thiamine and potassium.

Coffee and tea cause the loss of calcium through urine, reduce the absorption of iron and destroy thiamine, inositol, biotin and potassium.

Cough syrups, especially those containing alcohol, can drain all B vitamins, especially folic acid and B12, as well as iron, magnesium and zinc.

Oral contraceptives diminish, destroy and interfere with folic acid, Vitamin C and Vitamin B6.

Refined/white sugar diminishes, destroys and interferes with biotin, chlorine and Vitamin C.

Refined/white flour diminishes, destroys and interferes with niacin and magnesium.

Tobacco diminishes, destroys and interferes with Vitamin C, thiamine, folic acid and phosphorus.

Helpful Hints

❖ Rotate and vary your foods to make sure you are getting balanced amounts of all nutrients.

❖ Avoid calcium when eating foods rich with iron. Pumpkin seeds sprinkled on your salad, or a 'green' juice every day, are great ways to boost your iron levels.

❖ Be careful that you are getting enough Vitamin B12 in your diet. Eat a little dairy, egg or foods that have been fortified with Vitamin B12 every day.

❖ Drink a glass of orange juice a day for that vitamin C antioxidant!

❖ Get out in the sun once a day to increase your production of the important Vitamin D.

❖ Make sure you are eating a good source of omega 3 essential fatty acids every day: linseed oil, ground linseeds and walnuts are some of the best options.

❖ Eat sea algae a couple of times a week, or use a natural sea salt, to prevent a deficiency in iodine.

The Chef Recommends...

❖ Pineapple Orange Smoothie / **205**

❖ Carrot and Almond Salad / **210**

❖ Celery Leaf and Roasted Peanut Dressing / **219**

❖ Guacamole / **227**

❖ Sunburgers / **290**

CHAPTER 4

Life Force Be with You!

A Contemplative Question

Food, water, sunshine and oxygen are generally considered to be the fundamental elements that keep us alive. This, however, is only partially true. If a man who has just died is put in the sunshine, his stomach filled with good food and his lungs inflated with oxygen, he nevertheless will not live. Furthermore, a comparison of a chemical analysis of this man and a man who is still living will reveal no differences: the skeleton, organs, cells and even the molecules will show identical results. Even the bodily temperature, immediately after death, is likely to be the same. And yet, one man is dead and the other alive.

What is it then that the living man has, that the dead man is missing?

The answer: 'Life Energy' or 'Life Force', in Sanskrit known as *'prana'*.

> "IT MAY THUS BE SEEN THAT MAN *is not only a*
> *bundle of nerves, muscles, and bones: the dead man has these*
> *too. The difference between a dead body and a living one is*
> *the absence or presence of this Cosmic Life Force. Living man*
> *is so because life energy sparkles in the bulb of eyes, ears, all*
> *the senses, stomach, liver, brain, and all organs."* **P.Y.**

Understanding Life Energy

Life Energy is a conscious, intelligent energy that exists in every living organism. It is Life Energy that is responsible for giving life. An interesting note is that, in Sanskrit, the word prana not only means 'energy' but also 'life'. Prana, or Life Energy, can be considered similar to electricity, filling your body battery with life. Life Energy, however, is much more subtle than electricity or any other vibratory force existing in nature. It is also, as mentioned above, a conscious and intelligent energy.

Life Energy gives you the power to think, move, feel and will. Without it, you could not lift your arm, blink your eyes, get excited, feel happy, digest your food, think thoughts or interact with others. In short, you would not be able to do any of the things that a living person can do but a dead person cannot.

Life Energy is available to you in limitless amounts. The more Life Energy you have flowing harmoniously through you, the better you feel: physically, emotionally and mentally. Every individual, depending on his lifestyle and habits, manifests a different amount of Life Energy. It is easy to recognise people with a lot of Life Energy by simple observance: they tend to have rosy cheeks, strong bodies and a glow of good health; be positive-minded, good humoured and cheerful and be willing and enthusiastic, with an energy of readiness to greet life's challenges. Their bodies are held erect, their shoulders back and chest open in a gesture that welcomes life. Even the way they walk reveals a bounce in their step. People with very little Life Energy, on the other hand, are usually frail and weak and often ill. They are unenthusiastic, lethargic and can also be depressed. It seems that they are barely existing. Life is just something that 'happens' to them but is not really 'lived'. These are, of course, two ends of the spectrum. The amount of Life Energy manifested in a person can be to various degrees in between.

Physical Illness and Life Energy

Physical illness is nothing more than the result of a deficiency of Life Energy. The French scientist André Simoneton, after 20 years of research, scientifically demonstrated this principle in a field in which it was possible to conduct objective measurements: that of the bioelectricity emitted from human beings and other objects. Simoneton was an engineer with expertise in electromagnetism, who in the 30s and 40s collaborated in the vibratory theory of objects. He was able to demonstrate that the human organism emits a radiation of about 6200-7000 ångström (a unit of length equal to one ten-billionth of a millimetre), used to measure the wavelengths of electromagnetic radiations. He also demonstrated that when the wavelength of bioelectricity decreases to 6500 ångströms or less, the organism can no longer keep itself in good health and the body becomes ill.

> "DISEASE IS GENERALLY CONSIDERED *a result
> of external material causes: few realize that it comes through
> the inaction of the Life Force within. When the cell or tissue vehicle
> of the Life Energy is in any way affected, the Life Energy withdraws
> from that place and trouble consequently starts."* **P.Y.**

Physical symptoms are a warning that your body battery is running low on

Life Energy and urgently needs recharging. Annoying but relatively harmless symptoms, such as coughs, colds or sore throats, are the first signs of low energy and should be acted upon immediately. If ignored and your level of Life Energy continues to decrease, you can become extremely susceptible to more serious illnesses. On the other hand, when you keep your Life Energy high, illness is less likely to touch you. An experiment done by an American doctor, Thomas Powell, demonstrates this fact. For several years, bacteriologists did everything possible to make Doctor Powell's body ill (with his permission of course!). Germs of deadly diseases like the plague and cholera were introduced into his body through food, as well as through injections, and diphtheria germs were applied directly into a wound on his throat. Yet in all these years, Doctor Powell never got ill. Why? Because he knew how to keep his Life Energy, his 'inner healer', strong.*

How to Access Life Energy

Now we come to the big question: "How am I able to access this limitless source of energy that is capable of keeping me in perfect health and protecting me from disease?"

The most effective and direct way to access Life Energy is, quite simply, through will. Paramhansa Yogananda, understanding this relationship between will and energy, developed a series of 39 simple exercises, in which Life Energy can consciously be brought into the body through the medulla oblongata, the main door through which energy enters. This is done by tensing and relaxing individual muscles through the use of will. He called these exercises the 'Yogoda' exercises, later known as the 'Energisation Exercises'.†

---

* Gala D.R.; Gala, Dhiren; Gala, Sanjay. *Panacea on the Earth: Wheat Grass Juice*. Navneet Publilcations (India) Limited, pg 11.

† These exercises can be learnt from any Ananda retreat or meditation centre, or from a demonstration DVD, available for order from Crystal Clarity: www.crystalclarity.com

"THE YOGODA SYSTEM TEACHES ONE
*to harness and direct the will to assist the actual
vibrating Life Energy to any body part required.
Neither physical culture methods nor mental
healing can equal the marvelous results of Yogoda,
which employs the will and the Life Energy directly.
It is not imagination: one can feel the tingling
energy throughout the body by the use of
the Yogoda exercises."* **P.Y.**

Although a lot more could be said on this subject, it is not the specific argument of this book, so we'll leave it here. As a general rule, however, remember: the greater the will or willingness, the greater the flow of energy. When you meet life with enthusiasm and positivity, it works as a kind of magnet which attracts even more Life Energy.

Just as the sun supplies plants with energy through the process of photosynthesis, it also supplies the human body with energy. When the sun's rays enter the body though your skin, the Life Energy already existing there converts the energy of the sun into usable Life Energy. The same is true for oxygen: when you breathe in air, the Life Energy in your body transforms the oxygen into usable Life Energy. For this reason, it is important to make sunshine and oxygen an important part of your daily diet. Whenever you feel tired, down or mentally unclear, go out in the fresh air, take a few deep breaths and let the sun's rays penetrate your body. More will be said on the subject of sunshine and oxygen in the chapter "The Benefits of Fasting" in Part Three of this book.

Life Energy and Food

Now we come to the role that food plays in all this: food too, contains Life Energy. When you eat food, your own Life Energy, as well as being used for assimilating, digesting and eliminating the food, is also required to extract the food's Life Energy and convert it into usable energy for your body. An enormous amount of Life Force, therefore, is consumed every time you eat.

> *"...IT IS LIFE ENERGY that converts oxygen, solids, and liquids into the force that keeps us alive; solids and liquids develop into what they are by this same energy and when you put them into your stomach, they must again be converted into energy before they are of any use to the body..."* **P.Y.**

All foods contain greater or lesser amounts of Life Energy; some foods contain virtually none. If the food you eat contains less Life Energy than that which is required to assimilate, digest and eliminate it, it becomes a burden on your system: instead of recharging you with new energy, it is actually depleting you of energy. In this case, you will find yourself often tired and prone to illness. The word 'aliment' (i.e. food) is defined in the dictionary as "something that feeds, sustains or supports something else." The Latin root of "food" is alere, which means 'to nourish'. Foods that contain low amounts of Life Force do not feed, sustain, support or nourish your organism and cannot, strictly speaking, be considered foods. These include overcooked, chemical, devitalised and 'junk' foods..

> *"IT IS THE INTRICATE TASK OF THE LIFE FORCE to distill more life force from the nourishment taken into the body. Therefore, one's diet should be confined to foods which are easily converted into energy, or which are productive of fresh energy."* **P.Y.**

The scientist Simoneton, mentioned earlier as measuring the amount of radiation emitted by human beings, also tested the radiation emitted from different foods. Fresh fruit and vegetables, including juices made at home and drunk immediately, emitted a staggering radiation of 8000-10,000 ångströms! Among all the vegetables, he found that those with green leaves had the highest amount of bioelectricity. As you read in the last chapter, the green pigment, chlorophyll, allows plants to absorb the sun's rays which, as mentioned, are full of Life Energy.

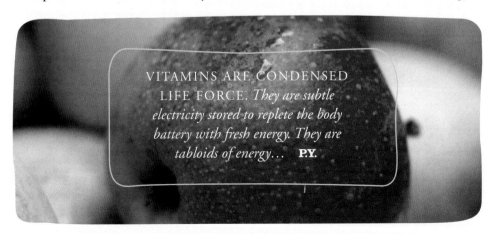

VITAMINS ARE CONDENSED LIFE FORCE. They are subtle electricity stored to replete the body battery with fresh energy. They are tabloids of energy... **P.Y.**

Other foods Simoneton found to have a high radiation were: sprouts, unrefined grains, freshly ground (unrefined) flours, dried fruit (especially sun-dried), nuts, seeds, cold-pressed oils, bee pollen, propolis, honey and natural yoghurt. You have probably noticed that all these foods are protective foods, as listed in the previous chapter, "Mother Nature's Garden". All protective foods contain a high amount of nutrients as well as Life Force. Interestingly, the nutrients themselves provide the food with a lot of its Life Energy. Yogananda says that vitamins, especially, are full of Life Energy. The word itself, vita-mins, suggests this, as it can make us think of 'mines of life' (vita being the Latin for 'life').

The Vital Role of Water

Water constitutes about 50-65% of your body. If eating vital food is important, then drinking vital water is essential. Ordinary tap water, by the time it has gone through the maze of processing and filtration required to turn it into 'drinking water', is practically devoid of Life Energy. Spring water, on the other hand, when obtained directly from the spring (not bottled), is absolutely full of Life Energy. Because water absorbs the energy of the material that surrounds it, spring water

should always be stored in glass containers, never in plastic.

If you are unable to obtain water directly from a spring, do not lose hope! Ordinary tap water or bottled water can be re-energised in the following way: place a handful of rock crystals, rose quartz crystals or amethyst crystals in a large glass jug (these crystals have energising properties). In the evening, fill up the jug with adequate water for the next day. In the morning, the water will be re-energised with Life Force.

N.B.: This method does not remove any harmful substances that may be present in the water.[*]

[*] More about the energetic properties of water can be found in the book *Water and Salt* by Doctor Barbara Hendel and Peter Ferreira, INA Verlag AG, 2003.

Helpful Hints

❖ Feel a cold coming? Increase the amount of your Life Energy.

❖ Prevention is better than cure: avoid junk foods as much as possible and enrich your diet with vitalising foods.

❖ Think 'LIFE!' when you are planning your meals. Include fresh fruit and vegetables in every menu.

❖ Have a high-energy green vegetable juice every day.

❖ Get your water from a natural spring or energise tap water with rock crystals. Avoid keeping your water in plastic containers.

❖ Remember: the greater the will, the greater the flow of energy.

❖ Get out in the sun every day and feel the rays permeating your skin. Take a few deep breaths and inhale Life Energy into your lungs.

The Chef Recommends...

❖ Soya Yoghurt / **187**

❖ Vitality Drink / **198**

❖ Mixed Sprouts Salad / **212**

❖ Avocado and Tomato Dressing / **221**

❖ Coconut Milk / **375**

CHAPTER 5

Vitamins Are Crunchy!

The following are guidelines that will help to ensure that the protective foods you eat are as beneficial for your health as Mother Nature intended, meaning untainted and unscathed by the alimentary errors of modern times.

Eat Raw

Many nutrients are sensitive to heat and can be destroyed though cooking. One of the world's leading researchers on the topic, Dr. Viktoras Kulvinskas, in his book *Love Your Body*, states that there is an average overall "nutrient destruction of approximately 85% from cooking".* For example, up to 96% of thiamine can be lost when food is boiled for a prolonged time. Similarly, up to 72% of biotin can be lost, up to 97% of folic acid lost and up to 80% of Vitamin C lost. Antioxidants can diminish by as much as 50%, all enzymes are obliterated, and many proteins are destroyed or converted into forms that are not easily digested. To underline the point, when you eat cooked food, you may be eating as little as only 15% of its original nutritive properties. Isn't that a waste of the wonderful medicines that Mother Nature has given you to keep you in perfect health? A diet lacking in raw food can have consequences for just about every aspect of your health.

> "DO NOT EAT VITAMIN-KILLED BOILED DINNERS.
> *Vegetables have been ripened and cooked in Nature's kitchen*
> *with the cosmic-fire–ultra-violet rays. Why do you want*
> *to cook them again? Scientific experiments show beyond*
> *question that cooking destroys the vitamins."* **P.Y.**

Cooking also destroys the Life Force of the food. This can be demonstrated with a simple example: a raw apple, when planted in the ground, (under the right conditions) will grow into an apple tree and will, in turn, bear its own fruit. It is

---

* Kulvinskas, Viktoras, M.S. Love Your Body, OMango d'Press, 1972, pg 6.

the Life Force in the apple that gives it the energy it needs to grow. A cooked apple, on the other hand, will never grow into a tree. Cooking has destroyed its Life Energy, which is the principle ingredient necessary for it to become a tree. As you read in the previous chapter, your Life Force is your 'inner healer'. If your diet includes too many cooked foods and not enough raw foods, your body is in danger of having insufficient Life Energy to be able to ward off illnesses and protect you against physical and mental imbalances.

A diet rich in raw foods, and therefore rich in nutrients and Life Energy, will go a long way to keeping you in good health. Many clinics even use raw food as their main form of healing therapy. This is what Hippocrates, the father of medicine, meant when he said, "May food be your medicine!"

In the winter time, you may be able to eat up to 50% raw food and in the summertime, much more. This does, of course, depend upon you. Listen to your body and try and establish what percentage of raw food is comfortable for you.

When you do eat cooked food, lightly steaming is preferred to other methods of cooking as it will damage the nutrient content the least. 'Lightly steaming' means about 5 minutes. Studies show that when steaming is kept to less than 5 minutes, the nutrient content remains relatively unharmed. When steaming time is increased to over 5 minutes, however, the nutrient content steadily diminishes.

Boiling food will result in the loss of some minerals in the water (minerals are water-soluble). Whenever you boil vegetables, grains or legumes, keep the mineral-rich cooking water for soup stock.

When sautéing and stir-frying, the trick is to cut or slice the vegetables small or thin enough so that the heat penetrates them quickly, thus preserving better their nutritional value.

The use of microwaves should be limited or avoided. Although research is not conclusive, many studies show that microwaves damage the molecular structure of food, decrease the bioavailability of many nutrients, affect the immune system and cause the formation of carcinogenic substances.[*]

> "BE SURE TO EAT MORE NATURE-COOKED
> *raw vegetables, fruits, dates and nuts. Above all,*
> *eat rightly, think rightly, and meditate and*
> *live in Divine Joy, night and day."* **P.Y.**

In Part Four of the book, "Table Talk", Mary and Nalini tell us about their experiences of having followed a raw food diet. See: "100% Raw" and "Raw Food".

---

* Newell, Lawrence; Wayne, Anthony. *Microwave Ovens – The Proven Dangers*. AlkalizeForHealth, 2000. Disponibile all'indirizzo http://www.alkalizeforhealth.net/Lmicrowaveovens.htm.

A couple of tips for shopping:

❖ Oils are often heated during processing. Look for oils that say 'cold-pressed'. Olive oil should always be 'extra virgin'.

❖ Honey, has also often been heated. Look for keywords such as 'unheated', 'unfiltered' and 'live enzymes'. You can usually recognise unheated and unfiltered raw honey by its cloudy appearance. Minimally processed honey is full of healthy live yeast, enzymes and pollen.

❖ Fruit and vegetable juices found in supermarkets are never really fresh: all commercial fruit and vegetable juices are heated in order to preserve them.

Chew Properly

Chewing food properly is of utmost importance. There are two main reasons for this. Firstly, chewing breaks the food down. In order for food to be absorbed into your blood and used by the body as nutrients and energy, it must be broken down into very small molecules. Secondly, chewing produces saliva. Saliva is the first of several separate digestive fluids in your body that are necessary to digest and assimilate the foods you eat. Contained in your saliva are certain enzymes (the most well-known being ptyalin) which are responsible for the partial digestion of carbohydrates. When you don't chew your food sufficiently, as well as placing unnecessary strain on your body by causing it to expend a great deal of Life Energy in the stages of digestion which follow, it's also probable that incomplete digestion will occur. If digestion is incomplete, not only are nutrients not extracted from the food but the undigested food can cause bacterial overgrowth in the colon, as well as flatulence and other symptoms associated with indigestion.

Chewing your food properly, therefore, is of utmost importance. As well as doing as much as 50% of the work of digestion, thus allowing your Life Energy to be used for other important things, it also ensures that nutrients are better extracted and indigestion more easily avoided.

Even drinks should be assimilated and digested. There is a saying: 'Chew your drink and drink your food!' When you gulp your fruit and vegetable juices down quickly, you bypass the important act of creating saliva. Take one small mouthful at a time and swish it around it your mouth for a couple of seconds (as you would with a mouth wash) before swallowing. You will be surprised at how much more you enjoy the drink – it even lasts longer!

Think Fresh

Protective foods are often conserved, for example, by tinning or freezing. Methods of conservation can negatively affect the nutritional content and even more importantly, the Life Energy.

Tinned food is conserved through heat. As aforementioned, heat destroys about 85% of the food's nutritional content as well as its Life Force. Because the food is actually boiled in the tin itself, it also tends to develop a strange texture and taste. Freezing, although not recommended, is better than tinning. Freezing destroys several nutrients, including Vitamins E and C and also affects the Life Force of the food. As with tinning, the taste and quality of the food is dramatically altered though freezing.

Besides frozen and tinned food, processed food in general (anything that has been altered from its natural state) should be limited where possible, as every act of processing destroys nutrients as well as Life Energy. Whole almonds, for example, are better than almond butter; whole wheat kernels are better than whole wheat flour or pasta; whole soya beans are better than soya milk, etc. Whenever processed food is desired or necessary, it is best to do the processing yourself at home. This will better preserve the amount of Life Force and ensure that no artificial preservatives or flavour enhancers are added (see below).

Because the majority of *protective foods* you buy will be fresh, you need to know how to store them properly. Even within a few days of being harvested, a food can lose up to half of its nutritional content unless it is stored in the correct conditions.

Fresh fruit, vegetables and fresh herbs should generally be stored in cool, dark places and eaten within a few days. Withering is a sign that the food is dying, losing its Life Energy and nutrients. Leafy green vegetables wilt very quickly and should be kept in the fridge; vegetables such as squash, potatoes and carrots last longer and can be kept in a cool, dark cupboard.

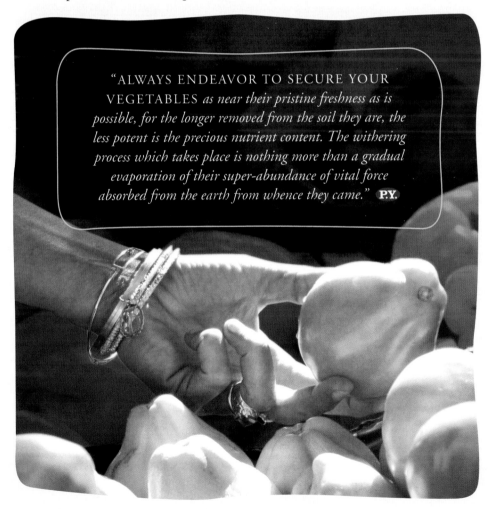

"ALWAYS ENDEAVOR TO SECURE YOUR VEGETABLES *as near their pristine freshness as is possible, for the longer removed from the soil they are, the less potent is the precious nutrient content. The withering process which takes place is nothing more than a gradual evaporation of their super-abundance of vital force absorbed from the earth from whence they came."* **P.Y.**

The next step, when dealing with fresh foods and the preservation of their precious nutritional content and Life Force, is to form the habit of preparing them as near to the time at which you need them as possible.

Since almost all nutrients are sensitive to light and air (as well as heat), as soon as you cut a food open, its nutrients rapidly disintegrate or lose their effectiveness. Life Force, because it is contained within the molecular structure of the food, is also easily lost through cutting, by which the molecular structure is damaged. Ideally, therefore, all foods should be prepared only when they are ready to be eaten (or to be cooked). Fresh fruit and vegetable juices should be drunk immediately, even before you clean the machine.

Similarly, the outer skin or shell of foods such as nuts and seeds works as a protection against the loss of nutrients. Buying walnuts in their shell, for example, is preferable to buying those already shelled.

Be Natural

Most packaged foods found in supermarkets contain chemical additives. There are more than 3000 food additives legally allowed for preserving food, as well as for changing and enhancing its colour, texture and flavour. As Dr. Gillian McKeith states in her book *You Are What You Eat*: "Just because many of these additives and chemicals are deemed safe, it does not mean that they are." Repeated studies have linked various additives to hyperactivity in children, allergies, migraines, behavioural problems, infertility, weakened immune system, liver and kidney damage, central nervous system disturbances and even cancer.[*]

Of particular note is monosodium glutamate, commonly known as MSG. MSG is added to enhance the flavour of food. It works in a different way than salt, herbs and other flavourings, in that; it doesn't actually change the flavour of the food or have a distinct flavour of its own. It excites and increases the sensitivity of your taste buds and 'tricks' your brain into thinking that the food you are eating tastes good. It's used to disguise the tinny taste of tinned products and to give a fresh taste to frozen or freeze-dried foods. Most commonly, manufacturers use MSG to make inferior-quality ingredients seem tasty, thus cutting their production costs. Excessive use of MSG is thought to cause lesions on the brain, causing cognitive, endocrinological and emotional abnormalities. In children, it is said that excess MSG could seriously damage their cognitive skills and cause learning difficulties.[†]

Many processed foods, for example, soya sauce, dried soup mixes, vegetable stock and crackers contain MSG. Restaurants also frequently add MSG to their menu items.

> "THE ORDINARY FIGS AND RAISINS ARE
> MUMMIES. *They are so fixed that they do not decay, but have
> no life. These figs and raisins you can write in your will and
> leave to future generations as heirlooms. Sun-dried figs only live
> three months. In the mummy kind, the sulphur fumes are passed
> through them and kill all the vitamins. Isn't it too bad to
> preserve things and kill the good part? Four un-sulphured figs
> and prunes and a few raisins a day are good."* **P.Y.**

You can tell if dried fruit contains added sulphites from the colour: bright orange dried apricots or bright red dried cranberries, for example, will usually have sulphites.

From a more spiritual perspective, chemical additives have a dulling and stultifying effect on the mind. This topic will be discussed further in the chapter "Spiritualising Your Diet". For now, let it suffice to say that when the mind is

---

* McKeith, Gillian, Dr. *You Are What You Eat*. Michael Joseph, an imprint of Penguin Books Ltd, 2004, pg 26.
Food Additives ~ Food Safety. Washington: Centre for Science in the Public Interest. Available at http://www.cspinet.org/reports/chemcuisine.htm
Food additives and their associated health risks. Food Democracy, 2008. Available at http://fooddemocracy.wordpress.com/2008/06/08/food-additives-and-their-associated-health-risks
Starr Hull, Janet, Dr. *Food Additives to Avoid*. Dr. Janet Starr Hull, 2002. Available at http://www.sweet-poison.com/food-additives-to-avoid.html

† *Monosodium Glutamate (MSG) Health Effects*. HealthDangers.com, 2003-2008. Available at http://www.healthdangers.com/drugs/MSG/msg-health-effects.htm

dulled and stultified, it loses its power to direct and control the flow of Life Energy in your body. As you read in the previous chapter, when the Life Energy in your body is low, blocked or uncontrolled, illness can easily enter.

> "...NATURAL FOODS INDIRECTLY PRODUCE
> HEALTH *by keeping the mind calm, thus permitting*
> *the normal flow of life energy to flow unobstructed.*
> *Unnatural and gross foods have the opposite effect."* **S.K.**

As a general rule, the best way to avoid chemicals is to get into the habit of reading the label before you buy anything.

Choose Organic
or Biodynamic

"Organic" refers to any food that was grown in a natural way, without the use of chemical pesticides and fertilisers. Organic agriculture does not use genetic modification and emphasises the utilisation of renewable resources, as well as the conservation of land and water. Biodynamic agriculture, developed by the Austrian philosopher Rudolf Steiner, goes one step further. While organic agriculture mainly looks at cultivation from a physical standpoint, biodynamic agriculture also considers the Life Force. Methods such as following lunar cycles are used to increase the Life Energy of food, as well as of the soil in which it is grown.

A growing body of scientific evidence supports the claim that both organic and biodynamic foods are superior in nutritional value to ordinary, commercially-grown foods. A study performed in 1993 by the Doctor's Data Lab in Chicago (published in the *Journal of Applied Nutrition*, Vol. 45, Issue #1) showed that organic food had, on average, TWICE the nutritional element content of regular commercial food on a fresh weight basis. Early results of the ongoing Quality Low Input Food (QLIF) study, a study involving 33 academic centres across Europe and the largest ever of its kind, reinforce this evidence, showing significant positive nutritional differences in organic food compared to non-organic, commercial food. The study indicates, for example, that organic fruit and vegetables contain as much as 40% more antioxidants than non-organic fruit and vegetables. Antioxidants are produced in plants as a defence against environmental stresses, such as insects or competing plants. Chemical pesticides and fertilisers, used by commercial farmers to make their crops more resistant to disease, insect attacks and weather variables, remove the need for plants to defend themselves and thus, to produce antioxidants.

In order to have a prolonged shelf life, commercial foods are often genetically modified to contain fewer enzymes (enzymes are the reason why food, once aged, starts to rot. It is, quite simply, a natural process of self-digestion). Organic and biodynamic foods are never genetically modified. The enzyme content remains as nature intended.

Apart from being superior in terms of nutrition and Life Energy, organic food is also a much safer choice for health reasons. Residues of chemical pesticides and fertilisers in commercial food create toxins in your body; your body will store these toxins until it has time to eliminate them. This can lead to many health problems; many of the pesticides used in farming have even been found to be carcinogenic. Reducing your exposure to these toxins by choosing organic or biodynamic is a definite step towards improved health.

As a side issue (but a none-the-less important one) the abundant use of chemical fertilisers and pesticides is an immense burden to nature. It is said that conventional agriculture contributes to more than a third of all environment and water pollutants.

To sum up, organic and biodynamic foods contain more vitamins and minerals, more enzymes and antioxidants, as well as more Life Energy, than commercially-grown foods do. They have been grown without the use of chemicals. Although organic and biodynamic foods may have the occasional blemish or bug and may even cost a little bit more, they are a guaranteed healthier and safer option. Consider the extra cost as an investment for your health. As a bonus, their taste is superior to commercially grown foods. Organic and biodynamic foods often contain less water and thus have a more concentrated flavour. As they are also usually grown locally, they ripen on the vine, making them taste fresh and filling them with Life Energy.

In Part Four of the book, "Table Talk", Helmut tells us about the joy of having his own vegetable garden. See: "Homegrown Food Has More Pep!".

Buy In-Season

To guarantee the best results for your health, in-season fruit and vegetables are preferred to those out-of-season. Eating out-of-season fruit can upset the natural balance of your body, which, being a part of nature, has different alimentary needs for each season: foods to help you confront the cold of winter, the heat of summer, the activity of spring and the slowing down of autumn. Eating in-season foods ensures that you are getting the correct combination of vitamins, minerals and enzymes that you need for that season. Eating out-of-season foods creates imbalance and stress. As a bonus, in-season food always tastes better and costs much less than out-of-season food. A chart of various fruit and vegetables and their corresponding seasons can be found in the appendix.

Helpful Hints

❖ Eat raw as much as you can. Grains and legumes can also be sprouted and eaten raw.

❖ Invest in a steamer to preserve the mineral content of your cooked vegetables.

❖ Practise chewing your food at least 30-50 times before swallowing.

❖ Substitute fresh foods for tinned and frozen foods.

❖ Buy a few plant boxes in which you can grow fresh kitchen herbs, such as parsley, rosemary and thyme.

❖ Read the label before you buy anything. Check for additives and unwanted ingredients.

❖ Choose organic foods whenever possible: the foods you can consume raw should be your priorities.

The Chef Recommends...

Gingerly Carrot / **197**

Waldorf Salad / **208**

German Cabbage Salad / **210**

Gazpacho / **239**

Lemony Fruit and Nut Balls / **356**

CHAPTER 6

Carbohydrates and Gravity

Carbohydrates exist in two different forms: simple and complex. Simple carbohydrates have a very simple molecular structure and are, in essence, sugars. Sweeteners such as honey, malt, maple syrup, corn syrup, molasses and white and brown sugar all contain simple carbohydrates. Complex carbohydrates have a more complicated molecular structure. All grains, including wheat, rye, spelt, oats, corn, barley and buckwheat; all legumes, which are beans, peas and lentils (legumes are a combination of carbohydrates and protein); tubers, such as white and sweet potatoes; and tapioca (a starch obtained from the roots of the cassava plant), contain complex carbohydrates.

The main role of carbohydrates is to provide you with energy. Glucose, the sugar that carbohydrates break down into is, in fact, the principle fuel that powers your body and brain (an astonishing 25% of the glucose produced in your body is consumed directly by your brain). Carbohydrates, therefore, form an important part of a healthy and well-balanced diet. However, as you will remember from the chapter "What is a Balanced Diet?" carbohydrates should be limited to only 20% of your overall food intake. Here are some of the reasons why:

The Acid-Alkaline Balance

The main reason that carbohydrates should be limited to only 20% of your overall food intake is that, in general, carbohydrates (especially white sugar and refined and processed grains, such as white pasta and white bread) are acidic and, when eaten in large quantities, can create a state of acidosis in the body.

In order to help keep the correct acid-alkaline balance in your body, stick to the following guidelines:

- ❖ Keep carbohydrates in general limited to only 20% of your overall diet.
- ❖ Choose whole grains rather than refined and processed grains.
- ❖ Choose unrefined, natural sweeteners, such as malt, honey and maple syrup rather than sugar.

Carbohydrates and Breath

Another reason to limit carbohydrates is that they contain large amounts of carbon, the excess of which must be cleared from your body in the form of carbon-dioxide. The more carbon-rich foods you eat, the harder your heart and lungs, and therefore your Life Force, have to work to expel the carbon. If you start to observe your breathing, you will easily notice this relationship between carbohydrates and breath. If you meditate, limiting the amount of carbohydrates in your diet is especially important: with too much carbon in your body, your over-active heart and lungs will never allow you to meditate deeply.

> "...PEOPLE, WHO EAT STARCH AND MEAT
> *all the time, have to breathe like bellows and have*
> *to keep their Life Force and mind constantly busy*
> *with the physical functions of breathing and with*
> *the heaviness and motion of the flesh."* **P.Y.**

For the same reason, if you want to have deep and restful sleep, eating carbohydrates at night time should be avoided. If the heart and lungs are busy pumping carbon out of your body, you will find that perfect rest is impossible.

The Sugar Bomb Effect

Simple carbohydrates, as mentioned at the beginning of the chapter, have a very simple molecular structure. As a result, they digest very quickly. While this may seem to be a plus, in reality, it creates a large quantity of glucose that literally floods your blood with sugar. This is known as the 'sugar bomb effect'. A hormone called insulin is produced in your pancreas to escort the glucose from your blood into your body cells, where it can be burned up as energy. Large amounts of glucose in your blood are toxic to your kidneys and other organs; the pancreas responds quickly to this emergency situation by immediately releasing large amounts of insulin to take the glucose away. This is known as the 'insulin effect.' Both the

'sugar-bomb effect' and the 'insulin effect' have consequences for your health, some of them severe. Here are just a few of them:

* ❖ The rapid production and burning up of glucose does give you a boost of energy, but it is always short-lived and usually goes as quickly as it came. The result is that you are left feeling sluggish, mentally as well as physically. You can feel tired, fuzzy-minded and experience difficulty concentrating. This sudden swing in energy also plays with your emotions. It can make you irritated, angry and depressed.

* ❖ The 'insulin effect' (unnaturally large amounts of insulin in the blood) increases the risk of heart disease, diabetes, Alzheimer's and many other diseases.

* ❖ A strain is placed on your body. It struggles to keep up with the demands of the glucose and insulin overload and, as a result, the aging-process is accelerated.

Simple carbohydrates, if taken in excess (and excess is not very much), will have this effect on your body. If you like sweet things, first, try to limit the amount that you eat; and second, choose natural sweeteners, such as honey, maple syrup and malt, which are minimally processed. Minimally refined natural sweeteners contain some nutrients which help your body to metabolise them without creating an imbalance. Highly refined sweeteners have been stripped of these nutrients. White sugar is highly refined; even brown sugar is only slightly less refined than white. The refinement process involved in making white sugar is an unnatural chemical process, in which sugar cane is stripped of its natural nutrients. The various stages of this process can be found in a chart in the appendix. Of all the sugars, unrefined raw cane sugar, Demerara, Mascobado (Mosavo) and Panela sugar are the best options.

> "...SUGAR SHOULD BE THE NATURAL BROWN
> QUALITY *which is hardly recognizable as to color, taste,*
> *and nourishing properties when compared with the anaemic*
> *white sugar used in the average home..."* **P.Y.**

Complex carbohydrates, as mentioned at the beginning of the chapter, have a more complicated molecular structure than simple carbohydrates. For this reason, foods that contain complex carbohydrates, as long as they are left in their natural form, take much longer to digest than foods with simple carbohydrates. Instead of creating fatigue to your system, this long digestion actually produces an efficient energy system. Because they are broken down slowly, glucose is released gradually into your blood stream, instead of all at once. This gradual release of glucose, and consequential, gradual burning up of glucose in the cells, provides you with long-lasting and steady energy, instead of a burst of short-lived energy.

Grains, unfortunately, are rarely left in their natural form. Refined grains, as well as creating an imbalance in your blood sugar level, are a poor substitute for whole grains for a variety of other reasons. These are discussed below.

Grains:
The Whole Story

> "THROUGHOUT HISTORY, *we gather that grain was*
> *the main form of nourishment, and raising it the chief occupation*
> *of the peoples, but the deplorably artificial substitutes that are*
> *stupendously advertised by unscrupulous commercial exploitation*
> *at the expense of humanity's physical well-being, are anaemic*
> *reminders of the fields of grain mentioned in the Bible, which*
> *were the sustenance of the nations and their herds."* **P.Y.**

Whole grains are an excellent source of vitamins, minerals and other nutrients. Brown rice, for example, is an ideal source of manganese (1 cup of cooked brown rice provides you with 88% of the Recommended Dietary Allowance), a very good source of magnesium and selenium and also contains phosphorus, iron, Vitamins B1, B3 and B6 and essential fatty acids. Whole oats are also an excellent source of manganese (1 cup of cooked oats provides you with 68.5% of the RDA) and a very good source of selenium, phosphorus, Vitamin B1, magnesium and protein. There is, however, a big difference between *whole* grains and the refined and polished grains more commonly found in the shops these days.

Grains have several layers. With whole grains, only the outermost layer, the *hull*, is removed, which is least damaging to the nutritional value of the grain. Refined grains, however, in order to extend their shelf life, are further processed to remove the bran and germ layers. This removal of the bran and germ can diminish the grain's nutrition by up to 80%. The process that converts brown rice into white rice, for example, destroys 67% of the niacin, 80% of the thiamine, 90% of the Vitamin B6, half of the manganese, half of the phosphorus, 60% of the iron and all of the essential fatty acids. The result is simply a starch that is largely bereft of its original nutrients. White flour, white bread, white rice, white pasta, etc., have all been refined.

"YOU MAY EAT A WHOLE DINNER,
*very palatable, very satisfying and filling, and yet
you may be eating a dead meal. Experiments show
that mice can live eight weeks on water alone,
but only six weeks on white bread."* **P.Y.**

As well as containing many nutrients, the bran is also the fibrous part of the grain. It can lower high cholesterol levels, protect against heart disease, decrease your risks of colon cancer, support your immune system and prevent disorders of the digestive tract. In addition, fibre is important for normalising blood sugar levels. Soluble fibres, in fact, slow down the absorption of the food, thus ensuring that glucose is released gradually into your blood stream after a meal. The result of removing fibre through processing is that grains are broken down and digested far too quickly. This quick digestion, as with simple carbohydrates, causes an over-flow of glucose in your blood and brings about the previously described sugar bomb and insulin effects. Have you ever felt tired and sluggish after an over-dose of white pasta or rice? This is why.

> *"DURING DIGESTION STARCHES*
> *are gradually converted into sugar and thus*
> *the digestive tract is not suddenly flooded with*
> *a concentrated solution of sugar as is the case*
> *when refined devitalized foods are eaten."* **P.Y.**

Another advantage of dietary fibre is that because it slows down the rate at which food passes through your digestive tract, you are left with a sense of satiety after a meal, which helps prevent you from overeating. The disadvantage of refined grains is that, because they leave your stomach quickly, you will probably feel tempted to eat more. Eating too many carbohydrates can make you gain weight. During digestion starch is converted into glucose. Glucose that is not used immediately is stored in your muscles and liver as glycogen, ready for when you need it. Your muscles and liver, however, are only able to store a certain amount glycogen: the rest gets turned into fat. If you have a little more fat than you perhaps should, maybe you are eating too many carbohydrates.

Although a little white pasta or pizza now and then doesn't hurt, whole grains are, in general, the best option. Many different types of whole grains are available, some of which you may never have heard of, each one with its own distinct taste and texture. If you vary the types of whole grains you eat, it is very unlikely that you will ever get bored! Remember though, whole grains should also be eaten in limited quantities.

As well as using grains in cooked dishes, for added nutrition, they can be sprouted and eaten raw. More will be explained about sprouts in the chapter "The Protein Myth". In the recipe section you will find detailed instructions on how to grow sprouts.

The Grain Family

- Amaranth
- Barley
- Basmati rice
- Brown rice
- Buckwheat
- Corn
- Kamut
- Millet
- Oats
- Quinoa
- Red rice
- Rye
- Spelt
- Wheat
- Wild rice

Helpful Hints

❖ Eat more dried fruit instead of things sweetened with sugar. Dried fruit and nuts can easily be made into delicious and nutritious biscuits.

❖ Substitute sugar with honey, agave, malt or maple syrup. Look for the key words such as 'unprocessed' and 'natural'. Many sugar-free desserts can be found in the recipe section.

❖ Fruit is much better for you than a packet of biscuits, but if you do feel like nibbling on biscuits, choose ones made with wholemeal flour.

❖ Increase the amount of fruit and vegetables in your diet, and you will naturally eat fewer refined and processed grains.

❖ Broaden your experience of whole grains. Buy a few that you have never used before and experiment with some recipes from the "Rice and Other Grains" chapter in the recipe section.

❖ Try wholemeal pasta (wholemeal wheat, wholemeal spelt, buckwheat) instead of white; it's more substantial and flavourful.

❖ Save the pizza for a 'once-in-a-while' treat.

The Chef Recommends...

❖ Chappatis / **246**

❖ Brown Rice with Squash and Tomato Stew / **268**

❖ Quinoa Summer Salad / **273**

❖ "Spelt-otto" with Butternut Squash / **277**

❖ Healthy Cake! / **354**

CHAPTER 7

The Protein Myth

"BEHOLD, I HAVE GIVEN YOU *every herb bearing seed,*
which is upon the face of all the earth, and every tree, in that which
is the fruit of a tree yielding seed; to you it shall be for meat."
GENESI 1,29 *(King James Authorised Version)*

Getting Enough Protein with a Vegetarian Diet

Many people who are vegetarian, or who are thinking about becoming vegetarian, worry about how to include enough protein in their diet without eating meat. Let your mind be at peace: an abundance of high-quality vegetarian and vegan proteins are available for those who choose to follow this life-style. Details about the most important sources of vegetarian proteins are given below. You will also find some information about the effects of eating meat towards the end of the chapter.

Contrary to popular belief, your body requires less protein than you may think. The Recommended Dietary Allowance (RDA) for protein is 0.8 grams for each kilo of your body weight (i.e. a person weighing 60 kgs would need 48 grams of protein a day). This, however, includes a generous 'margin of safety': in reality, the average person's true need is lower. Many say that the RDA provides for nearly twice the daily need of protein. Several studies have shown that people can lead healthy, active lives while consuming around 20 grams of protein a day for an adult male and even less for an adult female.*

Eating too much protein is actually detrimental to your health. Too much protein creates a build-up of toxins called ketones, which must be flushed out of the body through your urine. This puts an enormous strain on your kidneys and can lead to reduced kidney function and disease. The large amounts of water used to

N.B.: Growing children, pregnant and lactating women, as well as athletes and people performing strenuous physical activity may need more protein.

flush the ketones out of the body also cause dehydration. Dehydration can make you feel weak and dizzy and give you bad breath. As well as this, as you will remember from the chapter "The Secret of an Alkaline Body", proteins are generally acidic. Eating too much protein creates a state of acidity in your body, giving rise to an internal environment that is conducive to disease.

Animal sources of protein, which include meat, fish, eggs, cheese, butter and milk, are the first types of protein foods to reduce in your diet. As well as being highly acidic, they are also full of saturated fats. Plant-based sources of protein are generally much less acidic than animal ones, are low in saturated fats and besides protein, contain many essential nutrients. Plant-based sources of protein, for this reason, can be eaten more freely than animal sources of protein but still always in limited quantities.

A chart with specific protein contents of various types of foods can be found in the appendix (you may be surprised to see just how easy it is to obtain protein with a vegetarian diet).* At first, you may find this chart useful to help you to calculate the approximate amount of protein that you are eating each day and see whether this amount needs to be adjusted. After a while, however, forget about specific charts and calculations: limiting your intake of protein foods to only 20% of your overall diet, as recommended by Yogananda, (as long as you do not overeat) will make sure that you are eating neither too much nor too little protein.

What is Protein and how is it Formed?

Protein is responsible for an amazing 16% of your total body weight. Your muscles, hair and skin are mainly made of protein. In addition, protein functions in several other important ways: it forms antibodies to combat invading bacteria and viruses, carries oxygen throughout your body and forms part of the enzyme and hormonal system.

Protein is formed when amino acids, the 'building blocks' of protein, are united. Just as the 26 letters of the alphabet combine in many different ways to make an endless amount of words, amino acids combine together to create many different types of proteins. However, while words contain only a few letters, some protein chains contain as many as several hundred amino acids. The scope for variety is immense.

* If you eat meat, you will find the protein contents of beef and chicken in the appendix chart, "Soya Compared to Meat and Eggs".

Twenty-two different amino acids have been discovered so far: fourteen of these can be produced by your body; the remaining eight cannot. These eight are called 'essential amino acids'. Because your body cannot produce them, you must obtain them through food. The eight essential amino acids are: tryptophan, lysine, methionine, phenylalaine, threonine, valine, leucine and isoleucine.

Complete and Combination Proteins

"Complete protein" foods are those which have all eight of these amino acids in the correct quantities for your body. Complete proteins are found in all animal sources of protein, as well as some plant-based sources.

"Combination protein" foods contain only some of the eight essential amino acids but can be harmoniously combined together to form complete proteins. While in the past it was believed that combination protein foods (grains and legumes, for example) needed to be eaten in the same meal in order to ensure that they combined together to form complete proteins, protein combining within the same meal is now known to be unnecessary. Protein requirements can be met by consuming a variety of plant sources of protein during the span of the same day.

Soya Beans and Soya Foods

Soya beans and soya foods are an excellent source of plant protein. They contain all eight essential amino acids in the correct combinations for your body, making soya a complete protein food. Soya has the added benefit of being very alkaline and low in saturated fats. This means that, through soya, you can easily satisfy your protein requirements, without the side effects of acidosis and high cholesterol. In addition to being an excellent plant source of complete protein, soya foods contain such a wealth of fibre, vitamins, minerals and other nutrients that it is nothing short of astounding.*

Soya is one of the foods most widely researched for its health-promoting properties. While some issues have not yet reached a consensus, the claim that a regular consumption of soya foods can lower cholesterol and reduce the risk of heart dis-

---

* In-depth nutritional information on soya beans can be found in the appendix, "Soya Compared to Meat and Eggs".

ease has now been declared as fact by the Food and Drug Administration (FDA). In 1999, after a yearlong review of the available human studies, the FDA allowed this health claim on food labels: "A daily diet containing 25 grams of soya protein (also low in saturated fat and cholesterol) may reduce the risk of heart disease." Other claims relating to the health benefits of a regular consumption of soya foods include the possible reduced risk of diseases such as osteoporosis, prostate cancer, breast cancer and colon cancer, as well as the possible reduction of menopausal symptoms in women.

Some people avoid soya foods because of the claim that soya beans are one of the top genetically-modified food crops. This is true, but what most people don't know is that genetic modification is completely prohibited in the production of any certified organic food. The solution then is quite simply to use organically-certified soya foods only.

Like all foods, soya should also be incorporated into the diet in a balanced and moderate way. In Japan, where soya is a dietary staple, individuals seldom consume large quantities of soya at any one time.

Soya beans (soya in its least processed form) are one of the more nutritious forms of soya. A 170 gram serving of cooked soya beans provides about 28 grams of complete protein. Soya beans are delicious when mashed and used as a base for burgers or slightly stir-fried and dressed with toasted seeds and soya sauce.

Tofu, also known as soya bean curd, is the most common form in which to enjoy soya. A 100g serving of tofu contains about 11.5 grams of complete protein; more than twice the amount of protein in an egg. Tofu does not have a distinct taste of its own and takes on the flavours of the foods and spices it is cooked with. This works to its advantage because it means that tofu can be used in just about any dish, sweet or savoury, with great success. Tofu can easily be made at home: The recipe is given in the "Basic Recipes" chapter of the recipe section (page 190). Alternatively, tofu can be purchased from most supermarkets and health food shops. A whole chapter is dedicated to tofu (and seitan) in the recipe section.

Tempeh is a fermented soya bean product, containing approximately 17.5 grams of complete protein in a 100 gram serving. The process of fermentation converts the soya beans into a more digestible and nutrient-rich food, making fermented soya even better for your health than non-fermented soya. Because tempeh is made with a Vitamin B12 synthesising fungus, it is commonly recommended as a Vitamin B12 source for vegans.

Tempeh can be substituted for tofu in many of the recipes given in the "Tofu and Seitan" chapter of the recipe section.

Miso is a fermented soya bean paste with a salty taste and buttery texture. One large tablespoon provides between 2.5 and 3.5 grams of complete protein (depending on the type). Most types of miso also contain rice, barley or wheat. Miso is renowned as being an excellent food for promoting healthy intestines. Like tempeh, it is also commonly recommended as a Vitamin B12 source for vegans. Miso is most commonly used as a type of stock to give flavour to soups but can also be used in condiments and sauces. A recipe using miso is given in the recipe section: "Miso-Tofu Soup" (page 236).

Soya milk is an alkaline, low-in-saturated-fat alternative to regular cow's milk and can be used as a substitute in any recipe. A 250 ml glass of soya milk contains about 10 grams of complete protein. Although soya milk can be easily obtained from the shops, homemade soya milk costs less and has the advantage of having no added ingredients. The recipe for homemade soya milk can be found in the "Basic Recipes" chapter of the recipe section (page 182). Many other recipes in the book call for the use of soya milk.

Soya yoghurt, like regular yoghurt, is very beneficial for maintaining healthy intestines due to its large content of friendly bacteria. A 250 ml portion of soya yoghurt contains 10.5 grams of complete protein. Homemade soya yoghurt is easy to make, economical, natural and really tasty. You also get the added satisfaction of witnessing the miracle of milk being turned into yoghurt! The recipe for homemade soya yoghurt can be found in the "Basic Recipes" chapter of the recipe section (page 183).

Seitan

Seitan, another wonderful source of plant protein, is made with the gluten from wheat flour. It is, for this reason, also known as 'wheat-meat' or 'gluten'. Seitan contains seven of the eight essential amino acids. With the addition of soya sauce, tamari or the sea vegetable kombu during cooking, it acquires the missing eighth amino acid, making it a source of complete protein.

Seitan is low in saturated fats and without cholesterol: a 100 g serving contains about 118 calories, more than 25 grams of protein and less than 1% of saturated fats. The same amount of beef (depending on the cut) has anywhere between 220-360 calories, 18-30 grams of protein and is high in saturated fats.

Although seitan is readily available in most supermarkets and health food shops, its taste and texture bears little resemblance to homemade seitan, and the price is unacceptably high for the quality of seitan you receive. Seitan can be prepared at home, quickly and easily, for virtually no cost: 300-500 grams of seitan has the cost of only half a kilo of Manitoba flour (about 80 pence). The recipe is given in the "Basic Recipes" chapter of the recipe section (page 191).

Because seitan's consistency is very similar to meat, it is often used to make vegetarian versions of traditional meat recipes. Many such recipes are given in the "Tofu and Seitan" chapter of the recipe section (page 315). Like tofu, seitan has a neutral taste and takes on the flavours of the foods and spices it is mixed with. At Ananda, we often flavour our seitan with soya sauce and garlic before mixing it with the other ingredients.

N.B.: Seitan should be eaten in moderation (once a week) to avoid creating a gluten intolerance.

Sprouts

Perhaps the most amazing of all of the plant-based sources of protein, and indeed of all plant foods in general, are sprouts. All sprouts contain large amounts of high-quality protein; several, such as alfalfa, wheat grass, soya, linseed, chickpea, green pea and mung, contain all eight essential amino acids. Lentil sprouts contain all of the essential amino acids apart from tryptophan.

Sprouts are the first step in the life of a plant. A seed, once removed from the mother plant, remains in a dormant state. This seed contains all of the genetic information and nutrients necessary to become a new plant. The process in which a seed re-awakens is called 'sprouting', or 'germination'. During this phase, the seed is at the height of its nutritional and energetic potential. As well as having benefits for your physical body, recent studies in the field of psychosomatic science have found that eating these little reawakening seeds introduces a similar re-awakening energy into you; an energy that regenerates, renews and helps you to let go of the old.

During sprouting, the seed's vitamins multiply enormously: Vitamin C can increase by up to 600%, Vitamin B12 by 200-700%, Vitamin B5 and B6 by up to 100% and Vitamin B2 from anywhere between 400 and 1462%. Mineral salts also increase noticeably. Calcium, iron, phosphorus and magnesium increase by up to 100%. The protein content also multiplies; in lentils, for example, by up to 40%. What's more, during sprouting, the sprout's protein gets broken down into individual amino acids, a process which your body is usually required to do during digestion, making sprouts a kind of 'pre-digested' food. Each type of sprout also contains the specific vitamins needed to assimilate its amino acids. This makes sprouts one of the easiest foods to digest and assimilate.

Alfalfa sprouts are considered to be superior to most other sprouts. They contain 35% protein, as well as phosphorus, calcium, potassium, magnesium, iron and Vitamins A, B, C, D, E and K. Like all sprouts, they are also a rich source of enzymes and have an alkaline effect on the body.

> "MY STUDENT, *and personal friend, the late Luther*
> *Burbank, famous plant wizard, said that alfalfa contained*
> *some of the most important nutritive substances known,*
> *and would become the future food of man. The ancient*
> *Arabic name for it is 'Alfalfa' or, 'Father of all foods."* **P.Y.**

Growing sprouts is extremely simple, requiring only a couple of minutes of your attention a day. A full guide can be found in the "Basic Recipes" chapter of the recipe section (page 162-174). Serving suggestions and recipe ideas are also included. In the appendix you will find an easy-reference nutritional chart for sprouts (page 398).

The best thing about sprouts is, because they are eaten raw, without being picked, harvested, cut, peeled or treated in any way, they remain alive and vibrant with nutrients and Life Energy, even as you chew them in your mouth!

Legumes

All legumes, which are beans, lentils and peas, are packed with protein. They are combination protein foods, meaning that they must be combined with other protein foods to make complete protein. An excellent combination is with grains, nuts or seeds. Many tasty grain-legume combinations can be found in the recipe section. One portion of a grain-legume combination is, in fact, enough to provide you with the main part of your daily protein needs.

Legumes provide one of the best sources of dietary fibre and therefore come with all the health benefits of fibre-rich foods. They are packed with numerous vitamins and minerals and all with virtually no fat.

"SINCE HERBIVOROUS ANIMALS are able to build up complete proteins from plant food, it is assumed that seed proteins supplement those derived from the leafy or green parts of plants. Therefore, it is important, especially for vegetarians, to include both parts in their diets. The seeds are, of course, grains, peas, beans, lentils, etc." **P.Y.**

In the recipe section you will find a complete guide on how to cook legumes successfully ("Basic Recipes" chapter, pages 179-181), as well as a whole chapter dedicated to legume recipes.

Grains

All grains have a surprising amount of protein. They are combination protein foods, meaning that they need to be combined with other protein foods to make complete protein. Most commonly, they are combined with legumes. Whole grains, of course, contain more protein than refined grains.

Nuts

Nuts (almonds, walnuts, hazelnuts, Brazil nuts etc) are an excellent plant-based source of protein, many containing over 20%.

Because large pieces of badly chewed nuts often pass undigested through the alimentary canal without the nutrition being assimilated, Yogananda recommends eating nuts as nut butters or milks. Recipes for almond butter (page 228), peanut butter (page 229), almond milk (page 374) and coconut milk (page 375) can be found in the recipe section. If you do eat nuts whole, chew them thoroughly.

> "THROUGH EXPERIMENTATION *it has been found that the digestibility of nuts is increased as much as ten per cent when they have been made into nut butters before eating."* **P.Y.**

Nuts are best eaten in the morning and in small quantities. Combining them with dried fruit not only balances the nutritional content but also helps you to eat less.

Seeds

Seeds (sunflower seeds, sesame seeds, pumpkin seeds, linseeds etc) are high-quality plant proteins. In addition to their protein content, a handful of seeds provide a wide array of vitamins, minerals and other nutrients.

Many of the recipes in the recipe section call for various seeds or tahini (sesame paste). You might try looking up: "Sunburgers" (page 290), "Mixed Seed Crackers" (page 251) and "Tahini Sauce" (page 224).

Green Algae

Green algae contain amounts of protein ranging from 20%-65%. Of all the green algae, spirulina has the most; an incredible 65%, which is more than twice that of meat and soya. Because of this, spirulina has earned the name 'green meat'.

In addition to their high protein content, green algae are one of the plant kingdom's richest sources of vitamins, minerals, enzymes and the blood-enriching chlorophyll. Sea algae are an especially invaluable source of iodine, which is hard to find in the plant kingdom. As if this weren't enough, they have the added bonus of being highly alkaline. They are, in fact, considered a super food.

Algae can be taken as natural supplements, either ground or as capsules or tablets. Dried algae, such as kombu, can also be added to soups and rice to give a delicious flavour, as well as a boost of nutrition. Iodine, when taken in excess, can upset your thyroid gland. A moderate quantity of 3-5 grams can happily be taken daily.

Dairy Products

Milk, yoghurt, ghee and fresh cheese are traditionally included as part of the yogic diet. All milk products are sources of complete protein (apart from ghee which does not contain milk proteins).

"MILK IS ALSO VERY IMPORTANT in giving a well balanced mineral content to the diet, when the cows have the right food ....[and] are exposed to sunshine and feed on green pasture. Calcium is the mineral most often deficient in the ordinary diet and milk furnishes a high percentage of this element besides some potassium, sodium, magnesium, phosphorus, sulphur, silicon, and chlorine." **P.Y.**

Unfortunately, in the West, it is very difficult to find good quality milk from cows that have been treated well and raised naturally, i.e. under the sun in green pastures, as Yogananda advocates in the above quote. Nowadays, the majority of the dairy products in the West come from farms where cows live a pitiful life in horrific conditions and where male calves become a by-product, sold for meat. More information on this subject can be found in the appendix "The Birth of Factory Farms".

Apart from the moral issues, milk that comes from 'zero-grazing' cows (which more farms are adopting) lacks the nutrition of milk that comes from cows grazing in green pastures. Most of the vitamins and minerals in milk come from the cows' diet of green grass and sunshine (vitamin D is produced in the body through sunshine). Cows that are kept indoors and fed an unnatural diet do not produce nutritious milk.

Another issue is that, while everyone can digest milk in infancy, most of the world's population lose that ability sometime between the ages of two and five years. The reason is that the body stops producing an enzyme called lactase, necessary for digesting the lactose sugars found in dairy products. Although it is true that in countries where dairy is consumed the body has adapted to a certain extent, many people still have problems digesting milk and consequently develop milk intolerances. Symptoms include gas, stomach aches and often diarrhoea. Many people are more tolerant of yoghurt because a) the lactose is mostly converted into lactic acid, which is what gives the yoghurt its acidic taste, and b) the bacterial cultures used to make the yoghurt produce the enzyme lactase.

A final issue is that dairy products contribute to a glue-like substance called mucoid plaque on the walls of the intestine. The build up of this mucus can create several problems: indigestion, prevention of the assimilation of nutrients, intoxication of your body and even the housing of unwanted organisms.

If you include dairy products in your diet then here are some guidelines to follow:

❖ Buy your produce from local, small-scale farms where you can go and see for yourself if the cows are treated well. Buying organic does not ensure a natural and loving environment for the cows, although it is an improvement to conventional farming. If you can find a biodynamic source for your dairy products then this is the best option. Biodynamic farms treat their cows humanely and lovingly (although the male calves are still a by-product and sent for slaughter, which cannot be avoided in any dairy production). All biodynamic products will be labelled as such.

❖ If you want milk that has some life in it, as well as choosing milk from ethical sources, try and purchase micro-filtered raw milk, recently becoming more readily available on the market. Otherwise choose fresh milk (pasteurised) and avoid long-life milk (UHT, Ultra High Temperature). While fresh milk is only pasteurised (heated to about 63°C), UHT milk is sterilised (heated to 145°C). The high temperatures used in sterilising destroy the milk's nutritional properties as well as its Life Energy.

❖ Eat small amounts of yoghurt and try to limit other forms of dairy, such as milk, butter and cheese.

❖ Choose fresh cheeses rather than matured cheeses.

❖ Instead of using butter, use ghee, which is better for your health. The method for making ghee can be found in the "Basic Recipes" chapter of the recipe section.

A note for vegetarians about cheese: although the use of plant-based or bacterial rennet is common these days, some cheeses contain animal rennet, which is extracted from the inner lining of calves' stomachs when they are slaughtered. For this reason, they cannot strictly speaking be considered vegetarian. In the UK, cheese made with plant based or bacterial rennet is labelled 'suitable for vegetarians'. In the "Basic Recipes" chapter of the recipe section you will find two recipes for fresh homemade cheese made without any rennet: "Yoghurt Cheese" (pg 187) and "Paneer", which is similar to cottage cheese (pg 189).

Eggs

Eggs are another source of complete protein. Unlike dairy, however, eggs are not included in the traditional yogic diet. This said, Yogananda spoke highly of eggs and recommended that his students eat them as part of their vegetarian diet. Eggs are a valuable source of iron and phosphorus and are rich in vitamins A, B and D.

"EGGS ARE MODERATELY RICH *in both protein and fat.*
Both the yolk and white of eggs contain complete proteins....
Eggs are also rich in minerals which are in organic compounds and
very easily absorbed. Because they contain no carbohydrate,
eggs are a good supplementary food to use with carbohydrates." **P.Y.**

Yogananda did, however, also say that chickpeas are better than eggs and encouraged his students to eat less animal foods and more nuts. To those who didn't eat eggs he said to continue not to do so and to substitute them with other protein foods. Whether Yogananda would still advise eating eggs, in a day and age where so many alternative vegetarian proteins are readily available, is unknown. The issue with egg production is much the same as with milk production. Although most people are becoming aware of the pitiful conditions of caged hens, it is lit-

tle known that barn, free-range and organic egg farming are not much better, and by no means a solution. More information on the life of these hens can be found in the same appendix as mentioned above, "The Birth of Factory Farms".

If you choose to eat eggs, the best solution is to buy directly from a small, local farm, where hens live a longer life in more natural conditions.

Meat

There are many different aspects to take into account when considering meat-eating as part of the human diet: health risks, environmental impact, moral questions and even spiritual reflections. The spiritual side will be addressed in part two of the book in the chapter "Spiritual Vegetarianism".

At the core of the moral issues is ahimsa or non-violence, a well-known term thanks to the life-long mission of Mahatma Ghandi. Ahimsa means to wish no harm to any living creature on earth. It comes from the wisdom that we will never be at peace with ourselves if we are not at peace with all that surrounds us, of which we are a part. It is the practice of love and respect for every expression of the Divine on Earth.

> *"WHEN WE OURSELVES are living tombs*
> *of animals that have been killed, how can we then*
> *expect ideal conditions on earth?"* LEO TOLSTOY[*]

The way in which animals destined to become meat are raised and treated (especially in factory farming), the slaughtering of animals in general and the participation in these acts by eating meat, all go against the practice of ahimsa. These issues are explained more in depth in the appendix "The Birth of Factory Farms".

Morally, we can also question whether it is right to eat meat, or so much of it, when millions of the world's population are dying from hunger. Much of the arable land in the world is used to grow crops to feed livestock instead of people. The West cannot produce enough crops to feed their own livestock, and therefore they import much of it from developing countries. The sad truth is that, while people in developing countries starve, crops are being grown in those same countries to be exported to the meat-eating countries of the West. This is dramatically illustrated by the Ethiopian Famine in 1984. While millions starved to death, Ethiopia was growing linseed cake, cottonseed cake and rapeseed meal to feed livestock in Europe. The reality is that there is more than enough plant-based food in the world to feed each one of its 6 billion inhabitants, but as long as these crops are used to feed livestock, there will continue to be hunger in the world.

In the context of the environment, the negative footprint left by animal agriculture is alarming. Every year gigantic amounts of rainforests are being cut down, most of which are used for cattle grazing pasture. The Amazon rainforest (which alone holds about 20% of the world's freshwater, emits about 20% of the world's oxygen and is home to 10% of all known plant and animal species on earth) has already had one fifth of its forest destroyed. Global warming is arguably the most serious challenge currently facing the human race. Deforestation for animal agriculture is a major contributor due to the increased amounts of carbon dioxide that are being released into the atmosphere. According to the 2006 UN FAO report, "Livestock's Long Shadow", the livestock sector is responsible for 9% of CO_2 emissions. Deforestation is not the only way in which the livestock sector is contributing to global warming. Again, according to the 2006 UN FAO report, animal agriculture is responsible for 37% of methane gas (23 times the global warming potential of carbon dioxide) and 65% of nitrous oxide (296 times the global warming potential of carbon dioxide). It is also responsible for 64% of ammonia emissions, one of the significant contributors to acid rain.

The large amount of water used in animal agriculture is also a cause for concern. It is estimated that it takes over 20,000 litres of water to produce one kilo of beef. In contrast, a kilo of wheat can be produced with just 2,000 litres. The world's

[*] Parham, Barbara. *What's Wrong with Eating Meat?* Ananda Marga Publications, 1979.

freshwater supplies have been created over millions of years but are being depleted faster than they can be replenished. The Ogallala Aquifer in the U.S., one of the world's largest stores of fresh groundwater, is being depleted by a staggering 13 trillion gallons a year. Interestingly, a water saver on your kitchen faucet can save up to 23,000 litres of water per year, more or less the same amount that could be saved by eliminating just a kilo of meat!

Above are mentioned just some of the environmental concerns around animal agriculture. Other concerns include water pollution, degradation of topsoil and threats to biodiversity and ecosystems. As the 2006 FAO report concludes, "The livestock sector emerges as one of the top two or three most significant contributors to the most serious environmental problems, at every scale from local to global… The impact is so significant that it needs to be addressed with urgency."

The health risks involved in meat-eating are many, cancer being one of the more serious risks. There are several different reasons for this:

In order to maximise profits and produce as much meat as quickly and as cheaply as possible, the animals raised in factory farms are given antibiotics, stimulants to increase their appetite and chemical feed mixtures. Many of these chemicals, left as traces in the meat, have been proven to cause cancer in humans.

Secondly, meat is often imported from abroad; it is days after the animal has been slaughtered before the meat reaches the shop. The meat is then bought by the consumer, taken home and placed in the fridge, before it is finally consumed. During this process, the meat is in a continuous state of decay and bacteria continue to infect it. To counteract this, meat is often exposed to high doses of radiation, as radiation kills all known bacteria, good and bad. The process of irradiation, however, creates carcinogenic substances. These include benzene and formaldehyde, as well as several other unidentified chemicals that have not yet been tested for safety. Apart from the risks of cancer, radiation also kills nearly all nutrition. Vitamin B complex, for example, is destroyed by up to 96%. Interestingly, irradiation does not kill mad cow disease, foot and mouth disease or viruses like hepatitis, which are an ever-increasing danger to the meat consumer.

As well as being irradiated, nitrates, colourings and other preservatives are used to make the decomposing greenish-grey meat red again. Chemicals and preservatives, as explained in the chapter "Vitamins Are Crunchy", are known to be a cause of cancer.

Finally, many animals themselves develop cancer while living. (This next part is unpleasant but important.) Often, when animals in factory farms are found to be diseased with cancer, the cancerous part of the corpse is simply chopped off and the rest is sold as meat. In America, for example, after a routine inspection, it was discovered that 25,000 cows with an eye tumour had been sold as beef. Yogananda said he had actually seen butchers doing this. He also clearly says that meat-eating is one of the prime causes of cancer, and that those who continue to eat meat three times a day will almost certainly develop tumours.

Apart from the risks of cancer, meat and animal products are responsible for 95% of food poisoning.*In the UK alone, food poisoning makes millions ill every year and kills hundreds: Salmonella, which is caught from chicken, pork and eggs, is responsible for half a million human illnesses and hundreds of deaths every year; campylobacter, the number one food poisoning bug, found in half of all chicken on shops' shelves, infects millions and kills 80 to 100 people per year; clostridium perfringens, a bug that sheep pick up from infected soil, causes over 50,000 cases of food poisoning a year; and E Coli 0157, found in the gut of cows, is the most common cause of acute kidney failure in children. In Scotland, meat from one butcher's shop killed 20 and made hundreds ill in a single outbreak a few years ago. BSE, still found in hundreds of cattle every year, causes Creutzfeldt-Jakob Disease (CJD) in humans, which is invariably fatal. The reason for all this disease is, quite simply, the unsanitary and filthy conditions the animals are forced to live in. Animals are crammed into small enclosures and made to live in their own excrement. Sick animals often remain in the enclosure with the rest of the animals, and dead and decomposing animals are often left just lying around. All in all, an ideal breeding ground for disease.

The slaughterhouse is another contributing factor to diseased meat. Terrified animals in slaughterhouses defecate uncontrollably. At slaughter and during gutting and processing, faeces and intestinal contents infect the flesh used for meat. Equipment, water and people working there easily become contaminated, spreading parasites, bacteria and viruses.

Yogananda says that pigs, especially, carry a lot of disease, and if you look at the meat through a microscope, you will see it is filled with germs. He says that pigs eat angleworms, which have been found to carry pneumonia, and pork tastes so sweet because of the pus in the pig's system.

Fish meat can also be a danger to health. Fish are contaminated by all the pollutants we dump in the sea: mercury, dioxins, PCBs (Polychlorinated Biphenyl) and other toxic substances. Many

* *Viva! – Vegetarians International Voice for Animals.* Bristol, UK: Viva! Available at http://www.viva.org.uk/campaigns/dirty meat/expanded.htm

fish also carry parasites, and farmed fish, such as salmon, are dosed with drugs in an attempt to keep disease at bay.

What happens when you eat meat and it comes into contact with your digestive system? Human beings have very long digestive tracts, about 10-12 times the length of their bodies, resembling those of frugivorous or fruit-eating animals. Carnivores have very short digestive tracts, only about 3-5 times the length of their bodies, designed to expel decomposing meat from the body as quickly as possible. Meat passes unnaturally slowly through the human digestive tract; it takes about five days before it is fully digested and expelled. During this time, the poisons, chemicals and diseases that the meat contains are in constant contact with your digestive organs. It is not surprising that cancer of the intestines is so common among meat eaters.

"MEAT... IS HIGHLY CONSTIPATING
*and acts as a retainer of body poisons
and a harbinger of disease..."* **P.Y.**

Apart from risks caused by chemical feeds, antibiotics, irradiation, nitrates, colourings, preservatives, bacteria, viruses and disease, meat is also high in saturated fats. Saturated fats are the main cause of high blood cholesterol levels which, as you may know, can lead to serious problems. Cholesterol is a wax-like substance. When there is too much cholesterol in your blood, deposits build up inside your arteries. These deposits, called plaque, can narrow your arteries enough to slow or block blood flow. This is the cause of high blood pressure, heart attacks, heart disease and strokes. It is a well-known fact that vegetarians suffer much less from these diseases and generally have longer life spans than meat eaters have. Populations, in fact, that live principally on meat have a shorter average life span: The Kirgese, a nomadic meat-eating tribe in Eastern Russia, rarely live to be over the age of 40. Among primarily vegetarian populations, it is not unusual to find people living for over 100 years.

The common belief that it's necessary to eat a large amount of protein and that animal protein, such as meat, eggs, fish and dairy, is the best choice, constitutes 'The Protein Myth' described in this chapter. As you have read, plant proteins can provide you with all your protein needs. Plant proteins are full of nutrition, meaning that they are actually strengthening your health, instead of putting it at risk.

Fact Boxes

In Part Four of the book, "Table Talk", Christina relates her experience of how she became vegetarian. See: "A Single Matchstick".

- Incidences of **the most common tumours** (colon, breast, prostate, pancreas) are much higher among people who eat meat (70% of all people inflicted with these tumours) compared to vegetarians (only 30%).

- Vegetarians in Western countries have lower incidents of **obesity and diabetes** compared to non-vegetarians.

- In the UK, every three minutes someone dies of **heart disease**, one of which the main causes is an excessive consumption of fats and animal proteins. A vegetarian diet reduces the risk of death by heart disease by 24%.

- **High blood pressure** in vegetarians is one third to one half that of meat eaters.

- 95% of all **food poisoning** comes from meat and animal products.

- Vegetarians perform better on **endurance tests**. They can perform an endurance task from two to three times longer and can recover five times faster than meat eaters can.

- **Ed Moses,** two-time Olympic gold medalist for 400 m hurdles, is vegetarian!

- **Martina Navratilova,** legendary tennis champion with 166 titles and nine-time Wimbledon winner, is vegetarian!

- **Carl Lewis,** nine-time Olympic gold medallist and eight-time World Championships gold medallist for 100 m, 200 m and long jump events, is vegan!

- **Dave Scott,** the only man to win the Ironman Triathlon (2.4 miles swim,112 miles cycle, 26 miles run), more than twice (six-time winner), is vegetarian!

- **Sixto Linares,** world record holder for the 24 hour Triathlon (4.8 miles swim, 185 miles cycle, 52.5 miles run), is vegetarian!

- **Elephants and rhinoceroses,** two of the world's strongest animals, are both vegetarian!

- Throughout the world there are already **over 500 million vegetarians**.

Helpful Hints

❖ Feeling dehydrated? It could be that you are eating too much protein. Try reducing your protein intake to only 20% of your dietary intake.

❖ Substitute regular milk with soya, oat or almond milk and regular yoghurt for soya yoghurt. And when you eat dairy, buy biodynamic!

❖ Include tofu and seitan in your diet at least once a week. Making them at home is really fun and easy!

❖ Try making some traditional meat recipes with seitan instead of meat.

❖ Make sprouts an essential part of your daily diet. They can be eaten in salads, juiced in a juicer or squeezed into a sandwich! Even if you don't like the taste, think of them like a medicine.

❖ Try some traditional grain and legume combinations, such as rice and dhal, or pasta and chickpeas.

❖ Make your own homemade nut butters and have a spoonful every day.

The Chef Recommends...

❖ Yoghurt Cheese / **187**

❖ Red Lentil and Tomato Dhal / **305**

❖ Tofu Burgers with Lemon-Parsley Sauce / **322**

❖ Seitan-Sunflower Salad / **323**

❖ Almond Butter / **228**

PART TWO

Feeding the Soul

CHAPTER 8

Spiritualising Your Diet

"IT IS NECESSARY *to eat the proper food
in order to make a proper brain as well as a proper body.
All food has some relation to the mind.*" **P.Y.**

Until now, we have looked at food from physical and energetical standpoints; of how eating the correct foods can help you to have physical health and a high level of Life Energy. Correct food, however, is important not only for the health of your body; it is also important for your mental, and also spiritual, well-being.

Sattwas, Rajas and Tamas

The Hindu scriptures say that everything in this world contains vibrations of (latent) consciousness. Three levels of consciousness exist: sattwas, or elevating consciousness; rajas, or activating consciousness; and tamas, or darkening consciousness. The whole universe is a product of the mixture of these three qualities, known as gunas.

Each human being also manifests these three qualities. Your level of consciousness is influenced by your surroundings and the information you receive from them through your senses. If you expose yourself to sattwas, you will experience an elevation in your consciousness; if you expose yourself to rajas, you will experience restlessness and agitation; if you expose yourself to tamas, you will experience inertia and dull-mindedness. Although everyone manifests all three of the gunas to some degree, you are likely to manifest one quality more than the others. Let's take a closer look at how these three qualities are manifested in people.

Sattwic people tend to be calm, centred and peaceful yet full of bubbling joy. Their gestures are slow and graceful; their eyes are shining and full of love; their

thoughts are clear and their words are wise. Sattwic people are kind and generous and find their happiness in the happiness of others. The Dalai Lama is one such person who manifests predominantly sattwas.

> "THE SATTWIC PERSON *hears goodness*
> *and purity in all things, sees it reflected in all*
> *things, finds reminders of God in everything that*
> *he feels, tastes and smells. What he is in himself,*
> *he projects onto the world around him."* *

Rajasic people are over-stimulated. They can be restless, agitated, stressed, nervous, impatient, dismissive, domineering and centred in ego-power and ego-desire. The business world is full of rajasic influences (telephones, computers, deadlines, money and competition) and, as such, many business people manifest rajasic qualities. Because a rajasic mind is so used to being stimulated, rajasic people often feel uncomfortable with silence and stillness. They seek their happiness instead in adventure, excitement, 'fun and games' and physical or material challenges.

> "THE RAJASIC PERSON... *sees a beautiful mountain brook*
> *and thinks only, 'how much electrical power could I harness*
> *from this flowing water to make me rich?' He sees a beautiful*
> *painting and asks only, 'Monetarily, what is it worth?' He hears*
> *beautiful music and thinks only, 'It needs a more sensual beat.'*
> *He tastes delicious food, and thinks, 'It needs more spicing.'*
> *And so it goes for him with every sensory experience."*

Tamasic people can be dull-minded, unenthusiastic and lazy, or negative, irrational and even evil. They express contractive attitudes, are selfish and self-involved and seek their happiness solely through pleasure, ease or whatever pleases them personally. The classic 'coach potato' is tamasic. A drunkard, lying intoxicated on the street, is also tamasic.

> "TAMAS *is that quality in human nature (born, however, of*
> *cosmic nature) which attracts misery of all kinds. It creates such*
> *a thick wall around the ego that it causes one to view himself and*
> *his own interests as quite unrelated to anybody else's."*

This quote, as are the next two quotes, is taken from *The Essence of the Bhagavad Gita Explained by Paramhansa Yogananda* by Swami Kriyananda, Ananda Sangha Publications, 2006.

Reflecting the Moon within You

In truth, your soul, being a reflection of Spirit, is already perfect. Your level of consciousness, therefore, can only be described as your ability (or the ability of your mind) to perceive and reflect that perfection within you. To illustrate, a metaphor can be used. Imagine it is night time. Now imagine a lake; a beautiful, clear, calm lake. Nothing and nobody are around. Everything is still, everything is peaceful. The lake too, is perfectly still. Now look into the lake. Do you see the reflection of the moon? Because of the stillness and clearness of the lake, the moon is reflected in its full glory; whole, complete, undistorted. The calm and clear lake is the sattwic mind.

Now imagine the same lake a few minutes later. A group of teenagers come to take a midnight swim. They get into the lake and start splashing around, screaming and shouting to each other, causing numerous ripples on the surface of the lake. Now look at the reflection of the moon. Do you see that it is distorted, appearing to be agitated but only so because of the agitation of the lake itself? The agitated lake is the rajasic mind.

Once again, imagine the same lake. It is several years later and the lake has been forgotten and abused. People no longer come here to enjoy its beauty but to dump their rubbish. The lake is full of paper, plastic, rotten food and empty beer cans. Now look in the lake. Can you see the reflection of the moon? The lake is so full of dirt and rubbish that, even though the moon is shining in the sky, it is impossible to see its reflection. The polluted lake is the tamasic mind.

The information that you receive through your senses is sent as an impulse through the nerves to the brain, where it is turned into specific thoughts, feelings, ideas and perceptions in the mind. Some impulses have a calming and harmonious effect on the mind, allowing the moon to be reflected perfectly. These impulses are sattwic. Some impulses agitate and irritate the mind, distorting the reflection of the moon. These impulses are rajasic. Some impulses numb and dull the mind, clouding completely the reflection of the moon. These impulses are tamasic. This is why, if you are interested in experiencing your true Self, it is important to receive sattwic impulses, by keeping sattwic company, living in a sattwic environment, listening to sattwic music and reading sattwic books, etc.

The Important Role of the Food You Eat

As with everything in this universe, food also carries specific vibrations that, when you eat, are transmitted to your brain through your nervous system. All food, therefore, according to the type of vibration that it contains, can be classified as sattwic, rajasic or tamasic.

> "THE QUALITY *of the food's taste and color is all reported to the brain through the nerves of taste and sight, and is experienced as specific pleasant or unpleasant sensations. These sensations are elaborated into perceptions and conceptions. Repeated conceptions about food form definite mental habits and manifest themselves as material, active or spiritual qualities."* **P.Y.**

The influence of food on the mind should not be underestimated. Many spiritual teachers say that it is the easiest and most direct way to influence your mind. Your thoughts, actions and health are, to a large extent, determined by the foods you eat. Rishis, the ancient seers of India, lived on only fruit and raw food. This helped purify their minds and enable them to perceive deep spiritual truths.

Sattwic Food

Protective foods (fruit, vegetables, nuts, seeds, sprouts, grains, legumes, etc.) have a harmonious and strengthening effect on your mind and permit Life Energy to flow freely through your body.* All protective foods, therefore, in their natural state, are sattwic. A little milk or fresh milk product from cows treated with love and wisdom is sattwic, but too much becomes rajasic. Of all the sattwic foods, fruit is said to manifest the sattwa guna in its purest form.

Sattwic foods, as described by Yogananda, each vibrate with

> "FOODS, TOO, *are subject to the Law of Vibration, and it is incumbent upon us… to cultivate the Quality of discrimination in our choice from among those having the highest rate of vibration, thus taking our fate out of the hands of Chance."* **P.Y.**

A strong mind = a strong will. The greater the will, the greater the flow of energy.

a specific spiritual quality. As such, eating specific foods can help you to develop specific spiritual qualities. Bananas carry a vibration of humility, rooted in calmness; grapes, of devotion and divine love; lettuce, of calmness; and corn, of mental vitality. A full list follows at the end of this chapter. More generally, nuts help deep thinking and are good for brain power and concentration; fruit develops heart and spiritual qualities; vegetables give power of management over the bodily adjustment to physiological conditions; grains produce strength of character; and milk and milk products give enthusiasm and fresh energy.

Rajasic Foods

Excessively hot, spicy, salted or otherwise strongly flavoured foods are irritating and disturbing to the equilibrium of your mind and obstruct the normal flow of Life Energy in your body. They are, therefore, rajasic. These include horseradish, mustard, black pepper, soya sauce, onions, garlic and chilli. Fish, fowl, lamb, eggs, coffee, black tea, chocolate and sugar are also rajasic.

Sattwic foods, when over-flavoured, become rajasic. They also become rajasic by overcooking and processing. Habitual eating of heavily-flavoured, overcooked or processed foods, therefore, will make you irritated, restless, changeable and ill-balanced.

> "FORGET THE CREAMED SAUCES
> *and the white flour gravies, as well as the salt and*
> *pepper cellars, in preparing vegetables. Eat your vegetables*
> *as near their natural state as a wise Mother Nature*
> *presented them to us, merely adding a bit of fresh sweet*
> *(unsalted) butter, olive oil, home-made salad dressing,*
> *minced or powdered garlic, thyme, or any other*
> *of your favorite flavoring herbs."* **P.Y.**

Rajasic foods, because of their irritating effect on the mind and nervous system, are usually excluded from the yogic diet. This said, in the West, where the demands of the environment are themselves so rajasic, a little of the right kinds of rajasic foods can be desirable. The right kinds include foods which have medicinal and nutritional properties, such as onions, garlic and eggs. Yogananda, in fact, fed his students these latter three foods.

Tamasic Food

Odorous, putrefied, artificial, devitalised, chemical-containing, fatty and overly starchy foods are unnatural to the body and have a stultifying and dulling effect on the mind. They are, therefore, tamasic. Beef, veal, pork, matured cheeses, white sugar, coca-cola, typical fast food and deep-fried foods are all tamasic.

Fresh food left to go stale or rotten becomes tamasic as well as cooked food left to go cold.

"PEOPLE WHO TRY TO *boost their production by chemical means don't understand that life depends on the life-force, and not on that which is lifeless.*" **S.K.**

Too Much Food Is Tamasic

"THE CHIEF ABUSE OF THE BODY *lies in overloading it with unnecessary food.*" **S.K.**

Some unwelcome news for most of us. All food, when eaten in excess, blocks the energy flow in your nerves and has a dulling effect on your mind. This means that, unless eaten in moderation, even fruit (or any sattwic food) becomes tamasic.

These days, in a society where we have been trained to eat for pleasure and not for hunger, overeating is not uncommon. As a great Indian master, Satya Sai Baba has said, "We do not breathe more air than is necessary nor drink more water than is necessary to satisfy our thirst, but we don't think twice about overfilling our stomachs with unnecessary food." Even the most health-conscious people often overeat. A good guide is to stop eating before you are completely full: at least one quarter of your stomach should remain empty. This, perhaps, is the most difficult piece of advice given in this book.

Another good habit is to omit at least one meal every day as often as you can. Three meals a day are not always necessary. Try to skip breakfast, lunch or dinner either completely or by substituting that meal with a glass of fruit or vegetable juice or a hot cup of herbal tea. This is very purifying for the digestive system, as well as for the mind.

"USE YOUR WILL POWER *to resist the temptation of eating three meals every day, by which the whole system, including the cells, the heart, the nerves, the stomach, has to work continuously. Give your intelligent machine occasional rest by cutting off breakfast, lunch or dinner every day.*" **P.Y.**

Finally, while it is good to eat at regular times, it is not good to eat unless you are hungry. If you are not hungry at mealtimes, then wait until later to eat or skip the meal completely.

To sum up, by eating protective foods in moderate quantities, you will not only notice benefits and positive changes on a physical level but also on a mental level. As your thoughts, emotions and behaviour become gradually calmer and quieter, you will start to appreciate things around you that you may never have noticed before, whether it be the little bird that sweetly sings to wake you up in the morning or the elderly man down the road who smiles at you with warmth and understanding.

Sattwic, Rajasic and Tamasic Food

Sattwic	Rajasic	Tamasic
Nutritious	Refined	Chemical
Natural	Processed	Artificial
Fresh	Overcooked	Devitalised
Organic	Frozen	Odorous
Raw	Tinned	Heavy
Lightly cooked	Excessively-flavoured	Starchy
Light		Stale
Simple		Rotten
Mildly flavoured		Deep-fried or fatty

Sattwic	Rajasic	Tamasic
Fresh and dried fruit	Poultry	Beef
Nuts	Lamb	Veal
Coconut	Fish	Pork
Seeds	Eggs	Fast food
Vegetables	Too much dairy	Fizzy drinks
Sprouts	Potatoes	Matured cheese
Soya	Brown sugar	White sugar
Whole grains	Chocolate	Leftovers
Fresh dairy *(in small quantities and from cows treated with love and wisdom)*	Hot spices	Alcohol
	Pepper	Too much food
Legumes	Onions	
Cold-pressed oils	Garlic	
Algae	Black tea	
Natural sweeteners	Coffee	
Carob	Tobacco	
Lots of still water		

In Part Four of the book, "Table Talk", Tejindra tells us about how he first started to observe the effect that different foods had on his consciousness. See: "You Are What You Eat".

Spiritual Qualities of Some Foods

(as taught by Paramhansa Yogananda)

Almonds	Self control and moral vigour
Apples	Peaceful clarity
Avocados	Good memory
Bananas	Humility rooted in calmness
Beetroots	Courage
Blackberries	Purity of thought
Cherries	Cheerfulness
Coconuts	Uplifted spiritual awareness
Corn	Mental vitality
Dates	Tender sweetness
Figs	Flexibility, self-acceptance
Fruits of the Forest	Help to calm thoughts
Grains	Strength of character
Grapes	Devotion, divine love
Honey	Self control
Lettuce	Calmness
Maple syrup	Mental freshness
Milk	Enthusiasm, fresh energy
Oranges, lemons	Enthusiasm, hope
Peaches	Unselfishness
Pears	Peacefulness and for emergencies
Pineapples	Self-assurance
Raspberries	Kindness, compassion
Rice, brown	Sweetness, mildness
Spinach	Simplicity, guilelessness
Strawberries	Dignity
Tomatoes	Mental strength and endurance
Wheat	Refinement of good principles

In the 1970s, Lila Devi, a member of the Ananda community near Nevada City in California, was guided by Swami Kriyananda to create the *Spirit in Nature Essences*. *Spirit in Nature Essences* are essences made from the blossoms of fruit and vegetables, which, when taken internally, stimulate specific spiritual qualities in you (according to the above list by Yogananda). Lila Devi uses only the most pure and perfect blossoms and prays and meditates before she picks them. The resulting essences are very powerful and have helped many people to bring about important changes in their lives.

Helpful Hints

❖ Eat less cooked food. Raw food will help to calm your mind.

❖ Cut back on spices and heavy flavourings.

❖ Cultivate moderation: try to eat smaller meals and skip a meal whenever you're not hungry.

❖ Resist the temptation to 'binge' on junk food when you're emotionally upset; it will only make matters worse.

❖ Surround yourself with calming pictures, colours, music, books and friends.

❖ Observe your mind; how does it change in correlation to the food you eat?

❖ Eat lots of fresh fruit, one of the most sattwic foods.

❖ Try to ensure that the highest percentage of the food you eat is from the sattwic list.

The Chef Recommends...

❖ Carrot-Pineapple Cocktail / **199**

❖ Apple Seedy Smoothie / **203**

❖ Avocado, Kiwi and Walnut Salad / **209**

❖ Creamy Yoghurt Cheese Salad / **214**

❖ Almond-Cardamom Balls / **356**

CHAPTER 9

Spiritual Vegetarianism

Yogananda advises those who wish to follow a spiritual life to refrain from eating meat. Meat, especially beef, veal and pork, is harmful to the mind and to spiritual development.

"SINCE THE EXPRESSION of the soul of a person is dependent upon the condition of his body, and his body is dependent upon food, it is desirable to know not only the physical, but also the spiritual and psychical effects of food." **P.Y.**

Who am I?

As discussed in the last chapter, when we eat food, we absorb the vibrations of consciousness contained within it. Man has been given the gift of self-awareness. It is this self-awareness and the ability to enquire, "Who am I?" and "What is my purpose?" that gives him the potential to realise the Divinity within him. Animals are much less evolved than humans and live more by instinct than by self-awareness. When you eat meat, you absorb the vibrations of that animal consciousness. The more your mind is pulled towards animal consciousness, the less you will experience spiritual consciousness.

What's more, as Yogananda explains in the following quote, the consciousness that you possess works like a magnet. This magnet will attract to you people and situations that vibrate on the same level.

"...TOO MUCH MEAT causes you to lose your magnetism because animal magnetism tampers with your spiritual magnetism. Meat causes you to concentrate upon the physical plane too much, and you attract more or less physical companions instead of spiritual ones." **P.Y.**

The Aggressiveness
of the West

Animals, when they are slaughtered, feel intense anguish, fear and anger. We have already discussed the fact that these emotions fill the animals' bodies with toxins. More than this, however, the emotions are implanted in the animals' bodies as vibrations and hence, absorbed into the consciousness of the person who eats the meat. It is no coincidence, Yogananda says, that aggressive tendencies are more prevalent in nations where people eat a lot of meat and that more peaceful tendencies prevail in nations where the common diet is vegetarian.

> "ANIMALS, *when killed, leave vibrations*
> *of fear, anger and suffering in their meat,*
> *which affect the mind of the consumer."* **P.Y.**

Meat, because of the (aggressive) emotions contained within it, can inhibit you from experiencing two fundamental goals of the spiritual path: inner peace and harmony.

Changing Habits

We have established that the information that you receive through your senses has a definite effect on your level of consciousness. The other half of the story is that your level of consciousness determines the things to which you are attracted and want to experience through your senses. The sattwic person, for example, loves to be in nature, listen to beautiful music and be with spiritually-minded people. The rajasic person loves to be in bars, nightclubs and busy places, listen to music with a heavy (sensual) beat and be in the company of other rajasic people. The tamasic person likes to stay in bed, watch television and argue.

So it is with food: your level of consciousness determines the very food to which you are attracted. The *Bhagavad Gita* says:

> "FOODS THAT INCREASE VITALITY,
> *endurance, health, cheerfulness, and good appetite;*
> *and that are sweet, soft, substantial and agreeable are*
> *liked by the pure-minded (sattwic) persons."* **P.Y.**

> "FOODS THAT ARE BITTER, *sour,*
> *saltish, excessively hot, pungent, harsh, and*
> *burning are preferred by rajasic men and*
> *produce pain, sorrow and disease."* **P.Y.**

"FOODS THAT ARE STALE,
worthless, putrid, refuse and impure
are liked by tamasic persons." **P.Y.** *

Sudden changes in diet are usually unsuccessful because the mind still craves the food you used to eat. The body, being connected to the mind, can also suffer withdrawal symptoms. Giving up meat can be one of the hardest challenges. Although some people have become vegetarian from one moment to the next, most people find it easier to give up meat gradually. There is an interesting story about Yogananda's first disciple in America, Dr. Lewis. Wanting to follow the vegetarian diet that Yogananda recommended, Dr. Lewis gave up eating meat. Soon after, he began to suffer mysterious aches and pains in his body. He went to numerous doctors, but none were able to diagnose the cause. Finally, he asked Yogananda if he knew what the cause might be. Yogananda replied that the pains were because his body had been accustomed to eating meat and out of past habit, his cells were crying out for it. He recommended that Dr. Lewis eat a little meat once a week and the pains would disappear. Dr. Lewis followed his advice and was almost immediately cured. Some years later he was able to give up meat completely.

> "BAD HABITS OF EATING *make the*
> *human system demand wrong foods. In such*
> *cases the right food, although disagreeable*
> *to the system, should be taken in very small*
> *quantities, and then gradually increased until*
> *the system responds to normal food."* **P.Y.**

Cows and pigs have a much more developed nervous system than lambs, chickens and fish. Because of this, they feel pain more easily, and therefore, resist death more. Pork, beef and veal carry the strongest vibrations of fear, anguish and anger and should be the first categories of meat to omit. Lamb, chicken and fish can be given up gradually, according to individual needs.

In Part Four of the book, "Table Talk", Rashmi and Tejindra relate how giving up meat helped them to regain their serenity. See: "The Power of Food" and "Vegetarian Fearlessness".

---

* *Bhagavad Gita* 17, 8-10. These three quotations are taken from *The Essence of the Bhagavad Gita Explained by Paramhansa Yogananda* by Swami Kriyananda, Ananda Sangha Publications, 2006.

Helpful Hints

❖ Think of small steps you can take to make your life more sattwic. Start to apply these steps today.

❖ Visit the VIVA (Vegetarians International Voice for Animals) website, www.viva.org.uk or the European Vegetarian Union website www.euroveg.eu for more information on becoming vegetarian.

❖ If you eat meat, start to incorporate a little tofu and seitan into your menus. Find recipes that make them just as appealing to you as meat.

❖ Again, if you eat meat, experiment by giving it up for a week or two and see if you notice any difference in your behaviour.

❖ Stand back and be objective; in what way could meat be influencing your mind?

The Chef Recommends...

❖ Creamy Mushroom, Leek and Tofu Pastries / **316**

❖ Roast Vegetable Tofu "Sandwich" / **320**

❖ Seitan Steaks / **326**

❖ Seitan and Mushrooms in Nutritional Yeast Gravy / **326**

❖ Seitan and Roast Pepper Kebabs with Tahini Sauce / **329**

CHAPTER 10

Good Vibrations in the Kitchen

"MOMMY'S OUT IN THE KITCHEN,
she's making our dinner, I hear by the clink of the pans,
That she's happy, just cooking and knowing we're near her:
Her happiness flows from her hands."

Song by Swami Kriyananda

Food is, in its essence, sattwic, rajasic or tamasic. Just as your own level of consciousness is influenced by the things that surround it, so it is with food and indeed everything in this world. Every person coming into contact with the food – those who cultivate it, harvest it, process it, package it and sell it – all these people infuse it with their own level of consciousness or vibration.

The person who cooks the food, more than any other who comes into contact with it, has the power to influence its vibrations. Why is it that mum's cooking is always more satisfying than even the best food served in high-class restaurants? She's not necessarily better at cooking than the professionals but, when she cooks, she infuses her food with the love she feels for her family, and it's these special vibrations that make her food "the best".

In India, great importance is given to the vibrations with which food is prepared. Cooks are often from the Brahmin caste, traditionally considered the purest caste. Many highly developed spiritual people choose their own personal cook, who they trust to prepare their food with love. If the cook must go away for a few days, the person may even fast, rather than eating food cooked by someone else who is unknown to them. The great master, Sri Ramakrishna, for example, would not accept food prepared by worldly people. If such food was given to him unknowingly, he would feel that his whole body was burning.

"ACTIVITY *is not so much a time for*
receiving energy as for giving it…" **S.K.**

Cooking for others is one of the easiest and most direct ways to affect their consciousness. When you cook, therefore, it's important to keep your thoughts and feelings as uplifted as possible so that the vibrations you put into the food are pure and sattwic. If you find yourself in a bad mood one day or upset emotionally, it would be best not to cook for others.

Outlined below are some guidelines that you can use to keep your mind uplifted while you cook.

Becoming Centred

Before cooking, take a few moments to sit quietly, close your eyes and be inwardly calm. In those few moments, inwardly ask to be a channel of love and joy for all those who will eat the food. Once you feel calm and your heart feels open, you are ready to begin.

Concentration

Concentration is of utmost importance. Your soul, as an expression of Spirit, exists in the eternal Now; not in the past nor in the future. When your mind is still, completely absorbed in the present moment, you are able to reflect the Divine within you (remember the example of the calm lake), and soul qualities will fill your food.

When cooking, therefore try to concentrate on the task at hand. If you are peeling carrots, for example, focus on them and consciously infuse them with love and joy.

Practising concentration in the kitchen will help you to become more concentrated and therefore more successful in every aspect of your life, including meditation.

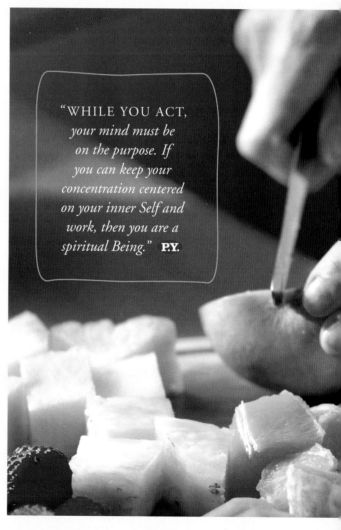

"WHILE YOU ACT, *your mind must be on the purpose. If you can keep your concentration centered on your inner Self and work, then you are a spiritual Being.*" **P.Y.**

Japa

Another practice that helps to focus the mind is japa. Japa is the continuous repetition of a sacred or uplifting word or phrase, whether repeated mentally or out loud.

Many people choose to repeat Sanskrit mantras when doing japa. A mantra is a sacred word, or a combination of sacred words, that carry a specific spiritual vibration. The ancient rishis (seers) of India declared that all creation is a manifestation of sound vibration, Aum* being the sound from which all other sounds come forth. Through deep meditation, they were able to experience the effects of different sounds on their consciousness and, in doing so, they developed the ancient language of Sanskrit. Sanskrit words, therefore, due to them being created purely because of their vibratory influence, are particularly powerful. Even if the Sanskrit words have no significance to your mind, the vibrations of the words have a transforming effect on every level of your consciousness. Some popular mantras are:

❖ **Om Sri Ram, Jai Ram, Jai Jai Ram**
(Lord Rama! Victory to Rama! Victory, Victory to Rama! Aum)

❖ **Om Namo Bhagavate Vasudevaya**
(Aum, I Bow to the Lord Vasudeva, or Krishna)

❖ **Om Namah Shivaya**
(Aum, I Bow to Lord Shiva, Destroyer of Evil)

❖ Simply the word *Aum*

Although Sanskrit words have the most powerful influence on your consciousness, words of all languages carry vibrations. The word peace, for example, has a calming effect on your mind. You have probably heard of the many experiments done by the scientist Masaru Emoto on water crystals and how they are influenced by words and thoughts. In this way science is proving what the ancient rishis declared thousands of years ago! Whatever language you choose for your devotional phrase, japa will have an uplifting effect on your consciousness.

An important side issue is that the food you are preparing, as well as being indirectly influenced by the uplifting of your own consciousness, will also be directly influenced by the vibration of your devotional words. The practice of japa while cooking, therefore, carries double benefits!

*Aum Amen

Uplifting Music

*"ONE CANNOT listen to music sensitively without
soon becoming aware that it conveys more than sounds,
that it is a vehicle for moods, for states of consciousness.
Sound has power. It is vibration."* **S.K.**

Along the same lines as japa, music, being sound, carries specific spiritual vibrations. Playing music that is sattwic while cooking is an excellent way to attune yourself to your soul qualities. What is sattwic music? Sattwic music can be defined in the following way: it is always uplifting and fills you with a sense of expansion. A lot of classical music, music used for Reiki and other healing techniques, music based on the sounds of nature and the music of Swami Kriyananda, are all examples of sattwic music. Rajasic music, on the other hand, may seem to uplift you but, in fact, only stimulates and aggravates your nervous system. Most pop and rock music with a fast, heavy beat is rajasic. Tamasic music is negative and depressing and has a darkening effect on your mind. Heavy metal music, for example, is tamasic.

Similar to the experiments done on water crystals, in order to see the effect that sound has on matter, science is also taking a keen interest on the effect that music has on matter: Numerous experiments have been conducted on the reaction of plants. When classical music is played, as if wanting to absorb the sattwic vibrations of that music, the plant starts to grow in the direction of the speakers. When rajasic or tamasic music is played, the opposite effect occurs: as if trying to escape from harmful vibrations, the plant starts to grow away from the speakers. These experiments clearly demonstrate the beneficial or destructive vibrations that music can have and transmit.

Singing along with, or simply listening to, sattwic music opens you to the vibration contained within it. That vibration could be joy, devotion, friendship, harmony, beauty or any other soul quality. These vibrations, through the change in your consciousness, will be infused in your food. As with japa, the music will also have a direct influence on the vibration of your food.

Conversations

Chatting and talking while cooking can be distracting. The ideal is to remain in peaceful silence, filled with sattwic thoughts and feelings, which expand into the food you're preparing. If you do choose to engage in conversation with others, be conscious of what you are talking about. Heavy political discussions, conversations about war and gossip about other people, for example, have a depressing effect on your consciousness. Try to keep the conversation on pleasant and cheerful topics. In the Ananda kitchen, we love to share spiritually uplifting stories with each other, from the Indian epics, for example, or of saints and devotees or our own inspiring experiences on the spiritual path. Stories that make you laugh are especially good to share while cooking!

Television and radio can also be included as conversations. In general, they carry rajasic vibrations and are distracting to the mind that is trying to stay focused. Listening to recorded spiritual discourses while you cook would be a good alternative.

A Sattwic Kitchen

The environment in which you cook has a strong influence on your consciousness. Lots of windows, good lighting, colourful curtains, inspiring pictures and fresh flowers or potted plants can help to make your kitchen sattwic. Surfaces should be kept clean, organised and free from clutter.

Picking at Food

Continuous picking at the food you're preparing lowers its vibration. Taste the food only when necessary and do so with the consciousness that you want it to taste as nice as possible for those who will eat it. Most Indians don't taste the food at all while cooking, preferring to be guided by intuition and experience.

Yogananda had a special method that he used for cooking, without tasting or measuring. He would first produce the exact taste of the dish he was about to prepare in his mouth. He then gathered together the ingredients needed to reproduce the same taste in the food. By using his intuition he never made mistakes in the kitchen and always knew how the food was going to turn out.

The Flipside of the Coin

Given above are many ways in which you can make sure that the food you prepare for others is as sattwic as possible. The flipside of the coin is: has the food that you eat been infused with sattwic vibrations? If you often eat in public places, the answer is: probably not. As practised by previously mentioned spiritual persons of India, it's wise to stick to food prepared by hands you know and trust. Once you have become more aware of the vibrations contained in food however, you will naturally find that food prepared with unsattwic hands is unappealing.

Sattwic Vibrations Help Digestion

The vibrations the cook puts into the food also have a definite influence on how easily it is digested. Have you ever noticed how sometimes, even though tastily prepared, the food you eat sits heavily in your stomach for hours? And how the same meal prepared by someone else seems to be digested easily and quickly? The difference is nothing more than the cook's vibrations.

Ananda: the Vibration of Joy!

The Ananda kitchen is renowned for its food. Sometimes the food we serve is original and creative, combining together ingredients that people may never have tasted before. Just as often, however, we love to serve simple, traditional recipes, such as mashed potatoes or pasta with tomato sauce, which everyone has eaten hundreds of times before. No matter what we prepare, however, people often comment that there's something different about our food; that it tastes 'special'. That is the vibration. By following the above guidelines, people will feel that your food is also 'special'. An interesting fact is that, even when the recipe doesn't turn out as well as you had hoped, because of the good vibrations you put in it, people will still think that it's delicious!

In Part Four of the book, "Table Talk", Namasya tells us about her experiences of cooking with this higher consciousness at Ananda; and Manu about how she became aware of the difference it makes when food is cooked with love. See: "Nourishing the Soul" and "The Secret's in the Vibration".

Helpful Hints

❖ Try not to cook for others while you are angry or upset. Take a shower, a brisk walk or a few deep breaths; put on some uplifting music and begin to cook with fresh energy.

❖ Allow time for cooking. When you can work slowly, it is easier to be calm.

❖ Begin with simple menus and get to know them well. It will be easier to focus on *how* you are cooking, rather than *what* you are cooking.

❖ Choose a *mantra* that inspires you and use it from the moment you start to cook (or indeed, during any activity!).

❖ Keep a selection of uplifting music and spiritual discourses in your kitchen that you can listen to while you cook.

❖ Remove the television from your kitchen and replace it with something that reminds you to remain inwardly focused.

❖ Make your kitchen beautiful! Use flowers, potted plants, colourful curtains and joyful pictures.

❖ Choose restaurants that have an uplifting energy: lots of light, smiling faces and sattwic music.

The Chef Recommends...

❖ CD: *Secrets of Love*. Melodies to open your heart.

❖ CD: *Scegli la Gioia* (Choose Joy). Joyful songs by the Ananda Singers.

❖ CD: *Joy is God*. A series of beautiful instrumental pieces, recorded live at Ananda in 2005.

❖ CD: *Yogananda per il Mondo* (Yogananda for the World). Instrumental arrangements of Yogananda's Cosmic Chants.

❖ CD: *Mantra of Eternity*. The sacred sound of *Aum*, chanted by Swami Kriyananda.

These CDs and many more are available from Crystal Clarity Publishers (www.crystalclarity.com), or in Europe from Inner Life (www. innerlife.it).

CHAPTER 11

Good Vibrations at the Table

In the previous chapters we have looked in detail at how to select, as well as prepare food that is full of nutrients, Life Energy and sattwic vibrations. This is not the final story. Just as important as the food itself is the way in which it is eaten.

A Harmonious Environment

There are certain moments of the day when your energy goes into a heightened absorbing or receiving mode. At these times you are much more sensitive to, and much more easily influenced by, the vibrations that surround you. Eating is one of these moments. The environment in which you eat is very important. Yogananda, in fact, recommends not eating in public places. Public places are filled with countless vibrations from so many different people, most of which are not conducive to a calm and peaceful mind. In India, spiritual aspirants will seldom, if ever, eat outside of their own environment.

Make your usual eating place as sattwic as possible, by filling it with plants, flowers and other beautiful things. If you decide to eat out, choose a restaurant that's calm and quiet, with lots of light, uplifting music and few people. Green parks are good for eating packed lunches.

> "IF YOUR VIBRATIONS *are in harmony with Divine intelligence and love, you will express that harmony in your environment."* **P.Y.**

Spiritual Company

Along the same lines, if your energy is in a receptive mode while you eat, the company you keep is also important. Restlessness, negativity, egoism, pride, vanity and selfishness in other people will affect you more while you are eating than at other times.* When possible, choose to eat with people who are calm and centred and have spiritual qualities that you would like to develop.

Your energy is also receptive while you sleep.

*"ALWAYS REMEMBER that you need the inspiration
of better company to keep yourself constantly improving,
and you should share your goodness with people
of inferior qualities who need your help."* **P.Y.**

Television and radio programmes, as well as music, can also be considered as 'company'. However, television and radio, as mentioned in the previous chapter, usually carry rajasic vibrations and agitate and excite the mind. Music, on the other hand, can be very beneficial if sattwic.

Concentration for Better Results

When sunbathing, Yogananda says, if you concentrate upon the sun's rays as they enter into your skin and consciously feel them filling you with energy and vitality, the results of that sunbathe will be one hundred times greater than if you had done it absent-mindedly. The same principle can be applied to eating. When you eat with awareness of the nutrients, energy and vibration contained within the food, you draw more from it than when you eat absent-mindedly. Remember that your energy is in receptive-mode already; eating with awareness of what you are receiving, therefore, can be a very powerful exercise.

When you eat, let your main focus be on eating. Turning the television or radio on, flicking through magazines and the classic 'eating at your desk' prevent you from receiving the maximum benefits that the food has to offer. Try instead to sit down, relax and dedicate your time to eating only. As you chew each mouthful well (remember the importance of chewing?), visualise the food filling you with nutrients, energy and sattwic thoughts and consciously receive.

*"PEOPLE THINK ABSENT-MINDEDLY of events,
people, and situations in their lives. Or they occupy their
minds with fillers or with leafing through magazines,
turning on the radio, or gazing out the window at
whatever is happening outdoors. Absent-mindedness, and
fillers: Paramhansa Yogananda rated these two as among
the most insidious influences in the aspirant's life."* **S.K.**

Eating in Silence

Eating in silence is a good habit. It not only helps to turn your attention inward and focus on receiving, it also helps with digestion and assimilation. If you try and hold a conversation between mouthfuls of food, you certainly won't be

able to chew your food properly. As you read in the chapter "Vitamins are Crunchy", if you don't chew your food well, many nutrients will not be extracted from the food, and the undigested food could cause bacterial overgrowth in the colon, flatulence and other symptoms associated with indigestion.

Even when you eat with others, talking is not always necessary. Other spiritual people, especially, will usually be happy to share your silence. If you do talk, remember to keep your conversations on happy and uplifting topics.

A Happy Mind for Happy Digestion

It has already been mentioned that your ability to digest food well is related to physical factors (such as chewing properly, eating light and digestible foods and eating in silence), as well as spiritual factors (namely the vibration contained within the food). Psychological factors are also involved. Your state of mind and mental processes while you eat also play their part. Your digestive organs, Yogananda explains, are directly linked to your sympathetic nervous system, that is, the part of your autonomic nervous system that is active during stress or danger. Harmful thoughts, therefore, such as anxiety, fear and worry, will slow your digestion and make it more difficult. Happy and serene thoughts, on the other hand, will help to make digestion efficient and effective!

> "ALL WORRY, *care and thought of difficulties should be put aside, particularly while eating and one should always partake of food with a thankful, joyful heart. The mind must take control and master the environment to see that there is only calmness and pleasantness at meal time if the digestive system is to function normally."* **P.Y.**

Blessing Your Food:
The Purity of Prayer

Almost all spiritual traditions teach the habit of saying a prayer before partaking of food. This is no coincidence: saying a prayer causes you to stop, pause and turn your attention inwards. This moment of pause not only prepares your mind for receiving the food but also helps you to receive it with the right attitude. Food is, after all, a gift, given to sustain your body and spiritualise your mind. It is, therefore, right and appropriate to receive it with love, joy and gratitude.

These next words, I believe, contain the best bit of news in the whole book: You, as the last person who comes in contact with the food before it is eaten, have the power to transform its vibrations! As a human being you may be limited in your ability to do this but, by offering the food up to the Divine, from whence it came, your food becomes pure, blessed and sattwic. At Ananda we have a prayer-song written by Swami Kriyananda that we sing together before we sit down to eat. It goes like this:

Receive Lord in Thy Light,
the food we eat for it is Thine;
infuse it with Thy Love,
Thy Energy, Thy Life Divine.

The first line helps you to open your heart in gratitude, recognising that nothing you have belongs to you: everything belongs to Spirit and is given as a gift to sustain you. The second line asks that the food be transformed and made sattwic by infusing it with the Essence of Spirit. You too can use this song to bless your food or use any similar words that come from your heart.

Something else you can do, which will magnetise the effect of your prayer, is to use your hands to channel this Divine Energy into your food. Your hands are extremely sensitive and it is easy for you to feel energy there. Try this: Rub your hands together vigorously for a few seconds. Now turn the palms of your hands towards each other at a short distance apart. Can you feel a tingling sensation? That is the presence of Life Energy. To use your hands to channel Divine Energy, turn them towards your food, holding them a short distance away. Visualise or feel Divine Energy flowing through you, out of your hands and into the food. This is a very powerful technique for changing the food's vibrations. (This technique can also be used to send healing vibrations at a distance.)

Yogananda wrote the following beautiful prayer for eating food. You will also find a copy of this prayer at the end of the book, which you can tear out along the indicated line and hang in your kitchen or dining room.

Heavenly Father,

Receive this food. Make it holy.

Let no impurity of greed ever defile it.

The food comes from Thee.

It is to build Thy temple.

Spiritualise it. Spirit to Spirit goes.

We are the petals of Thy manifestation, but Thou art the Flower, its life, beauty and loveliness.

Permeate our souls with the fragrance of Thy presence.

In Part Four of the book, "Table Talk", Narya tells us how he was relieved from many food allergies by seeing the Divine Presence in everything he ate. See: "It's All in the Mind".

Helpful Hints

❖ Make your eating environment as sattwic as possible. Try to avoid eating in public places.

❖ Try to eat in silence at least once a day. During this time focus on receiving the energy and nutrients that the food contains.

❖ Instead of putting the television on while eating, try listening to sattwic music.

❖ Take time to eat: avoid eating 'on-the-go', on your feet and at your desk.

❖ Think positive thoughts when you eat and try to remain happy and cheerful.

❖ Always be inwardly grateful for the food you eat.

❖ Memorise Yogananda's or Kriyananda's prayer for blessing food before meals. Recite it with your family or inwardly, alone.

PART THREE

The Next Level

CHAPTER 12

The Benefits of Fasting

Once you learn how to eat correct foods in moderation, you are already making huge steps towards physical and mental health. You will feel strong, healthy, enthusiastic and full of energy! As the title of this part of the book suggests, there is, however, a 'Next Level': fasting belongs in this category.

Strictly speaking, fasting is the total avoidance of all solids and liquids, including water. More commonly, however, the term 'fasting' is used to refer to the avoidance of solid foods and the intake of liquids only. The most stringent form of liquid fasting is consuming only water; more liberally, fasting includes the use of fresh fruit or vegetable juices, as well as herbal teas. Yogananda recommends fasting for one day a week or three consecutive days a month, on orange juice (and water). Longer fasts are also beneficial but should not be undertaken without the supervision of a specialist.

Before looking at the benefits of fasting and how to undertake a fast, let's take a brief look at what's happening in your body when you fast:

As you read in the chapter "Carbohydrates and Gravity", your body's energy needs are principally provided by glucose. Glucose that is not used immediately is stored in your muscles and liver as glycogen and once these can contain no more, in your body as fat. When your body is deprived of food, due to the lack of incoming energy, it turns to its own resources, a process known as lipolysis. Lipolysis is the breaking down of fat stores in your body in order to produce energy.

Chemically speaking, a fast does not commence until your body begins to use its fat stores as an energy source. This will usually happen only after about 12 to 24 hours of going without food. For this reason, a one day fast should last for at least 24 hours and preferably 36 hours.

Give Your Organs a Well-Deserved Rest

The most obvious benefit of periods of fasting is that they give your digestive apparatus a well-deserved rest. Your stomach, intestines, pancreas, gallbladder and liver are amazing machines. They have been your faithful and humble servants all your life, silently labouring to digest the food you eat day after day, year after year. But they get tired. Can you imagine how tired you would feel if you had to work continuously, without ever having a day off? A day off allows you to rest and rejuvenate yourself and resume your normal daily activities with renewed energy. The same is true for your digestive organs; abstaining from solid food for at least a day gives them the rest they need to be able to resume their work with increased effectiveness.

> "COULD YOU FOLLOW A MUSICAL SCORE,
> *read, walk, write, talk, and meditate simultaneously, doing*
> *justice to them all? Well, that is just about what the digestive*
> *organs are called upon to do three times a day, year in and year*
> *out, through life, with an incompatible conglomeration of food-*
> *stuffs tossed into their mechanical apparatus…Business men*
> *and women would benefit their health very greatly by fasting or*
> *eating very little on Sundays and holidays. …Twenty-four hours*
> *fasting each week will give the digestive system a thorough rest,*
> *and you can start on your work with fresh vigor."* **P.Y.**

Your digestive organs rest the most when you fast only on water. However, fasting on fresh juices, because they are so easy to digest and assimilate, also allows your organs an effective rest.

Ridding Your Body of Toxins

Another of the wonderful benefits of fasting is the process of detoxification. Detoxification means the elimination of toxins from your body through your colon, liver, kidneys, lungs, lymph glands and skin.

Toxins are harmful or poisonous substances which accumulate in your body and cause disease. A small amount of toxins are produced by the normal metabolical processes of your cells; the rest are caused by unnatural diet, stress and chemicals

"WHEN YOU FAST on orange juice
it scrubs every cell. At least every month
you should give a thorough
house-cleaning to your body by fasting.
Do not let poison accumulate in your
system… Don't let yourself get sick." **P.Y.**

absorbed from the surrounding environment, among other things. DDT, for example, an insecticide that has been banned in many countries since 1974 because of its toxicity, has been found in the urine, faeces and sweat of people while fasting.

So, how does detoxification work? Toxins in your body are stored in your fat reserves. When your fat is broken down and used for energy during a fast, toxins that have accumulated throughout the years are released into your system and are then eliminated through the aforementioned organs.

Detoxification is not only a physical process. Everything physical is inseparably linked to the psychological. As you cleanse your body of physical poisons, you will probably feel that you are also letting go of many mental poisons, which are the thoughts and emotions that you no longer need.

Because of the complete lack of glucose, fasting on water is the most effective way to break down fat reserves and eliminate toxins (the less energy provided by external sources, i.e. food, the more your body turns to its own energy reserves, i.e. fat). Fresh juices, however, although they continue to provide your body with some glucose, actually have properties that help to stimulate the cleansing of waste products from your body. Both water fasting and juice fasting are therefore effective methods for detoxification.

A Natural Healing

> "MOST DISEASES CAN BE CURED *by judicious fasting.*
> *Unless one has a weak heart, regular short fasts have been*
> *recommended by the yogis as an excellent health measure."* **P.Y.**

Fasting is Nature's greatest remedy for overcoming disease and returning to a state of normalcy. As you know from the chapter "Life Force Be With You!", a great deal of energy is required to digest food every time you eat. With the absence of food, however, that same energy is diverted away from your digestive system and towards your metabolic and immune systems, where it is used to combat illness. This is one reason why animals instinctively fast when they are wounded or ill and why humans lose appetite during illnesses such as influenza, gastritis, tonsillitis and colds. Yogananda, in fact, taught that when you have a cold, you should fast for two days:

> "REMEMBER THAT DURING A COLD *the extra poisons*
> *of your body are being thrown off. If you add more food to your*
> *system, you help to obstruct the poison-eliminating system of*
> *Nature by clogging up the circulation with extra food chemicals…*
> *Fasting during a cold is very good, for it helps Nature to effect*
> *her own cure without interruption from any source."* **P.Y.**

Many people have been cured from serious physical ailments, even cancer, by periods of prolonged fasting. In fact, there are actually many clinics that use fasting as a therapeutic method. For many philosophers, scientists and physicians of ancient times, fasting was an essential part of life and health. Socrates, Plato, Aristotle, Galen, Paracelsus and Hippocrates all used and believed in fasting therapy.

Long Life and Youthfulness!

A scientifically proven advantage from fasting is the feeling of rejuvenation and extended life expectancy. Detoxification and an improved immune system, which have already been discussed above, are two of the main reasons for this. During fasting, moreover, a number of other incredible phenomena take place. It has been found that, during fasting, production of protein for the replacement of damaged cells (a process known as 'protein synthesis') occurs much more efficiently. Your DNA and RNA, which control this process of protein synthesis, have actually been found to make fewer 'mistakes'! A higher efficiency in protein synthesis naturally results in healthier cells, tissues and organs. A second phenomenon that takes place during fasting is a greater production of hormones. Specific hormones include the human growth hormone, as well as an anti-aging hormone. No wonder people who fast look so young!

"A THREE-DAY FAST *once a month on orange juice with a laxative each day, will expel almost all poisons, and will do much to make the body strong, healthy, and youthful to the last days of life.*" **P.Y.**

An interesting study* that demonstrates the extension of life due to fasting (even though I am not prone to encourage the use of animals for such studies) was performed on earthworms. The experiment was performed by putting an earthworm on a cycle of fasting and feeding. The worm was kept without food until the scientists saw its size decreasing (meaning that it had used up its fat reserves and was beginning to use its protein reserves). At this point it was given food, before commencing another period of fasting. The worm was able to survive on its own tissue for months, all the time showing great vigour and energy! What is more, the isolated worm outlasted its relatives by 19 generations, while still maintaining its youthful physiological traits. The life-span extension of the worm was the equivalent of keeping a man alive for 600 to 700 years!

* Carroll, Will. *The Health Benefits of Fasting/Serendip's Exchange.* Serendip, 1994-2009. Available at http://serendip.brynmawr.edu/biology/b103/f02/web1/wcarroll.html

Spiritual Benefits of Fasting

The fact that voluntary abstinence from food is a tradition in most religions clearly demonstrates that the benefits of fasting are not only physical but also spiritual. Throughout time, Christians, Jews, Native Americans and followers of the Eastern religions have fasted for a variety of reasons: penitence, preparation for ceremony, purification, mourning, sacrifice, the enhancement of knowledge and powers, and communion with God. The Essenes, a community of yogi-like mystics who lived in the Holy Land around the time of Christ, believed that all disease was the result of sins committed against the body and that it took three days of fasting on water to be purified from those sins.

> "I SHALL RECOGNIZE *all disease as the result of my transgressions against health laws and I shall try to undo the evil by right eating, less eating, by fasting, by more exercise, and by right thinking.*" **P.Y.**

The bible is full of stories about those who fasted. Moses, Elijah, Daniel and Jesus all employed the method of fasting, some of them for as long as 40 days.

So, what is it about fasting that supports the process of purification, sacrifice, mourning and knowledge? Yogananda has the answer: fasting assists in a greater spiritual awareness. The soul, he explains, is independent of food. Because of our attachment to food and the belief that life depends on food, we have developed what he calls 'gross-mindedness', or 'matter consciousness'. Because of its identification with the body, your soul has come to view life as mere physical existence; it has forgotten that its true nature is actually divine. Fasting helps you to break this delusion. Jesus, Yogananda says, fasted for forty days in order to convince himself that his soul had risen above bodily conditions. When he was tempted by hunger the words he uttered were, "Man shall not live by bread alone but by every word that cometh from the mouth of God." "Bread" in this case, explains Yogananda, refers to food; "every word" refers to Cosmic Energy, or Life Energy; and the "mouth of God" is the medulla oblongata at the base of the brain, the 'door' through which Life Energy enters. According to the Hindu scriptures, the man of the future will draw his nourishment almost solely from this Cosmic Energy.

> "GOD ORIGINALLY CREATED *Cosmic Vibration of Energy which, when once started, became perpetual, and you can, by your wireless will power, draw upon it and bring it into your body through the medulla. This Cosmic Energy, the same energy through which you and everything else in the universe were created, surrounds and permeates all Creation within and without all the time. It enters through the 'Mouth of God' and is the invisible 'Word' which sustains life of all kinds.*" **P.Y.**

When you deny your body food, your mind is impressed with the truth that there is something far greater than food which sustains it. The more you fast and meditate, the greater your realisation of this truth will be. Fasting, in other words, helps you to turn your mind away from physical matters, turning it inwards, towards a deeper, inner reality. This is why fasting is used in the various religions before important ceremonies; for purification and for communion with God.

Many advanced yogis and mystics have demonstrated their victory over body-consciousness by living without physical food for indefinite periods of time (without losing weight or becoming weak). Therese Neumann of Konnersreuth, Germany and Giri Bala of Ranchi, India, are two such women saints. The stories of Yogananda's encounters with each of these remarkable women are recounted in the appendix "Extraordinary Encounters".

Fasting for even short periods of time, such as one, two or three days, can help you to increase your spiritual awareness. Gradually you will feel yourself becoming less and less attached to food, and your food requirements will actually decrease. Here is an affirmation to practise while you fast:

"GOOD FOOD *or any kind of food or no food are all alike to me,
because my body emanates from my soul, which is unconditioned, and
I am above food, hunger, and decay. I am immortal, I am satisfied, all
my wants are fulfilled, hence I am above hunger, decay or death.*" **P.Y.**

Getting Started:
How to Fast

A one-day fast can last for between 24 and 36 hours, the latter being more effective. The 36 hours would include the night before the day you decide to fast. Let's say you choose to fast on a Wednesday. Your fast would actually begin after your evening meal on Tuesday and would continue through until breakfast on Thursday.

A three-day fast would also begin the evening before and could be broken on the evening of the third day or the morning of the fourth day.

Laxatives are an important part of fasting. During the process of detoxification, many toxins will collect in your intestines, which need to be flushed out daily. Take a natural herbal laxative the evening that your fast begins (even for a one-day fast) and then every evening until your fast ends. Herbal laxatives are readily available and can be obtained from any chemist or herbalist shop. They come as either capsules, lozengesor as herbs for making teas. Some of the most common herbal laxatives are: cascara sagrada, senna leaves,* liquorice root, buckthorn, rhubarb root and aloe vera. Alternatively, an enema can be used daily.

Water assists the detoxification process of fasting and should be consumed in abundance. Try to drink at least 2-3 litres a day.

Organic oranges (during an orange juice fast) are preferred to non-organic oranges. You want to keep your body as pure as possible and avoid the addition of any new toxins.

Deep breathing is an essential part of fasting for the inhalation, as well as the exhalation. As explained in the chapter "Life Force Be with You!", oxygen is easily converted into Life Energy and can be used to recharge your body. Inhaling deeply will revitalise you and banish any fatigue you may experience while fasting.

> *"JUST AS ELECTRICITY passes through a rod made of a conductive substance, and electrifies it, so the body battery becomes fully charged with life force derived from oxygen. People who perform breathing exercises always have shining, magnetic eyes."* **P.Y.**

The exhalation is equally as important: quite simply, when you exhale, you release toxins from your body in the form of carbon dioxide. The more you exhale, the deeper the level of detoxification.

During fasting, Yogananda recommends inhaling and exhaling deeply from six to twelve times every hour. Breathe in as slowly and deeply as you can and concentrate on the energy in the air as it fills your lungs. As you breathe out, feel that you are releasing both mental and physical toxins. This method is best practised outdoors but, when weather conditions necessitate, it can be practised indoors in front of a wide-open window.

Sunshine (if there is any) can also give energy while fasting. Like oxygen, sunshine is easily converted into Life Energy and can banish fatigue. Additionally, rays of sunshine are known to be able to cure diseases and sickness. Sit or stand in

---

* Senna leaves are known to be very strong laxatives. Be sure to follow the dosage instructions carefully or ask advice from a herbalist.

the sunshine as often as you can, from ten minutes to one hour, according to the strength of the sun. If you concentrate on the energy in the sun's rays as you feel its warmth on your body, you will find that you are able to draw several times more energy from it than if you were to sunbathe absentmindedly.

> "... SUCH FOOD SUBSTITUTES AS RAYS
> AND OXYGEN ... *can be easily assimilated*
> *and converted into energy by the latent life forces*
> *in the body. Magnetic foods* give energy*
> *more quickly than solids and liquids which are*
> *less easily converted into life force."* **P.Y.**

Yogananda's Energisation Exercises, for those who know them, are the best and most direct way of bringing energy into your body while fasting. As you practise them, feel that your body "... does not live by bread alone but by every word that cometh from the mouth of God."

Exercise is very beneficial for supporting the process of detoxification while fasting. As explained earlier, toxins are released from your body when you exhale. The more oxygen you have pumping around your body while you fast, the more carbon dioxide can be released. Toxins are also released through the skin in the form of perspiration. Walking, cycling, swimming or other gentle exercises are all recommended.

Baths and showers are very good for cleansing the skin during fasting. Steams and saunas are also good. As well supporting detoxification, they provide warmth.

Skin brushing will help clean your lymph system, improve circulation and keep pores open, encouraging your body's discharge of toxins. Clear pores will also absorb sunshine and oxygen more efficiently. Your skin is the largest organ of your body and is responsible for one-fourth of your body's detoxification. Skin-brush before showering or bathing, as your skin must not be wet. Brush all areas of your skin (except your face and any sensitive areas) with long strokes towards your heart. A soft, dry brush or bath gloves are best.

Alcohol, nicotine and **caffeine** should be avoided whilst fasting.

Silence and seclusion can be very beneficial during a fast. Fasting is usually accompanied by a feeling of inner freedom from bodily ties and a desire for spiritual expansion. Taking time out from worldly duties to be by yourself gives you the opportunity to meditate, pray, partake in self-examination and take long nature walks, etc.

* The sun's rays and oxygen.

*"THE SABBATH DAY must be used for the most part in real
Spiritual activity, which helps the Soul to be recharged by the greatest
power and wisdom of God...The real observance of the Sabbath
consists in spending it in seclusion, fasting, and meditation."* **PY**

"Clean up" is a motto used during fasting. As you 'clean up' your body, cleaning up your environment as well, will help you to bring about positive and beneficial changes on all levels of your life. You might want to clean up your desk, your wardrobe, your kitchen or your garage. Throw away anything that is no longer useful to you.

Symptoms You May Have While Fasting

The symptoms you may have while fasting depend on the toxicity of your body. If you have a lot of toxins, you are probably going to feel them being released. The good news is that the more you change your eating habits and fast on a regular basis, the less toxins there are to be released and the easier it all becomes. Do try to persist, even if you feel discouraged: the fact that you are suffering from symptoms while fasting is a good sign that you really need it.

Symptoms include:

❖ Headaches
❖ Fatigue
❖ Irritability
❖ Dizziness and light headedness
❖ White/yellow coating on tongue (this can be scraped or brushed off)

❖ Foul smelling urine and stools
❖ Bad breath and displeasing tastes in the mouth
❖ Skin odour, skin eruptions and small spots
❖ Nausea
❖ Vomiting

Symptoms are felt mainly during the first two days of a fast; on the third day you may feel so good and full of energy that you will even want to continue! After you have completed your fast, you will feel cleaner, healthier and more alive.

Some people experience hunger during fasting, while others experience no hunger at all. If you feel hungry, exercise, sunbathing and deep breathing will usually take the sensation away.

Coming Off Your Fast

The way in which you come off your fast is just as important as the fast itself, especially when you fast for more than 36 hours. Your first meal should be light and easy to digest; heavy foods should be avoided. Fruit, steamed vegetables, white rice and herbal teas are good.

Some people fast and then the next day eat twice as much, in order to make up for the meals they missed. This, of course, completely misses the point of fasting and undoes any good that may have been done.

Making Transitions

Fasting can be hardest for those who need it most. If you are accustomed to eating three meals a day, plus in-between-meal snacks, going without food or even skipping a meal can be an intimidating thought. Nevertheless, why don't you try it? If it proves too big a step for you, try fasting for a half day only or for one full day with only orange juice (or another type of fruit or vegetable juice when oranges are out of season).

It must also be said that some bodies find it more difficult to fast than others, especially those that are thin. If this is the case with you then try fasting initially for only half a day and, instead of drinking only water, include fresh juices too. If this still proves to be too difficult, try a diet of only fruit. Personally, I have found that my body reacts differently on different days: some days I have felt that fasting is just not appropriate, whereas on other days, fasting has filled me with a renewed strength. Hindus traditionally fast on the 11th day of the full moon and the 11th day of the new moon (Ekadasi). Yogananda explains that

> "… THERE ARE CERTAIN ELECTRICAL, PRANIC INFLUENCES *that operate on these days to keep the body supplied with subtle vitality.*" **P.Y.**

In my own experience, I have found this to be true. Even though my body is of slim build, when I fast on these days, I feel full of energy and very little hunger.

Daily Fasting

In general, everyone would benefit from returning to the habit of overnight fasting for 12-14 hours, or even longer if possible. If you eat dinner at 7:30 pm, try not to eat breakfast until at least 9:30 the next morning. If you can, resist until lunch time. Alternatively, try skipping dinner and fasting until breakfast. In general, learn to eat less. These daily periods of fasting, along with healthy and moderate eating, help your body to 'keep on top of things' and ease the amount of work that needs to be done on your weekly and monthly fasting days. The less you overload your system with food and the more you allow it to rest, the stronger, healthier and more youthful you will be. Remember the example of the little worm!

> "DO NOT THINK
> THAT SATISFIED HUNGER
> *means satisfied body needs.*
> *Learn the laws of rational,*
> *scientific diet, and live on simple*
> *and wholesome food."* **P.Y.**

In Part Four of the book, "Table Talk", Anand and Gurupriya relate their experiences of fasting. See: "Fruit and Nuts Are Good" and "20 Years of Fasting Experience".

Helpful Hints

❖ During your fast, take long, gentle walks, preferably in natural surroundings: it will take your mind away from food, and the fresh air will give you energy.

❖ Repeat to yourself the previously mentioned affirmation for fasting by Yogananda.

❖ Avoid places where people are eating or where food is being prepared.

❖ Use the time you usually spend eating to do something you enjoy that you never usually have time for.

❖ Make fasting a habit: choose a regular day to fast each week and stick to it.

❖ Reread this chapter during your fast to remind you of all the benefits you're receiving by doing it.

N.B.: The author states that, by promoting the benefits of fasting, she obviously doesn't intend in any way to encourage or induce dietary imbalances, such as anorexia and bulimia. For those who suffer from such ailments, fasting is absolutely discouraged, and it is advised to consult one's doctor or a health organisation dealing with such matters.

CHAPTER 13

The Nine-Day Cleansing and Vitalising Diet

In addition to fasting, you may want to try Yogananda's "Nine-day Cleansing and Vitalising Diet". This diet is designed to rid your system of accumulated toxins. Many Ananda members follow this diet once a year, often as a group, with great results. As its name suggests, the diet lasts for nine days.

Foods to Eat While on the Diet

Every day, the following foods should be eaten; no other foods should be eaten during the diet (including spices, oil or salt):

- ❖ 1½ grapefruits
- ❖ 1½ lemons
- ❖ 5 oranges
- ❖ 1 cooked vegetable with its juice (as much as you want)
- ❖ 1 raw vegetable salad
- ❖ 3 cups Vitality Beverage (see below)

If you feel the need of additional nourishment during the diet, a tablespoonful of thoroughly ground nuts in a half glass of water or in a glass of orange juice may be taken.

Vitality Beverage

In his Super Advanced Lessons, Yogananda states that the Vitality Beverage is a blood tonic and very effective against rheumatism, various stomach disorders (including acute indigestion), chronic catarrh, bronchitis and nervous "breakdown".

One cup of the beverage should be drunk with each of your three meals.

Yogananda gave two different methods for preparing the Vitality Beverage, both of which are given below. The first, he says, is preferable. Because of the larger quantities it makes, it is also much more practical. Some people, alternatively, choose to juice the ingredients. This is basically the same as the second method, only the yield is greater.

Ingredients:

* ❖ 2 stalks celery
* ❖ 5 carrots including part of the stem
* ❖ about 300 g dandelion leaves, turnip greens or spinach
* ❖ 1 bunch parsley
* ❖ (no salt or spices)

First Method (*makes about 1 litre*)

1. Using a food processor, mince the celery and carrots.
2. Lightly boil the celery and carrots in about one litre of water for ten minutes.
3. Add the greens and parsley and boil for a further ten minutes.
4. Strain the vegetable stock through a sieve into a bowl. This is your Vitality Beverage.

Second Method (*makes about 250 ml*)

1. Using a food processor, mince each of the ingredients.
2. Put the ingredients into a cheese cloth and squeeze out the liquid into a bowl. This is your Vitality Beverage.

Laxatives

A natural laxative must be taken every night while on the cleansing diet before going to bed. Yogananda recommends senna leaves,* which can be taken with a glassful of orange juice. To obtain the best results, take half a teaspoon at first and later increase to one teaspoon.

Taking Baths

Yogananda states that while on the cleansing diet it is very beneficial to take a salt bath every night, just before going to bed. 900 grams of some good bath salts can be dissolved in a quarter tubful of warm water.

Senna leaves are known to be very strong laxatives. Be sure to follow the dosage instructions carefully, or ask advice from a herbalist.

Ending the Diet

As with fasting, the way in which you end the nine-day cleansing diet is just as important as the diet itself. The first day after the diet you should be especially careful in the selection and quantity of the food you eat. Light and easy-to-digest foods should be emphasised. After the first day, your normal diet can be resumed gradually.

If you feel that you have not been successful in ridding your body of all its toxins, the cleansing diet may be repeated after an interval of two or three weeks.

It is very helpful to continue taking salts baths every now and then for several weeks after finishing the diet.

In Part Four of the book, "Table Talk", Mati and Dino tell us about their experience of The Nine-Day Cleansing and Vitalising Diet. See: "An Inner Journey" and "100% Purification".

Helpful Hints

❖ Do the diet together with a group of friends and take it in turns to prepare the Vitality Drink.

❖ Treat yourself to good-quality salad ingredients: try adding cherry tomatoes, rocket, avocado or fresh herbs to make your salad extra special.

❖ Blend a tomato with a little lemon juice and fresh parsley to use as a tasty condiment for your salad or simply use the lemon juice alone.

❖ Occasionally blend the cooked vegetable together with its cooking water to create a puree.

❖ Eat the oranges whole instead of juicing them: this will make them last longer and will keep you full for longer.

❖ Think of how alkaline your body is becoming by doing this diet!

❖ If 9 days seems like a long time, ask yourself, what are just 9 days in a whole lifetime?

PART FOUR

"Table Talk"

Introduction

I thought you might like to meet some of the Ananda family! It will, of course, be through the subject of food!

I asked a few of my Ananda friends to tell us about an experience they have had in the past that relates to something in this book. Real life experiences are always fun to read and often inspiring and helpful. Let's see what they have to say...

100% Raw!

Mary

From 1978-1982 I ate exclusively raw foods. It didn't happen overnight but took years to build up to it. After experimentation with different diets, cleansing techniques and struggling with eliminating cigarettes, I became a raw food enthusiast. The main focus was on wheat grass juice, then sprouts, baby greens (such as buckwheat and sunflower greens) and fermented foods (such as sauerkraut and seed yoghurts). The wheat grass juice with pure chlorophyll cleaned and purified my system whereas the sprouts and young greens fed my body with amino acids and living enzymes. I started to really feel good; better than I've ever felt. Eventually, I joined forces with two friends (James and Eddie), and we started the job of sharing information with others. We called our little group "Life Light", and we gave classes and workshops and travelled around the U.S. (mostly in California). We gave away samples of wheat grass juice and sold raw food meals and desserts at health food shows and conventions.

Though we rented a ranch outside of L.A., where we gave a lot of workshops, when we were on the road, we travelled in converted school buses! One was our travelling greenhouse (it housed over 100 trays of wheat grass, greens and sprouts and even had an automatic watering system); the other we lived and slept in. Eddie was the mechanic/technician/carpenter who kept the vehicles running, built our booths for the shows and manufactured our electric wheat grass juicers (which we also sold). James was the 'missionary', organiser, main teacher and kept it all together. I myself did all the food preparation, the planting and growing (with help from the boys when necessary) and some teaching. Because I like the taste of good food, I created a lot of delicious dishes. Once we catered a party in Beverly Hills: ALL RAW — even the carrot birthday cake!

It was a really beautiful time in my life, in which I learned so much and felt great. In time, however, personal differences and also my spiritual search divided us. Alas, little by little, I started again to eat a 'normal' vegetarian diet and even picked up some bad eating habits. Without the support of my friends, it was difficult for me to keep a lifestyle that was so extreme. The last few years, however, I've been getting back into eating a larger percentage of raw foods. I'm growing sprouts and sunflower greens for the Ananda Assisi community, and I'm glad to be able to share these wonderful foods with our community members and guests.

An Alkaline Miracle!

I had been suffering from tiredness for months, maybe even years. Especially in the morning, soon after breakfast, I would already be exhausted and sometimes even had to go and lie on the sofa. I had already tried eliminating wheat from my diet, which had helped somewhat. But the tiredness persisted, and I was starting to become worried. I decided to consult a specialist, and he told me that I was suffering from a very strong

Sahaja

case of 'metabolic acidosis'. Mahiya gave me some very helpful advice about simple changes I could introduce into my diet... and it worked immediately! As soon as the next day, that terrible fatigue had completely disappeared: a true miracle! For the first couple of weeks I was pretty strict and eliminated almost every acidic food. I started my days with fresh orange and lemon juice with ground almonds, followed by carrot and apple juice and a banana and soya milk smoothie (I like big breakfasts!). For lunch, I had a big salad with sprouts, followed by a little grain and cooked vegetables. For dinner, another big salad, a soup and some cooked vegetables. Not a hard diet at all! After the first week, I was already experiencing the joy of eating more raw foods, to the point that I was almost not attracted at all even to pasta and pizza, which, being Italian, I simply adore!

Now I've relented a bit with my discipline and occasionally eat a little pasta and pizza, but I make sure I always have my big, non-acidic breakfast and big salads with every meal to make up for the acid foods I sometimes like to eat. I feel soooo much better!! And it's such a joy to drink those juices; it's like drinking pure prana. They are alive and make me feel alive!

The Secret's in the Vibration!

When I was a young girl I had what you might call 'a stomach of steel'. I could eat anything I wanted and make the most terrible mixes. I honestly digested everything! With the years, the situation changed somewhat radically. I developed allergies to certain types of fruit and vegetables, and I had more and more difficulty digesting whole meals. The situation became so difficult that I decided to do a gastroscopy to verify if there was some physical problem but, fortunately, they didn't find anything.

Manu

After I began the spiritual path I gradually became vegetarian and, thanks to this new diet, my digestive problems greatly decreased, but they never went away. It always puzzled me, however, that when I came to stay at Ananda I was able to digest whatever I ate without any difficulties at all, even foods that were absolutely 'off limits' for me, such as peppers or certain combinations of foods that I would definitely have avoided if I were at home. During a vedic astrology consultation at Ananda, Drupada (a brilliant astrologist and friend) helped me to understand the reason why. He explained to me that I am incredibly sensitive to the vibrations in food. "For you it's better to eat a hamburger from MacDonalds made with love, than the best organic food prepared in a hurry or by a person who doesn't love his work." Now that I know this secret I always keep an eye on the vibrations in the food I eat, not only to avoid having digestive problems but also not to pollute my body. I've come to understand that energetically 'unclean' food is as if it had gone bad; it not only pollutes my physical body but my energy body too. Thank you Ananda!

Homegrown Food Has More 'Pep'!

Helmut

One of my first memories is with my mother in the garden, "helping" her to collect the veggies for our meals. My favourite soup was "Kreuz und quer durch den Gemüsegarten" (a bit of everything from the vegetable garden). I grew up on a farm, and we never bought any kind of veggies or food; everything was homegrown. My brothers, sister and I were all encouraged to have a little garden of our own as soon as we were old enough to do so. I was 'spoiled', so to speak, with good food from the beginning.

But then, as the saying goes, 'The grass is always greener on the other side." When I went to the city to study, I saw the supermarket food and thought: "Wow, that's the real thing!" I grew fond of it for a while... not long though. I came to realise that there was just not enough 'pep' (today I'd call it prana) in this kind of food, and I soon began to look for organic things. In those days, organic food was not that readily available, so whenever I had the chance to have a garden, I grew a few vegetables.

For the last 26 years, my wife and I have had a continuously expanding garden, in which we grow an ever-wider variety of fruit and vegetables. We had one at our house in Bad Homburg, Germany; at Ananda California; and now we have one here at Ananda Assisi. It takes time, and we spend every free hour there, but I tell you, it's not work but fun and very relaxing (to be completely honest I would add... most of the time). It's so recharging to put all of our attention and love in the little plants, prepare all the things they need to grow, tend to them, free them of weeds and give them, above all, our love. Whatever pessimists might say, we know that they do respond to this love, the mightiest force in the Universe. They show it to us through their beauty, their taste and the energy that they give us. It is not even necessary to have a garden to grow your own food: tomatoes, herbs and even a little bit of lettuce can be grown on a sunny balcony or veranda.

There is hardly anything more beautiful than saying grace over food that you have watched grow; that you have tended to and loved. Another benefit is the wonder you experience in the process of growing: you feel that God is the power behind planting, growing, harvesting and everything. To paraphrase the food-blessing song we sing at Ananda before meals:

"Receive Lord in Thy Light the food we
eat, grow and harvest, *for it is Thine.*
Infuse it with Thy Love, Thy Energy, Thy Life Divine."

The Power of Food

Rashmi

During the first 25 years of my life, my diet was mostly characterised by animal proteins. This means that for 25 years, up until I left home, I ate beef steak or pork chops for break-fast, lunch and dinner – every day. Such a diet was inevitable for a person like me with an Umbrian mother used to cook-ing typical Umbrian dishes, all based on various types of cold meats - game, rabbit, wild boar – and an Italian mentality of "the more you have, the more you eat."

Consequentially, it must be said that aggressiveness and restlessness were not lacking in the way I behaved; aggressiveness that I usually released by doing a lot of sport. Even when I started to look after my own diet and to limit my intake of red meat (eating only raw ham and game a few times a week), I noticed that when I decreased the amount of sport I was doing, my aggressiveness towards situations and people increased. This sometimes resulted in anger, causing damage to my re-lationships with relatives and friends.

When I came to work in Nocera Umbra on the post-reconstruction of the earth-quake in 1997, I completely abandoned every type of sport that, up until that time, was my main outlet for 'letting off steam'. I observed how my anger and aggres-siveness were increasing, even though, at that time, I was already practising relaxa-tion and psycho-physical techniques. The fact is that, in this period of nearly 10 years, I had started to eat pork and beef again on a daily basis, and they became a central part of my diet. During this time I also gained about 20 kg. Unfortunately, hand-in-hand with my increase in weight was an increase in the touchiness and ir-ritability I expressed in relationships with my colleagues at the local council where I worked. I have to admit that (even if it wasn't the only cause) this negatively in-fluenced my work performance, my health and my tranquillity.

After I came to know Ananda and the teachings of Paramhansa Yogananda (who gives a lot of importance to correct diet), I decided to put aside some of my dietary habits, many of which were dictated by greed. I completely gave up beef, pork and alcohol. This change in diet was very natural to me after all and, without a shadow of a doubt, strongly contributed to the re-development of calmness and serenity that had long ago abandoned me. This is how I directly experienced the influence of diet on the personality and, as Yogananda says, how important it is that the food we eat has a vibration that is in tune with Spirit (namely plant foods), without depleting ourselves of the correct quantities of protein that can be easily found in nuts, sprouts and legumes. It is likely that one day (I don't know how far away), we won't even have a need for plant foods but, while we are waiting for that day, it is definitely very healthy to nourish ourselves with these sattwic foods.

Nourishing the Soul!

Hello, I'm Namasya. At Ananda, my experience of 'karma yoga', that is, yoga in action, has mostly been in the kitchen. I have to say that the field of proper diet never interested me and even less so, cooking. I always ate whatever was on my plate (except for meat and fish, which my mum says I always refused, even as a child). I never thought about how to balance my diet, neither when I was little nor when I, so-to-speak, got bigger.* I have never given it much thought, which isn't anything to brag about!

Namasya

I really find it interesting to observe the people that accompany me on this adventure in the kitchen, where particular care is given to the nourishment of the soul, even before that of the body, and to the relationship between food and the mind. I've also noticed that little miracles can happen. A person such as myself, completely deprived of any cooking experience, who doesn't even give any particular importance to the taste itself of the food that she's preparing and eating… finds herself cooking for people with a somewhat different conception of food, much more elaborate and sophisticated. In any case, I've humbly observed that by keeping the right attitude of seeing the bigger picture, that is to say, the purpose that's at the root of every action, everything flows. It's surprising to hear that what you cooked was actually enjoyed, and it's a true JOY to share food made with the most flavourful of all ingredients: LOVE!

May my experience be an encouragement to all those who have no knowledge in the kitchen and demonstrate that, if I can do it… they can too! It's enough to nourish the essence of true existence, the soul, with the only ingredient that can nourish it: the LOVE of DIVINE JOY.

So, may there be ever new JOY among the stove, pots and forks so that the food you eat is permeated with this authentic and unique ingredient, where GOD is in everything and everyone. BUON APPETITE!

* Namasya expresses herself in this way because she is of short stature.

You Are What You Eat

Tejindra

For more than ten years I had the same routine: frying pan, oil, garlic and chilli… then I'd throw in the vitals. Spicy food was my favourite; the spicier, the better. Then I began meditating and one day, not long afterwards, I found that my life-long routine was evaporating, leaving me with a new found desire for steamed and raw vegetables and fruit. This was very strange to me. It wasn't a conscious decision at all, just an organic change. The few times I was tempted to re-turn to my old routine, I found my mind uncontrollable and blurry. This fren-zied mind-set – active and distracted – perfectly describes my way of life before I began to meditate – and I found that I no longer wanted to participate in it. Unconsciously, it seems I had made the connection between sattwic diet and the ability to focus on the present moment, and ever since then I have a new routine: steamer, water and vegetables.

Vegetarian Fearlessness

After about two years as a vegetarian, I travelled back to my home in the U.S. to stay with my family (all confirmed carnivores!). At one evening meal, we dis-cussed 'letting go of the world' and having more faith in the universe. My youngest brother, who up to that point had been quite receptive to the topic at hand, had a point to make: "That all sounds good, but what if someone walked into the room and wanted to cut your throat with a knife?" I looked at him strangely. "Where on earth did that thought come from? Why would anyone live their life with that type of hallucination in their head?"

I tried to recall the last time I had felt a sense of dread, a fear of dying a horri-ble, violent death. It had been about two years, just before I became a vegetarian.

A Single Matchstick

Christina

Up until the age of 19, I didn't know that some foods are good for us and others ruin our health. I was convinced that one could freely eat anything, as long as it was edible, with-out worrying about the consequences! The only thing I had been taught was that some food makes you put on weight, and some food makes you lose weight.

One fine day in July of 1988, I went to the swimming pool. Here I met a music teacher who told me he was a vegetarian. "What does that mean?" I asked in utter ignorance. "It means that I don't eat meat," he said. "What?" I cried out in astonishment, "Are there people who don't eat meat? Why?!" His reply was simple and kind: "Meat is not good for us," and then, "…poor animals." That was it: the conversation ended there. I noticed that there was a gentleness in him that infused his every word and gesture. There was also a deep sense of respect for every being: I could tell he didn't judge those who didn't think or behave in the same way he did. I felt something awakening in me.

That same evening my mum served me ham for dinner. As I was eating it, for the very first time, I started thinking about how it had arrived on my plate: the pig, the killing, the suffering involved… I contemplated that I was an accomplice in all of this, even though it would actually be possible to live without eating animals. I started to ask myself, "Why should we show affection for pets, such as cats and dogs, and not for other creatures, such as the funny pigs, the peaceful cows and the amusing chickens? No one would eat his pet animal. Does our affection depend, then, on the taste of the meat?" Suddenly, I realised that the reasons I was eating meat were only ignorance, unawareness and conditioning; I just didn't know any better. This awakening filled me with new energy. I put the plate aside and told my mum, "From this moment on I will not eat anything that comes from killing animals." She just smiled and didn't take me seriously, because she knew how much I relished eating meat… but that was the last time I ever ate it. From that day I stopped eating meat, fish, chicken and even eggs. Not bad considering that up until that same morning, I didn't even know what vegetarianism was! This is the miracle of awareness and of becoming more conscious of life. We start to ask questions rather than blindly following patterns acquired by the society and the environment in which we grow up; we feel the urge to understand life more fully; we become aware of the roots of the tree of our existence, even though they are not visible to the eye! That day was a turning point for me.

In the years that followed, I travelled a lot around the world, especially in Asia. With great joy, I discovered that the world is full of happy and healthy vegetarians! I realised that vegetarianism was not a new and trendy way of eating that belonged to a minority but the natural diet of man! In the West, we have strayed away from nature in so many ways.

During the five years I lived in India, in the ashram of Sathya Sai Baba, I had the opportunity to dedicate myself full time to the study of the spiritual aspect of life; its very roots. I read the words of many Masters, as well as the ancient sacred scriptures of India, and my awareness of the impact of food on us became deeper and deeper. I always tested whatever I read on myself before believing it fully. I wanted to have personal experience. I've tried all types of detoxifying diets: water fasting, juice fasting, lemon and maple syrup fasting, urine therapy, wheatgrass juice therapy… I even ate nothing but raw food for 18 months, living only on raw vegetables, nuts, sprouts and fruit! At this point, my mum was so worried about me that, to pacify her, I had a full blood and urine test to check the level of my proteins and vitamins, etc. The doctors were astonished at the perfection of the results! "How do you do it?" they asked me, "What do you eat?" That was one of my little victories over public opinion… and my mum finally managed to relax.

One of the most remarkable and interesting aspects of food that I've studied and experienced is its effect on the mind, feelings and personality. The first thing I noticed was the close relation between meat consumption and aggressiveness: I used to be victim to fits of anger over which I had no control… when I stopped eating meat, they never happened again. When I came to know about how the food is influenced by the people who handle and cook it, fifteen years ago now, I stopped going to restaurants and eating food cooked by strangers. I do, however, eat food cooked in ashrams and by people I trust. On those few occasions that I have eaten food in restaurants, I've noticed thoughts and feelings in me that I do not usually have, as well as strange dreams and images flowing through my mind at night time. The problem is that if you eat out all the time, you will be so full of other people's influences that you won't even notice them. You will probably even think they are yours and identify with them. But try to preserve your magnetism and cook yourself all the food that you eat for some time, and you will realise how true it is. Thank Goodness we have the power to purify our food through prayer! Of course, food is not the only way in which our minds and personalities can be influenced, but it can definitely be used to improve our lives on all levels.

My diet consists of very simple and plain food, mostly raw. When I do cook food, I do it very briefly so as to preserve all the nutrients and the life force. To explain it all in a sentence: I eat the food as close as possible to the way in which Mother Nature offers it to us. The more I do this, the more energy I feel flowing through my body and the more positive thoughts and feelings I experience.

I now live happily at Ananda Assisi where I serve as a cook. I have also shared my knowledge and experience of food through courses, as well as through articles in a yoga magazine. I've even ended up on a TV program to talk about diet!

Have you ever seen the film Back to the Future? It's all about how certain things would not be as they are now if some events had not happened in the past. Well, that music teacher I met one fine day in July at the swimming pool would be wonderstruck at the impact of his one simple and kind sentence: "Meat is not good for you" and "…poor animals." This reminds me of a saying: "One single matchstick can light a huge fire if the wood is dry!"

An Inner Journey

Mati

When I moved to the Ananda community, I heard about Yogananda's Nine Day Cleansing Diet and decided to try it. I felt the need to challenge myself and strengthen my will power, as well as remove toxins from my body and deeply cleanse on all levels. The diet appealed to me because it only lasts for nine days. In the beginning I was a bit worried. How would I feel? How would everything go? My mind gave me thousands of excuses not to do it, but I strongly felt it was the right thing to do. I asked God for help and felt that I was not alone throughout the whole nine days. In Italy we have a saying; "Help yourself and God will help you" and this is what I did. During the diet I wore a crystal (which gives strength and energy), and for a week before starting I took the flower essence corn,* which gives mental strength and determination.

The diet went well and I managed to complete it. The first 3-4 days were not easy: I felt weak and was easily tired. My body was working hard to expel all the toxins. I had a headache and some nausea but discovered that these symptoms went away by drinking a lot, especially hot water and lemon juice. From the fifth day I was full of energy and felt great. I didn't even feel hungry anymore! This was one of the most incredible things for me: I'd never had this experience before. It helped me to understand how to go beyond the body; how much more there is to discover besides the physical.

I found the diet to be a great opportunity for self-observation. Desires for foods that I was craving came periodically into my mind. When this happened, I tried to take a step back and be detached, watching my thoughts but not identifying with them. I began to see just how often I ate foods only because I had a mental desire for them, not because I really needed them. Now I realised that I didn't need them, and I was experiencing it firsthand! I had no desire for sweets, for example; they actually made me feel sick to look at, as if my body was rejecting any food it did not require. As I observed my mental desires and habits, I felt my consciousness become more aware, my actions guided from a higher level. It was truly a life-changing experience.

Afterwards, my body felt cleaner, lighter – as if brand new. The need to eat certain foods had either diminished or disappeared completely. Some desires, of course, came back, but with time and practice I know these too can be eliminated. I also found I could sense whether a food was good for me without even tasting it and I understood that what was good for my tongue was not necessarily good for my body and mind.

* One of *Yogananda's Spirit in Nature Essences.*

I was amazed at how the diet purified me on a psychological level too: my worries and anxieties disappeared. I felt like I had been wiped clean with a sponge. My outlook on life changed, like I had turned the page on a new chapter or as if I were a painter standing in front of a blank canvas. I felt more ready to face my daily life and the coming months.

I have never found any other diet that gave results on such a deep level. I felt much lighter and full of energy and strength, so much so that I could have continued for a few more days. But what I mostly felt was full of joy, probably because the food included in the diet is so sattwic. It was a wonderful experience and I recommend it to anyone. It will take you on an incredible inner journey and help to awaken your inner 'hero'! I am very grateful to Yogananda for the gift of this cleansing diet.

It's all in the Mind

Two years ago I had a very intense attack of asthma and had difficulty breathing, especially during the night. I had already tried homeopathic as well as regular medicine, but nothing had helped. One day, after another night of wheezing, my wife Laura encouraged me to see a doctor. The first thing the doctor said was, "You must be allergic to something." We did all the tests and found out I was allergic to nightshades (potatoes, tomatoes, aubergines, peppers), milk,

Narya

cheese and white and brown flour. I started on a very strict diet in which I basically couldn't eat anything that I was used to eating– only rice with a few other things. After a couple of months I felt much better.

It was at this time that Swami Kriyananda arrived in Italy from India, where he now lives. One night Swamiji invited me and some others out to dinner with him. Swami ordered his favourite pasta dish, pasta primavera, then turned to me, looked straight in my eyes and said, "You must have pasta primavera too: it's very good." Now pasta primavera means: white flour, tomatoes, cheese, aubergine and a lot (you have no idea how much!) of cream: all the worst things for my diet. Nevertheless, I said, "Absolutely Swami. I will have that." The plate of pasta was very large with so much cheese and cream, but Swami also grated some parmesan cheese on top! In my mind I was thinking, "Oh my God, this is it for my lungs!" but I started to eat. When I was finished and was feeling full, Swami turned to me and said, "I can't eat any more of my pasta. Will you finish it for me?" And so, not only did I eat my pasta, I also ate half of his. But that's not all…Swamiji then ordered mashed potatoes made with milk and butter and bruschette with tomatoes. At this point I was really thinking, "Tonight there's no way I'm going to sleep!" But that night a little miracle happened: I slept perfectly. I had a tiny bit of asthma but even less than the previous night. I was amazed. "Swamiji, you are teaching me a good lesson," I thought.

From that moment on, I realised that it's all in the mind and that the thoughts we project onto the food can make it good or bad. God is in everything but I was closing my mind to that every time I saw tomatoes or some other food and would think, "If I eat that I'll get sick." Certainly you should do your best to have a good diet but don't be too strict and don't close your mind. Especially when food is given to you with love and a lot of hospitality, receive it as a gift from Divine Mother and it will become prasad, which is to say, blessed food.

After this episode with Swamiji I ended my strict diet and became much more flexible about what I ate. After a couple of months, my asthma disappeared and my lungs became completely clean. Now I can eat pasta, I can eat tomatoes, I can eat potatoes, aubergine and everything with no problems. Certainly, if there is rice for lunch, then I eat rice, but if there is only pasta, I eat pasta. In this way I have seen that we can cure ourselves just by seeing that God is in everything and everything is made from the same energy.

Raw Food

After reading about the many benefits of raw food on health and vitality, I decided to follow a raw food diet for two months. Reading that cooking depletes so many of the nutrients convinced me that cooked food is dead and raw food is alive!

For breakfast I made delicious smoothies with bananas, strawberries, soaked prunes, nuts and sultanas. Mid-morning and mid-afternoon I juiced fresh fruit and vegeta-

Nalini

bles. I have to say, I was so full of energy that I didn't know what to do with it all! Luckily I have a huge vegetable garden and this expended most of it! In this garden I grew much of what I ate. I gave a lot of love to the vegetables as I was working, and I know that this made a big difference to the vitality of the food. I also ate a lot of sprouts. Sprouts, especially alfalfa sprouts, contain a wealth of nutrition. It is a myth that we cannot fulfil our nutritional needs through raw food.

For the whole two months I felt fantastic: my skin was clear and I lost some weight I'd gained in the winter. It's not that I ended up looking like a rabbit, but I stabilised at my ideal weight. The body really knows what it's doing. The other benefit of this raw food diet was that it really helped my meditations… In fact, the more I think about it, I'm wondering why I don't do it again this spring! I think that even if you can do it for a couple of weeks, you'll feel incredible.

Fruit and Nuts Are Good!

The first person I ever heard relate his experience about fasting was the Mexican Migrant Workers Rights activist, César Chávez. He was doing a fast to protest against the conditions of migrant farm workers and was being interviewed. The interviewer asked him what his experience was like and he said, "Well, one thing certainly is that all my senses are heightened by not eating. Like those children that you hear playing out-

Anand

side: I hear them very clearly." And the interviewer said "I don't hear any children." She had to go all the way downstairs, out of the house and into the middle of the street before she could hear the children playing. I was very intrigued by this and wanted to see if it was true, so I put a pack on my back and went out to the desert of Eastern Washington and fasted for five days.

This was the first fast I had ever done and so my body was obviously in need of cleansing. The first couple of days my urine was black, and I had all this plaque on my gums and teeth. After the third day my urine started to clear up, and I realised I'd gone through the classic 'three day cleansing'. After the fifth day, I decided that it was enough and I went home.

That day was the beginning of one year of eating nothing but fruit and nuts. I was a young man with a lot of energy, so I ate a lot. It was no small thing. I would buy good southern pecans, different whole nuts and a whole array of fruit. My friends thought it was a little strange: "Gosh, look at all the money you spend on these fruit and nuts," a friend commented one day. I brought his attention to the amount of money that he spent on a piece of steak!

When I ate only fruit and nuts I felt wonderful and was full of energy. It was a period in my life when I was physically working hard. I was a heating and household appliance technician and would go in and repair peoples' refrigerators and electrical heating systems, so it was a job that kept me on the move. That year I also noticed I didn't get any flu or colds.

As I got more associated with Ananda, I realised that you could have a good, healthy, vegetarian diet that was more varied and not only confined to fruit and nuts. I relaxed a little with my eating habits and started to eat other things, but I was still very drawn to fruit and nuts as my basic food groups.

When I first met Swami Kriyananda in Seattle in 1978, I was thinking that maybe my diet was a little too radical. "Maybe it's not good to eat only fruit and nuts," I thought. But Swami picked the thought out of my mind. During one of his discourses he started talking about diet: "Diet, of course, is very important to achieving inner states of calmness and relaxation," he said. And then, out of the blue, "Yes… fruit and nuts are good!" He then went on to talk about other aspects of a sattwic diet, but I thought it was intriguing and amusing the way he picked up on the question that I had in my mind about whether I was being too radical or not! So, fruit are nuts are definitely good!

20 Years of Fasting Experience

The first time I fasted was more than 20 years ago. I had already been practising *Hatha Yoga* for many years and had just started to meditate. It was also about this time that I first heard about Paramhansa Yogananda and Ananda.

I was already a vegetarian and my boyfriend was putting a lot of emphasis on changing his diet to a healthier one. He asked me if I would like to do a fast together with him, and I said yes! The fast that we did was based on fruit and vegetable

Gurupriya

juices and, if I remember correctly, lasted for 6 or 7 days, including one preparation day and two days to adjust back to a normal diet.

After this experience, fasting became an important part of my life and I repeated it once or twice a year. I discovered many new variations of fasting, including a fast with lemon juice, honey, cayenne pepper and water. Some of my friends were also fasting regularly, so we shared our experiences, challenges and benefits. One of my friends gave me a book about fasting with herbal teas as a method of self-healing. The book explained that different herbal teas support the body in purifying different body parts, the skin and inner organs, for example. I was never seriously ill in my life, and I am sure that these regular periods of fasting are one of the main reasons for this but, at this time, I had a neurodermatitis on my hands, definitely caused by certain wrong eating habits. With the help of regular fasting, I was able to change my diet and was eventually completely healed from this illness.

Knowing that fasting strengthens the body to be able to defend itself against all kinds of illnesses, I continued to fast at least once a year. The fact that the body and especially the digestive system (which is my most sensitive area), get a profound cleaning during fasting, is another reason why I continue to fast. Using fasting as a method of healing yourself, or even better, as a *prevention* against illness, is also a good way to save money usually spent on doctors' bills and medicine. For those who have decided to live a simple life, as we do at Ananda, this will be appreciated.

Since living at Ananda, I usually fast in the autumn or spring after an intense summer or winter period, when my body and mind can look forward to a calmer period (even though it will never be without challenges!). Spring and autumn are also good times to fast because fasting helps the body to adjust to the new season. To make the fast as effective as possible, I usually take time out from work. I consider myself fortunate to be able to do this, because I realise that, for others, it might not be that easy. Spiritually speaking, I have found that fasting is much more effective when I combine it with semi-seclusion. By immerging myself more deeply in my spiritual practices – yoga, meditation, affirmations, chanting, etc. – I have had endless inspirations, which always make these fasting times really special. Some of the benefits are that I feel stronger, more serene and full of self-confidence, stability and harmony on all levels. You can also use the time you usually spend preparing food and washing dishes, etc. to take walks and to enjoy nature.

And let me finish with another discovery, which is quite interesting to me:

I never feel hungry when I fast. This, along with many other aspects of fasting, is well worth experiencing.

100% Purification

Several years ago, about 18 or 20 of us in the community decided to do Yogananda's Nine Day Cleansing Diet together, although not everybody made it to the end. I think this cleanse is perfect for people who work long hours and tend to transgress a little in their diet, perhaps by eating too much cake because they don't have time to prepare anything more healthy and have to fill their stomachs. This, at least, was my experi-

Dino

ence. If you do it with a group or with another person, it's even better, because you can help each other. The first day goes well for most people but maybe the second day you might have the desire to eat something that's not included in the diet, and the third day you might be thinking, "Help! I can't make it. I've got a headache!"

For me this diet was 100% purifying: I truly found that it detoxified every-thing. It was wonderful to be able to do it. I was working on the construction of the Temple of Light at the time. While my work mates were huffing and puffing because they had eaten two plates of pasta and felt heavy, I, who had only eaten a cooked vegetable and a few oranges, felt light and full of energy. I wasn't thinking "Oh no, the cement mixer's arriving: I don't have enough strength to level the ce-ment out!" On the contrary, it was the others who didn't have enough energy after eating their pasta! The last few days I felt even better and could even do with less food. In fact, I almost felt like fasting! And I also lost weight – well, more precisely, I deflated – one, two or three kilos.

I recommend this diet to everyone and I thank Yogananda for it and for all his teachings.

Recipes

 ANNA DATHU SUKHI BHAVA

May the cook be happy! / *Vedic blessing for those who cook*

Contents

Introduction

The story of my beginning as a cook is quite fun and will give hope to anyone! I would like to share it with you.

It all began only shortly before I came to know of Ananda. I had been a vegetarian for several years, but I really had no idea of how to cook. My usual dinner was a plate of pasta with tomato sauce from a jar or maybe some tinned baked beans on toast (an English delicacy!). When I had more money, I treated myself to pizza, potato waffles and ready-made microwave meals. It never even occurred to me to that I could make my own food. One day, however, I don't know what came over me, but I woke up with the desire to learn how to cook. I went to the supermarket, bought every single herb and spice I would need, as well as several essential ingredients, and from then on, spent most evenings in the company of the kitchen stove and my recipe book!

Some of the dishes I remember making are: carrot and coriander soup, vegetable lasagne and houmous. Although I was enthusiastic, I was a complete novice in the kitchen and basically clueless. I didn't even know what salt was for or how to use it to make seemingly tasteless food taste good: needless to say, many of my dishes were lacking in flavour! My humble evening experiments were short-lived. Not long after my cooking transformation I set off for the Ananda Village guest retreat in California, *The Expanding Light*, and left the kitchen behind… or so I thought!

Like many others, instead of paying for my stay at *The Expanding Light*, I opted to do a work exchange programme. My duties included cleaning up after meals, housekeeping and… cook's assistant (to my delight)! For many weeks I quite happily cut lettuce, peeled carrots and sliced onions. Soon after, however, an event occurred that was to push me forwards in my cooking adventure: the two main cooks suddenly became ill and were unable to work. I don't know whether it was the enthusiasm that gleamed in my eye or whether they were just plain desperate, but somebody had the crazy idea to ask if I (as well as a couple of others) would be willing to take on the cooking duties. Talk about running before you've learnt to walk! I was assured, however, that it would be no problem, because everything was written down and calculated, and all I had to do was follow the recipes. And so, with all the courage I could muster, I decided to rise to the challenge. For the

next month or so I cooked two or three times a week for about 60 people. As they had said, it was not so hard: I simply read the recipe and did as it said. The food mostly turned out well, and if it didn't, I called Diksha, the kitchen manager, and she came and fixed it for me.

When I moved to the Ananda community here in Italy, I was immediately allocated to the kitchen- not as a main cook but as an assistant. Even in those days Ananda was famous for its food (although I have to say that it's even better now!). One of the things that struck me immediately was how differently the kitchen was run: here, nobody followed recipes, let alone planned menus! The cook would simply step into the walk-in fridge, look at what was available and invent a menu on the spot! Nobody ever weighed anything or measured anything: nothing was ever calculated mathematically. It was fascinating to watch.

After I had been assisting the cooks for several months, they entrusted me with making dinners. I was both excited and terrified. Although I had learnt several specific recipes from my time at The Expanding Light and learnt a few things from the main cooks here (Pasquale and Christina), my general cooking skills were still minimal. The thing that scared me most was the thought of having to cook without out a recipe. For the first few months, Pasquale and Christina decided the menus for me. They would tell me exactly what to make and how to make it. Their instructions, however, often seemed vague to me. Things that went without saying to them, like "add salt", were, for me, essential instructions! And they hardly ever told me specific quantities…

As I gained more experience in the kitchen, I steadily improved. Whenever Christina, Pasquale or one of the other cooks made a dish that I liked, I wrote down exactly what they had done. I would then try and reproduce the dish myself. In this way I began to understand how to combine different ingredients and seasonings. I soon gained the confidence and the experience to make my own creations. Walking into the fridge and deciding the menu based on the vegetables available is natural to me now. As it is with anything you do in life, the more you practise, the better you become.

So, whether you are a novice in the kitchen or an accomplished vegetarian cook, I hope you will enjoy these recipes and… *A Taste of Joy!*

Joy to you, Mahiya

Using the Recipes: Cooking is Creative

All the recipes in this book have been developed in a creative way. At Ananda, when cooking, the emphasis is always placed on experimenting with new ingredients, new styles and new tastes. When we do use a recipe, it is usually to draw inspiration and new ideas; we then change it according to our own tastes and style of cooking.

Depending on how much experience you have with cooking, I encourage you to do the same. If you are a beginner at vegetarian cooking, it is a good idea to follow the recipes as they are written until the ingredients, tastes and cooking methods become familiar to you. As you gain more confidence, you can gradually try experimenting. If a recipe calls for an ingredient that you don't have, try using a similar ingredient that you do have, for example, broccoli instead of cauliflower and millet instead of quinoa, etc. If a recipe calls for a spice or vegetable that you don't like, try substituting it with one that you do like. Gradually, as you gain more experience, you will see that new ideas come quickly and easily to you. Even if you already have experience with vegetarian cooking, I suggest that you follow the recipes as they are written at least once, in order to get a feel for the outcome intended. After that, make any changes you wish according to your own tastes and inspiration.

Although the recipes in this book have been thoroughly tested, there are many factors which can alter the outcome of the dish. These factors include the altitude at which you live, the cooking equipment you use and the freshness of your ingredients. Even the person cooking puts a certain amount of their own uniqueness into the food: it is not uncommon for the same dish to turn out differently depending on who cooked it, even if it was prepared in the same kitchen, with the same ingredients, following the same recipe. Therefore, use your common sense, as well as your experience. Get used to tasting the food while you prepare it, seeing if there's something that needs to be added or adjusted. You will, in time, develop the sensitivity to know exactly what needs to be changed in order for the food to be perfect.

And remember: when food is prepared with love and as an act of giving and serving, it becomes filled with sweet and devotional vibrations. These vibrations are, in the end, the most important ingredient. Even if you make mistakes, when food is prepared with love, it will taste wonderful to those who eat it.

Important Indications

V   **VEGAN**: Vegan recipe or vegan option given in the recipe.

G   **GLUTEN-FREE**: Gluten-free recipe or gluten-free option given in the recipe.

G*   These recipes easily become gluten-free by substituting the wheat pasta with rice, corn or buckwheat pasta; or the grain with rice, quinoa, buckwheat or any other gluten-free grain.

Q   **QUICK**: Quick recipe that can be made in 30 minutes or under or a quick option given in the recipe. The time given is for an average speed person. Bear in mind that the first time you make a recipe, you'll be a bit slower; but the more you make it, the quicker you'll become.

Q*   Quick recipes to carry out but require periods of waiting or soaking or that the oven is already pre-heated.

Tbsp   refers to a 15 ml measuring tablespoon. Ordinary tablespoons are usually only 10-12 ml.

tsp   refers to a 5 ml measuring teaspoon. Ordinary teaspoons are usually 3½-4 ml.

1 cup   16 Tablespoons = approximately 250 ml.

Basic Recipes

Sprouts and Baby Greens

Sprouts

To have a little sprouts garden in the corner of your kitchen and see a seed that awakens and changes into a sprout, is really to observe a miracle in progress. These miracles happen in nature all the time but especially if you live in the city, rarely do you get the opportunity to observe them so closely. The beauty of sprouts is that they grow right there in your kitchen! Every day you have the opportunity to see how much they have changed and developed from the day before. In a day and age when most people buy their food at the supermarket, already harvested and packaged, this connection with nature through sprouts can be really significant, especially for kids.

Including sprouts in your diet is one of the most cost-efficient, easiest ways to obtain a concentrated amount of nutrients, protein and Life Energy. A 500 gram container of alfalfa seeds costs about £5-8. This is enough to supply you with alfalfa sprouts every day for about three months. Apart from the seeds, all that is required to grow sprouts is about one minute of your attention each day, a few simple tools (described later) and four magic ingredients...

Water is the first and probably the most important magic ingredient. The moment the seed comes into contact with water, it awakens from its deep slumber, and the chemical reactions required to turn the seed into a plant are activated.

Correct temperature is the second magic ingredient. In general, an environment of 20-28°C works well for all seeds.

Oxygen is the third magic ingredient. In order for seeds to germinate, they need to be able to breathe. A container that allows plenty of fresh air to access the sprouts is therefore important..

Light is the fourth magic ingredient. Light, however, is not necessary for all sprouts, only to the leafy varieties (described later) and only after 3-4 days of germination. Light allows leafy sprouts to photosynthesise and produce the energy-

Leafy Sprouts

Legume Sprouts

giving chlorophyll. Sunlight should always be *indirect*, never *direct*. Direct sunlight is too strong for the delicate sprouts and will burn them.

Choosing Seeds

Sprouts vary enormously from one to the other in taste, appearance and texture as well as in their nutritional health benefits (a detailed nutritional chart, which includes all varieties of sprouts, can be found in the appendix).

Every sprout is, indeed, unique. In general, sprouts can be divided into three categories: *leafy sprouts*, *legume sprouts* and *grain sprouts*.

Some of the easiest and most popular seeds to sprout are:

Leafy Sprouts	Legume Sprouts	Grain Sprouts
Alfalfa 1	Red Adzuki 1	Oats 1
Radish 2	Mung Bean 2	Spelt 2
Red clover 3	Fenugreek 3	Wheat 3
	Lentil 4	Kamut 4
	Green Pea 5	Rye 5

Alfalfa is a good sprout to start with.

Seeds must be high-quality, preferably organic and look good in both their exterior colour and shape. Broken, damaged and unusually-coloured seeds will probably not sprout and could also easily rot or prevent the good seeds from sprouting.

Seeds are much cheaper when bought in larger quantities. This is no problem in terms of storage as, when stored in the correct conditions (in a cool, dry, dark place), seeds will last for years. Buy small quantities at first to see if you like the sprouts; if you do, you can invest in larger quantities.

Sprout seeds can be purchased from most health food shops.

Grain Sprouts

There are two main methods used for sprouting seeds:

❖ **The Jar Method**

❖ **The Sprouter Method**

Both are simple to use and economic. Each one has its own advantages. What follows is a step-by-step guide on how to grow sprouts with both the jar and the sprouter methods. The first four steps for each of the two methods are basically the same but differ in technique, whereas steps five, six and seven are the same for both methods.

THE JAR METHOD

This is the most economical of the two methods (although the sprouter method involves only the cost of the sprouter) and perhaps the best option for getting you started. To use the jar method, you will need:

❖ a few glass jars between 800 ml and 1500 ml

❖ a few pieces of mesh*

❖ some elastic bands

Step One: Soaking

Take a glass jar and place a small amount of your chosen seed inside. The amount of seed required depends on how much that variety expands when it grows.

❖ For *leafy sprouts* (such as alfalfa, radish and red clover etc.): Start with just 1 ½ tablespoons in a 800 ml jar or 3 tablespoons in a 1500 ml jar

❖ For *legumes* (such as green pea, mung, adzuki etc.): Start with ¼ of a cup in a 800 ml jar or ½ a cup in a 1500 ml jar

❖ For *grains* (which don't expand very much at all): Fill the container you use one third full with grain.

Place a piece of mesh over the top of the jar and hold it in place with a sturdy elastic band; this will remain in place until the sprouts are ready to be 'harvested'. It is important to cover the jar with a piece of mesh, rather than a lid, because it allows for good ventilation. As you will remember, air is one of the magic ingredients needed to grow sprouts successfully. The mesh will also act as a filter when it comes to rinsing.

* The material used for bridal veils works excellently.

Fill the jar with about twice the amount of warm water as there are seeds and leave them to soak for the required amount of time. Individual soaking times are given in the "Sprouting Specifics" chart at the end of this chapter (generally 8-12 hours). The soaking times given are the *ideal* amount of time that seeds should be soaked; there is, however, a little room for give and take.

Step Two: Initial Rinsing

When the required soaking time is over, take the glass jar to the sink and empty the water through the mesh. Rinse the seeds well by filling the jar with a little warm water, swishing it around so that the sprouts underneath also get a good wash and then emptying it. Repeat this process several times until you see that the water is clear. Empty the rinsing water one final time.

In order for seeds to sprout they must be moist but without excess water. To ensure that all excess water is drained from the jar, leave it upside down at a 45° angle for about 5 minutes.

Step Three: Finding a Home

Place the jar in a suitable corner of your kitchen. Leafy sprouts should be kept in semi-darkness for the first 3-4 days of germination and then in indirect sunlight for the last 1-2 days so that they can photosynthesise. Legume and grain sprouts should be kept in semi-darkness for the whole sprouting process. Remember that the surrounding temperature needs to be between 20 and 28°C for the sprouts to grow, and they must have good air ventilation.

Step Four: Daily Watering

In order to keep the sprouts moist, they must be watered 1-3 times daily until they are ready to harvest. Water the sprouts by repeating the process given above in "Step Two: Initial Rinsing". However, as you are watering this time, not rinsing them thoroughly as before, it is necessary to fill and empty the jar only once. Always leave the jar upside down at a 45° angle for about 5 minutes.

Each type of sprout has different watering requirements. These are indicated in the "Sprouting Specifics" chart at the end of this chapter. In general, leafy sprouts and legumes need watering the most and grains, the least. In fact, grains, which ferment easily if given too much water, often do better by being lightly vaporised, rather than being submerged in water.

Continue to water your sprouts daily until they are the desired length and ready to be harvested (see "Step Five: Harvesting Sprouts").

THE SPROUTER METHOD

The sprouter method is the most popular way to grow sprouts and also considered the most convenient. To use the sprouter method you will need:

❖ a bowl to soak seeds in

❖ a set of sprouter trays

Sprouters are available in plastic, terracotta and glass. The advantage of a sprouter compared to jars is that you can rinse all the sprouts you are growing in one go. In addition, the sprouter's trays stack one on top of the other, looking more orderly and taking up less space in your kitchen. Different varieties of sprouts can be grown on the different levels of the sprouter, as long as they have the same watering requirements.

When choosing a sprouter, make sure its trays have plenty of holes or slots in the bottom. Holes allow the proper drainage of water from one level to the next and supply a support for baby sprout rootlets. The base tray is not used to grow sprouts but to collect falling water. It should, therefore, have no holes.

Another important thing to look for when choosing a sprouter is that, when its trays are stacked one on top of the other, there is plenty of space between each level. This allows for correct air ventilation. A lack of space in between each level encourages the growth of mould.

Sprouters can be found in most health food shops. The sprouter I use myself is the 'GEO' sprouter (see photo).

The basic steps for growing sprouts in a sprouter are exactly the same as for the jars. The method used is slightly different:

Step One: Soaking

As with the jars method, all seeds must be soaked according to their specific requirements. Instead of soaking them in a jar, you can use a bowl or any other container.

Step Two: Initial Rinsing

When the required soaking time is over, strain away the soaking water with the help of a sieve and rinse the seeds several times until the water runs clear (as with the jars method).

When the water is clear, strain the seeds a final time, spread them out on the sprouter trays and then stack the trays one on top of the other. It's important not to overfill the trays with seeds as it could prevent correct drainage of water and air ventilation. (The only exception is for mung sprouts: the more you put the better they grow.) With practice, you will get used to the right amount of seeds for each tray.

Step Three: Finding a Home

Place your sprouter in a suitable, warm place, remembering that leafy sprouts should grow in semi-darkness for the first 3-4 days and then in indirect sunlight for the last 1-2 days; legume and grain sprouts should grow in semi-darkness for the whole sprouting process.

Step Four: Daily Watering

With the sprouter method, watering your sprouts is really quick and simple. There is no need to water each individual tray separately. The holes in the trays allow you to water all your sprouts by pouring water over the top level tray only. Excess water will pass down though the holes, watering the sprouts on the lower level trays as it goes. It will then collect in the bottom tray and can be discarded.

The best way to water your sprouts is to place the whole sprouter in the sink. Turn on the tap and put your hand under the flow of water to make a sprinkler effect. Be careful of small seeds for the first couple of days: until they are a little bit bigger, too strong a flow of water can wash them through the holes. Alternatively, use a watering can (with sprinkler) or a glass to pour the water over the sprouts, just as you would do with a plant.

The watering requirements for each sprout variety are the same as with the jars method (see "Sprouting Specifics" chart).

That's it! When your sprouts are the desired length, they are ready to be harvested.

Final Steps for Both Jar and Sprouter Methods

Step Five: Harvesting Sprouts

Harvesting time varies from sprout to sprout. In general, grain sprouts are the quickest sprouts to harvest, taking only 1-2 days. Although the white sprout of grains can be left to grow to about 2 ½ cm, most people prefer the taste when they are harvested sooner. Legume sprouts should be harvested before the leaf comes out, when the sprout is between ½ and 3 cm long (depending on the legume). Leafy sprouts, on the contrary, are at the peak of their nutritional benefits when they have a green leaf. They generally grow to between 2 ½ and 5 cm.

Specific lengths of different sprout varieties are given in the "Sprouting Specifics" chart. Sprouting time is also indicated in the chart, although it is approximate and can vary according to the environmental temperature.

Step Six: Hulling Sprouts

It is worth spending a few minutes to 'hull' your sprouts before eating or storing them. Hulled sprouts look better, taste better and keep longer. Hulling sprouts is easy. First remove them from the sprouter or jar where you have grown them, being careful not to break the roots, and then put them in a largish bowl or directly into the sink. Fill the bowl or sink with water and then swish it around gently with your hands in order to help the hull loosen from the sprout. Loose hulls will either float to the surface or sink to the bottom, whereas sprouts should float halfway. This will allow you to carefully remove the sprouts from the water, leaving the discarded hulls where they are or vice versa.

Some sprouts, such as grains, do not need to be hulled (they are already hulled) and can be eaten or stored straight away without any prior preparation.

Step Seven: Storing Sprouts

Sprouts can be stored in the fridge for about a week without losing nutritional value (unlike other foods once harvested), although they are always best eaten within the span of a few days.

Stored sprouts must be completely dry. If you have hulled your sprouts, dry them by spinning them around for a few seconds in a salad spinner. When they are dry, put them in a suitable container (glass is best) and keep them in the fridge.

Because sprouts can be stored in the fridge, a good method is to refrigerate enough of each sprout to last you the same amount of days that that variety takes to grow. This way, in the time that it takes you to consume your already-cultivated sprouts, you can be growing your next batch.

Avoiding Mould

Sprouts that are grown in the wrong conditions can develop mould. Mould flourishes in excessively damp environments with a lack of ventilation. Avoiding mould is therefore easy: simply take care to:

- ❖ drain sprouts in jars well after each watering
- ❖ avoid overfilling sprouters with too many seeds (which can prevent the drainage of water and ventilation)
- ❖ allow plenty of air ventilation to all varieties

Summary:

Step One: Soak a small amount of seeds.

Step Two: Strain and rinse the soaked seeds well.

Step Three: Find a home that has the correct temperature and light.

Step Four: Water your sprouts 1-3 times daily.

Step Five: Harvest your sprouts when they are the correct length.

Step Six: Hull your sprouts (vegetable and legume sprouts only).

Step Seven: Dry your sprouts well and eat them or store them in the fridge.

Sprouting Specifics

Sprout	Soaking	Watering	Length
Leafy Sprouts			
Alfalfa	8-12 hrs	2-3 times daily	2 ½-5 cm
Radish	8-12 hrs	2-3 times daily	2 ½-5 cm
Red Clover	8-12 hrs	2-3 times daily	2 ½-5 cm
Legumes			
Red Azuki	8-12 hrs	2-3 times daily	½-2 cm
Mung Beans	8-12 hrs	2-3 times daily	½-2 cm*
Fenugreek	8-12 hrs	2-3 times daily	2 ½-5 cm†
Lentils	8-12 hrs	2-3 times daily	½-1 cm
Green Peas	8-12 hrs	2-3 times daily	2 ½-3 cm
Grains			
Oats	1-5 hrs	Once daily	¾ cm
Spelt	8-12 hrs	Once daily	¾-2 ½ cm
Wheat	8-12 hrs	Once daily	¾-2 ½ cm
Kamut	8-12 hrs	Once daily	¾-2 ½ cm
Rye	8-12 hrs	Once daily	¾-2 ½ cm

*Although this is the ideal length for harvesting mung sprouts from a nutritional point of view, they can be grown as long as 7 cm (in a sprouter only, not in a jar) for use in Chinese-style dishes (see the recipe "Chinese-Style Spaghetti").

Sprouting Time	Particulars
5-7 days	Expose to indirect light a couple of days before harvesting.
5-7 days	Soft white hairs in first few days indicate incorrect quantities of water and can lead to mould. Rinse the hairs away under running water immediately and adjust rinsing routine. Expose to indirect light a couple of days before harvesting.
5-7 days	Expose to indirect light a couple of days before harvesting.
2-4 days	Grow in semi-darkness. Harvest before leaves develop.
2-4 days	Grow in semi-darkness. Harvest before leaves develop.
2-4 days	Grow in semi-darkness. Harvest before leaves develop.
2-4 days	Grow in semi-darkness. Harvest before leaves develop.
2-4 days	Peas must be non-cracked. Grow in semi-darkness. Harvest before leaves develop.
1-2 days	Over-watering can cause fermentation.
2-3 days	Over-watering can cause fermentation.
2-3 days	Over-watering can cause fermentation.
2-3 days	Over-watering can cause fermentation.
2-3 days	Over-watering can cause fermentation.

† Fenugreek, because of its appearance and length, almost seems to be a leafy sprout; it does, in fact, grow very well together with radish, red clover or alfalfa sprouts.

Sunflower and Buckwheat Baby Greens

Sunflower and buckwheat baby greens are similar to sprouts, the only differences being that they are longer, grown in soil and are cut when they are ready to be harvested. Baby greens, with their long, white stems and rich, green leaves, are two of the most appealing salad vegetables available. Not only are they beautiful to look at, they also provide a wealth of nutrition: they are an excellent source of protein, as well as phosphorus, potassium, calcium, magnesium and the blood-enriching chlorophyll. Like sprouts, baby greens are an invaluable source of Life Energy.

You Will Need:

❖ Sunflower or buckwheat seeds with hull (preferably organic and specific for growing sprouts)

❖ A flat tray (about 20 cm x 30 cm)

❖ Unfertilised soil

❖ Several wooden blocks

❖ A dark plastic sheet, large enough to cover the tray (a bin bag works fine)

❖ A watering can

Step One: Sorting Seeds

❖ Sort through your seeds to remove any damaged ones (damaged seeds don't sprout and have a tendency to rot).

Step Two: Soaking

❖ Soak the seeds for 12-15 hours.

❖ Rinse well and then strain the soaked seeds.

Step Three: Sewing

❖ Place a wooden block in each corner of your flat tray and one in the middle.

❖ Fill the tray with a layer of soil (the places where you put the wooden blocks remain without soil). Water the soil well.

❖ Spread the soaked seeds on top of the watered soil and cover with another light layer of soil. Spray this layer of soil with a little water.

Step Four: Initial Growing

❖ Cover the tray with a dark plastic sheet and leave the seeds to grow in the dark for 3-4 days until they are about 3 cm high (no need to water the soil further in this period).

❖ After 3-4 days uncover the baby greens, remove the wooden blocks and place the tray in indirect sunlight.

Step Five: Watering

❖ Water the greens once a day (more if you see the soil is getting dry) by pouring water in the holes where the wooden blocks were. When the rootlets grow longer they will form a type of mat which holds together the soil, allowing you to lift the soil up and water underneath. Never water on top of the soil as this will cause the seeds to rot.

❖ When the greens are about 8-10 cm high they are ready to harvest.

Step Six: Harvesting and Hulling

❖ To harvest your baby greens, simply cut the stems using a knife or scissors as close to the base as possible. Put the greens in a bowl of water and remove any remaining hulls. Wash well and eat fresh! (Baby greens should be eaten fresh because, having had their stems cut, they stop growing and start to lose nutritional value).

Eleven Great Ways to Serve
Sprouts and Baby Greens

❖ Eat them fresh and un-cooked in mixed salads or potato salads

❖ Blend into smoothies or juices *(leafy sprouts)*

❖ Juice them *(leafy sprouts)*

❖ Use in sandwiches, wraps and roll-ups instead of lettuce *(alfalfa, red clover, radish, baby greens)*

❖ Use in coleslaw *(red clover, radish)*

❖ Stir-fry briefly with other vegetables *(alfalfa, red clover, radish, mung bean, lentil)*

❖ Stir into soups or stews when serving *(mung bean, lentil)*

❖ Combine in rice dishes towards the end of the cooking time *(fenugreek, lentil, mung bean)*

❖ Sauté briefly with onions *(mung bean, red clover, radish)*

❖ Puree with peas or beans *(mung bean, lentil)*

❖ Steam a little and serve with butter *(mung bean, lentil)*

Recipes in This Book Containing
Sprouts and Baby Greens

Grains | v

All grains use essentially the same preparation and cooking techniques, although the amount of water and cooking times may vary. Here are some general guidelines:

- ❖ Measure the volume of grain you will need.

- ❖ Wash the grain well. Three times is usually sufficient, although some more dirty grains might need more. The water will be reasonably clear after the last rinsing.

- ❖ Leave harder grains to soak for several hours (see "Soaking Grains for Quicker Cooking" below); softer grains do not need to be soaked.

- ❖ Place the grain in a saucepan with fresh water and a little salt. The amount of water varies depending on the grain (see chart below).

- ❖ Cover, bring to the boil and then turn down to a simmer. Do not stir the grain or lift up the lid while it is cooking (if necessary, you can shake the pot once the water boils). When all of the water has been absorbed and the grain is very nearly cooked, remove it from the heat and leave it to stand. The grain will continue to steam on its own until it is perfectly done in another 5-10 minutes or so.

- ❖ Fluff the cooked grain with a fork and serve.

Grain	Amount (dried)	Amount of water	Cooking time once water boils	Yields
Amaranth	1 cup	2 cups	20 minutes	1 ¾ cups
Barley, pearl	1 cup	3 cups	30 minutes	4 cups
Basmati rice, white	1 cup	1 ¾ cups	8-10 minutes	4 cups
Brown rice	1 cup	2 cups	25-30 minutes	2 ½ cups
Buckwheat	1 cup	2 cups	15 minutes	2 ½ cups
Bulgur*	1 cup	1 ¼ cups	4-5 minutes	3 cups
Millet	1 cup	2 cups	10-15 minutes	3 cups
Quinoa	1 cup	A little less than 2 cups	20 minutes	3 ½ cups
Spelt, pearled	1 cup	2 cups	25 minutes	2 ½ cups

Grains soaked for 8 hours

Grain	Amount (dried)	Amount of water	Cooking time once water boils	Yields
Brown rice	1 cup	1 ½ cups	15 minutes	2 cups
Kamut	1 cup	3 cups	60 minutes	3 cups
Rye	1 cup	1 cup	25-30 minutes	2 cups
Spelt, hulled	1 cup	2 cups	50-60 minutes	2 cups
Wild rice	1 cup	3 cups	35-40 minutes	4 cups

*Bulgur can also simply be soaked in twice the amount of hot water for 2-3 hours or warm water for 8 hours.

N.B.: The indications given in the above table are approximate cooking times, and yields of grains can vary even from brand to brand.

Couscous

Because couscous is pre-cooked, it has a slightly different cooking process than the other grains.

Put 1 cup of couscous in a saucepan. Mix with a little olive oil and then add an equal amount of boiling water or vegetable stock. Cover immediately and leave to stand for about 10 minutes until all the water has been absorbed. No further heat is needed. Fluff the cooked couscous with a fork. The yield is 3 cooked cups for every dry cup.

Soaking Grains for Quicker Cooking

It is recommended to soak harder grains, such as hulled spelt, wild rice, kamut, rye and pot barley, before cooking. Medium-hard grains, such as brown rice, do not necessarily need to be soaked, but doing so will dramatically reduce their cooking time (cooking water should be adjusted accordingly). Soft grains, such as quinoa and amaranth, as well as refined grains, do not need to be pre-soaked.

As well as saving you time, soaking grains to reduce cooking time helps to preserve the nutritional and energetic content of the grain (the more you cook them, the fewer nutrients they retain).

Grains, as a general rule, should be soaked for up to 8 hours. Do not soak the grain for more than 12 hours, as it may start to ferment, especially if the surrounding temperature is warm. Refrigerating the grain while it is soaking is an excellent option.

Use the water the grain was soaked in to cook the grain, adding fresh water as required. If you soak a grain for more than 8 hours, change the water halfway through and use the second round of water to cook the grain.

Increase the Flavour by Dry-Roasting First

Dry-roasting grains enhances their flavour by giving them a rich, nutty taste. Dry-roasting also transforms the starch into dextrin, making the grain more digestible and fluffy rather than sticky. Grains such as quinoa, millet and amaranth are often dry-roasted before being cooked in water. Bear in mind, this will slightly reduce their cooking time.

To dry-roast: Place the grain in a frying pan (no oil). Dry-roast on a medium heat for 2-10 minutes (depending on the grain), stirring constantly until the grain is fragrant and lightly browned.

N.B.: Nuts and seeds can be dry-roasted in the same way.

Alternatives to Cooking with Water

Grains are usually cooked with water, but vegetable stock (page 192) can also be used to enhance the flavour and increase the mineral content. Oil, ghee (page 188), herbs and spices can also be added during cooking.

Cooking Large Quantities

Increasing the amount of grains you cook changes the grain-water ratio: as the amount of grain increases, the amount of water decreases proportionately. No formula exists that can be applied to all grains: experimentation is the only way to find out. Too much water, however, can easily be rectified by either straining and using the extra liquid as a stock, or by removing the lid and cooking the grain for a few minutes on a high flame. Too little water can be rectified by adding a little more.

The Difference between Hard and Soft Grains

Some grains remain slightly chewy when cooked; others become soft and fluffy. Harder-texture grains are: barley, brown rice, kamut, rye, wheat and spelt. Softer grains are: amaranth, buckwheat, white rice, bulgur, couscous, millet, oats and quinoa.

Serving Sizes

In planning a meal, prepare between 1 and 2 cups of cooked grain per person (you can use the chart to help you calculate the corresponding amount of uncooked grain). Robust grains, such as spelt, pot barley and brown rice, are more filling than lighter, fluffier grains like basmati, quinoa and bulgur and so, less is needed. Cooked grains will keep well in the fridge for 3-5 days.

Legumes | V G

As you read in the chapter "The Protein Myth", legumes are a great source of nutrition: combined with grains, they provide you with all of your protein needs. Every vegetarian's diet should include legumes.

Cooking soft, tender and easy-to-digest legumes is easy. Here's how to do it:

❖ Soak your chosen legume in plenty of water. (See "Two Different Methods for Soaking Legumes" below.)

❖ Strain the legume and rinse it well. Discard the soaking water (it is toxic).

❖ Put the legume in a large saucepan with 3-4 times its volume in water. Cover, bring to the boil, then turn down the heat and simmer for 1-2 hours until the legume is completely soft. The legume should be covered with water at all times. If necessary, you can add extra water during the cooking process.

❖ When the legume starts to foam, remove the foam with a tea strainer.

❖ When the legume is soft and fully cooked, remove it from the water. Keep the cooking water: it is excellent for soups, especially minestrone soup.

Two Different Methods for Soaking Legumes

The most common method for soaking legumes is the "Overnight Method":.

❖ Put the legume in a bowl and cover it with plenty of water. Three cups of water are required for every cup of the dried legume.

❖ Leave the legume to soak for 6-8 hours or overnight. If the legume is soaked for longer than 8 hours, it should be kept in the fridge to prevent fermentation.

An alternative method for soaking legumes is the "Two Hours Only Method":

❖ Put the legume in a large saucepan. Cover with three cups of water for every cup of the dried legume used.

❖ Bring to the boil and continue to boil for two minutes.

❖ Turn off the heat and leave the legume to soak in the boiling water for two hours. (Keep covered).

N.B.: Be sure to discard the soaking water and cook in fresh water.

Both methods have their advantages, so choose whichever one suits you best. Split red lentils, split peas and mung dhal are very small and do not need to be soaked before cooking. Lentils, in general, do not necessarily need to be soaked before cooking, but cooking time is greatly reduced if they are.

Why Legumes Sometimes Never Get Soft

The secret to soft and tender legumes is to avoid using legumes that have been sitting in your cupboard for more than 6 months. The older a legume, the longer it takes to cook. If the legume is too old, it may never get soft. If, however, you do get stuck with an old legume, adding a pinch of bicarbonate of soda to the soaking water will help it to become soft.

When to Add the Salt

Salt should never be added to the water while the legume is cooking: it blocks the cooking process and prevents the legume's skin from becoming tender. Salt, however, can be added to the water once the legume is completely soft.

In the case of legume salads, salt can be added to the cooking water a little earlier. This will help keep the skin of the legume intact.

Difficulties with Digestion?

If you have difficulties with digesting legumes, try these few simple tricks:

* Try incorporating legumes into your diet slowly. Start by eating reserved amounts of smaller legumes, such as lentils and white beans, one or two times a week. Your body will gradually grow accustomed to legumes and start to produce the enzymes necessary for their digestion.

* Add the algae kombu to the legume cooking water: It aids with digestion and also enhances the flavour.

* Fresh ginger is also excellent at helping with digestion and can be added to the cooking water. Cumin seeds, coriander seeds, fennel seeds, bay leaves and rosemary, can also be added to the cooking water to aid with digestion.

* Make sure the legume is cooked thoroughly: hard and chewy legumes are difficult to digest.

* Take care to remove the white foam from the cooking water when it forms on the surface. This foam is one of the main contributors to gas. You may even like to try discarding the cooking water once it foams and continue cooking your legumes in fresh water.

* Some people say that cooking legumes in distilled water prevents the problem of gas (although I have never personally tried it).

A Note about Soya Beans

Raw and undercooked soya beans contain a substance that inhibits trypsin, a key enzyme for protein digestion. Soya beans should be soaked for at least 12 hours and cooked in water for about 3-4 hours. During the first hour of cooking they should be boiled, after which the heat can be turned down to a simmer. Other soya products (tofu, tempeh, soya milk, soya sauce, etc.) are quite safe to eat.

Soya Milk | V G Q*

Obviously, you can buy soya milk at the supermarket, but homemade soya milk is much more natural and contains a higher concentration of soya than the ones in the supermarket, making it more nutritious. This recipe for soya milk requires only about 30 minutes to make. ▶ *Makes approximately 1750 ml of soya milk.*

Soak for about 12 hours in plenty of water:
   250 g organic soya beans

Strain the soya beans and rinse well.

In a large saucepan (5 litre capacity), bring to the boil:
   1 ½ litres water

Now, in a blender, blend the soaked soya beans together with 750 ml of water until you have a fine paste. Add the paste to the boiling water.

Bring the mixture back to the boil, removing the foam that forms on the surface. When it boils, turn down the heat, being careful that it doesn't boil over. Boil for about 10 minutes then turn off the heat.

Strain the milk through a sieve lined with a very thin cheese cloth (the thinner the better- it should pour right through).

Leave to cool and then refrigerate. Drink within 5 days.

🧍 *Soya milk is an excellent alkaline alternative to cow's milk and is virtually free of saturated fats.*

Soya Yoghurt | V G Q°

Soya yoghurt, because of the live cultures it contains, is excellent for keeping your intestines healthy. Soya yoghurt is really easy to make and tastes great in smoothies, with fruit salads or poured over desserts. It works best if you use homemade soya milk to make it. This is because homemade soya milk has a much higher content of soya beans compared to shop-bought soya milk. If you do use shop-bought milk, it's important that it contains no added salt. There is no need to add the water if you use shop-bought soya milk. ▶ Makes 1 ½ litres.

Bring to the boil:
   1 litre homemade soya milk
   ½ litre water
   3 tsp agaragar flakes or 1 tsp agaragar powder
and boil for 5-8 minutes, as indicated on the agaragar packet.

Let the milk cool down to 45-50°C (this will take a little while so find something to do in the meantime). At first you may need a thermometer to find the correct temperature but, with practice you can simply use your index finger. The soya milk should be a little hotter than the natural temperature of your finger.

Stir into the hot warm milk:
   6 Tbsp already-made soya yoghurt
   any sweetener to taste *(optional)*
   vanilla to taste *(optional)*

Transfer the warm soya milk into a glass jar. Put a lid on, and then wrap the jar in a woollen scarf or small blanket. This will keep the soya milk warm, creating the perfect environment for the cultures to multiply and transform the milk into yoghurt.

This process takes about 8-10 hours depending on the season and other variables. During this time, the jar should not be touched or moved. It is, therefore, ideal to make yoghurt in the evening and leave it to rest overnight when it will not be disturbed.

To know if the soya yoghurt is ready, tilt the jar. If the yoghurt falls away from the side of the jar, it is ready. At this point the yoghurt should be refrigerated.

Before you finish eating your yoghurt, remember to put a little bit aside to make your next batch with. This is your 'starter' yoghurt.

N.B.: Soya yoghurt has an almost solid consistency, but it also creates lots of whey: this is normal. Sometimes I blend my soya yoghurt to make a more homogeneous consistency.

◑ *Soya yoghurt is alkaline, full of protein and low in saturated fat.*

Yoghurt | G Q*

Yoghurt, because of the live cultures it contains, is excellent for balancing your intestinal flora and helping with digestion. Homemade yoghurt tastes so much better than the readymade yoghurt bought in the shops, and it is so simple to make. ▶ *Makes 1 litre.*

Bring to the boil:
  1 litre fresh milk*

Let the milk cool to 45-50°C (the lower the temperature, the more liquidy the yoghurt; the higher the temperature, the more solid).† At first you may need a thermometer to find the correct temperature but, with practice, you can simply use your index finger. The milk should be a little hotter than the natural temperature of your finger.

Stir into the hot milk:
  1 Tbsp already-made natural yoghurt

Transfer the hot milk into a 1 litre glass jar. Put a lid on and then wrap the jar in a woollen scarf or small blanket. This will keep the milk warm, creating the perfect environment for the cultures to multiply and transform the milk into yoghurt.

This process takes about 8-10 hours depending on the season and other variables. During this time the jar should not be touched or moved. It is, therefore, ideal to make yoghurt in the evening and leave it to rest overnight when it will not be disturbed.

To find out if the yoghurt is ready, tilt the jar. If the yoghurt falls away from the side of the jar then it is ready. At this point it should be refrigerated. If you delay refrigeration, the yoghurt becomes sour.

Before you finish eating your yoghurt, remember to put a little bit aside to make your next batch with. This is your 'starter' yoghurt.

🌀 *Remember, biodynamic milk is the best milk with which to make your yoghurt: it's more nutritious and energetic than regular commercial milk, as well as safer, and it also causes much less suffering to the cows.*

---

*Although UHT milk is not recommended, if you do happen to use it, note that it does not need to be boiled first: it has already been heated to high temperatures during processing. You just have to bring it to the necessary temperature of 45-50°C.

† It's fine to let the milk cool down completely and then heat it to the correct temperature several hours later. The important thing is that it has been boiled.

Yoghurt / Soya Yoghurt Cheese | V G Q*

This is a wonderful, creamy, fresh cheese, so simple to make. It can be spread on bread or crackers, used as a dip or eaten with salad or potatoes. There are two recipes in this book combining yoghurt cheese with other ingredients: Creamy Yoghurt Cheese Salad (page 214) and Open Jacket Potatoes with Yoghurt Cheese (page 347). On page 357 you will find the recipe Yoghurt Mousse with Berry Sauce, which uses sweetened yoghurt cheese.

Line a bowl with a cotton or linen cloth. Put at least 1 litre* of dairy yoghurt or soya yoghurt (this recipe does not work so well with homemade soya yoghurt so use a shop-bought one) into the cloth and then tie closed with a string.

Tie the string to a handle or piece of furniture which allows the yoghurt to hang suspended in the air. Put a container underneath to catch the liquid (hanging on a tap works well as the liquid drips straight into the sink).

Leave the yoghurt suspended for about 9 hours. During this time the liquid part of the yoghurt (whey) will drip out and leave a creamy yoghurt cheese.

After 9 hours, take the cloth down and use a spatula to remove the cheese.

The cheese can then be flavoured with salt, olive oil and fresh herbs. Garlic is also good. My favourite combination is garlic paste (page 193) and fresh mint.

The whey that comes out of the yoghurt also is very nutritious and can be used in soups or simply drunk as it is. It's very beneficial for upset stomachs and for your intestines.

Yoghurt Cheese contains all the properties of yoghurt but in a concentrated form. Remember that dairy products are high in saturated fats: small portions, therefore, are better than large ones. Soya, on the other hand, is low in saturated fats.

---

* The quantity of cheese that comes out will be about half the amount of yoghurt you hang.

Ghee
(clarified butter) | G Q

Ghee has a rich, sweet taste, and when added to vegetables, rice or chappatis (page 246), gives a wonderful yet simple flavour. Because ghee does not contain water or casein (the substance that makes butter go rancid), it lasts for years without going bad. It is, therefore, worth making large quantities. According to Ayurveda, ghee strengthens the digestive fire. For those who have digestive problems, a spoon of ghee with every meal is recommended. In my experience, not all brands of butter (usually the lesser-quality ones) have made good ghee. Buy good-quality butter, and if it doesn't come out well, change brands.

Put at least 500 g of butter in a heavy-based saucepan. Cook over a medium heat, stirring occasionally, until the butter starts to boil.

When you see the surface becoming covered with a white froth, turn the heat down as low as possible and continue to cook.

When the butter is a clear, pale gold and you can see the bottom of the pan, turn off the heat (see approximate cooking times below).

Strain the butter through a thin cheesecloth, into a jar or any other container. This is your ghee. The solids that you see left in the cheesecloth after straining are toxic residues that are usually deposited in the body when we do not clarify the butter. (These milk solids are only toxic when butter is cooked at high temperatures.) Unlike butter, ghee does not need to be kept in the fridge.

Be careful not to let any water come in contact with the ghee, for example, by using a wet spoon, as this will make the ghee turn rancid.

Quantity of Butter	Cooking Time	Quantity of Ghee
500 g	About 20 minutes	300-400 g
1 kg	About 40 minutes	600-800 g

Cooking times depend on several factors: the quality of butter used, the width of the saucepan and especially on the type of stove that is used (gas or electric).

The amount of ghee obtained depends on the water content of the butter: the more water, the less ghee.

🐄 *Using biodynamic butter to make your ghee, as well as being of higher quality and more flavoured than commercial butter, causes much less suffering to the cows.*

Paneer
(Indian cottage cheese) | G Q

This cheese is traditionally used in Indian cooking, but it can also be flavoured with olive oil, garlic, herbs or chilli to give it a more Western taste. Typically, the paneer is cut in cubes, fried in ghee or oil, and then mixed with vegetables. Very simple and quick to make.

Bring at least 1 litre of full cream milk to the boil, stirring occasionally to prevent a skin from forming.

When the milk boils, lower the heat to a simmer and then add vinegar, yoghurt or lemon juice. You will know the right quantity by the reaction: when enough vinegar, yoghurt or lemon juice has been added, the milk will separate into paneer and whey. The whey should be a clear yellowish colour. If not, add a little more vinegar, yoghurt or lemon juice.

Turn off the heat and leave it to stand for a couple of minutes. Then strain the paneer through a colander lined with cheesecloth.

To make a firm cheese that can be cut into cubes, leave the paneer in the cheesecloth and colander and press it under a heavy weight for about one hour. The cubes can then be roasted or fried

N.B.: Paneer does not melt when heated

Pasteurised milk (heated to 63°C) contains a lot more nutrition than sterilised/ long life milk (heated to 145°C).

Tofu | v G

Although tofu can easily be purchased in the shops, homemade tofu is much cheaper and absolutely delicious compared to the shop-bought one. In order to make homemade tofu, you will need to start with homemade soya milk (page 182). Once you have your soya milk, the extra step for making tofu requires only around 5 minutes - well worth the effort. Shop-bought soya milk has a very low quantity of actual soya and will make very little tofu. Many ideas for recipes are given in the "Tofu and Seitan" chapter. ▶ *Makes about 400 g of tofu.*

Make a double batch of homemade soya milk according to the recipe on page 182 (i.e. with 500 g of soya beans). This will give you approximately:
   3 ½ litres of soya milk.

Bring the soya milk to the boil. In the meantime, dissolve in 200 ml warm water:
   1 Tbsp nigari*

When the soya milk boils, turn off the heat and then slowly add the dissolved nigari: after a few seconds the soya milk will separate into tofu and whey. The whey should be a clear yellow. If not, add a little more nigari.
   Strain the tofu through a colander lined with a damp cheesecloth, or through a rectangular tofu mould lined with a damp cheesecloth - this will give you a block of tofu, like that which you find in the shops.†
   Press the tofu with a weight for around 30 minutes.

Tofu will keep in the fridge for up to a week. It should be kept immersed in water, and the water should be changed every couple of days.

N.B.: For an already-flavoured tofu, fresh herbs and spices can be added to the soya milk, just before you add the nigari. Some ideas are: chopped coriander leaves, chopped ginger, spring onions, green chillies and crushed garlic.

 Tofu is an excellent source of plant protein: alkaline, nutritious and low in saturated fats.

* Magnesium chloride. A coagulant that can be found in health food shops.
† Many simple ideas for how to make your own tofu mould can be found on the internet (a Tupperware box or milk carton with drainage holes, for example).

Seitan | v

Contrary to popular belief, seitan is very simple and quick to prepare. Many people, when I have showed them how to make seitan, have been surprised at just how easy it is. Out of the approximately 120 minutes needed to make the seitan, the actual working time is less than 20 minutes. The remaining 100 minutes are required for soaking and boiling, during which time you can be occupied doing other things. Seitan does not have a strong taste of its own but can be flavoured with garlic, soya sauce and herbs. Many ideas for recipes are given in the "Tofu and Seitan" chapter.

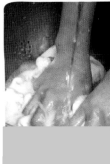

Mix together:

    1 kg Manitoba flour*, or 750 g Manitoba flour plus 250 g wholemeal wheat or wholemeal spelt flour

    water

to make a simple dough (as if you were making bread).

Put the dough in a bowl, cover with warm water and leave immersed for half an hour.

Remove the dough from the water and transfer it into a colander. Put the colander in the sink. Rinse the dough with *warm water*, squeezing it and kneading it continuously with your hands until the water runs clear. This will take about 10 minutes. The consistency, when it is ready, should be a little like chewing gum.

Make a long sausage shape with the seitan and then wrap it in a wet cloth. Close the cloth at both ends, and in the middle, with string or elastic bands. The seitan should not be wrapped too tightly, as it expands when cooked. If it is not able to expand, the final consistency will be hard and rubbery.

Cook the seitan for about 1 hour in boiling water.

The seitan is now ready. It can be flavoured and cooked straight away or stored in the fridge for up to a week. If stored in the fridge, it should be kept immersed in water, and the water should be changed every couple of days. Before using the seitan, squeeze out as much excess water as possible

Seitan contains seven of the eight essential amino acids. Adding kombu to the cooking water or soya sauce once it is cooked, makes your seitan a source of complete protein.

* A high protein Canadian flour. White flour can be used instead of Manitoba flour but will produce only about 300 g of seitan for every kg of flour used instead of the 600 g of seitan produced from Manitoba flour.

Homemade Vegetable Stock | v g

Homemade stock is really simple to make and will give added flavour to your soups and risottos. Make a few litres at a time and refrigerate or freeze.

▶ *Makes approximately 2 ½ litres.*

Sauté in a large (5 litre) saucepan:

2 onions, *cubed*	2 carrots, *cubed*
2 stalks celery, plus leaves, *cubed*	1 bay leaf
1 tsp dried thyme or a sprig fresh thyme	

for about 15 minutes, until the onion starts to brown.

Add to the saucepan:

4 litres water	1 medium potato, *whole, with skin*
2 tomatoes, *whole*	1 clove of garlic, *unpeeled*
few sprigs of parsley	salt *(optional)*

Bring to the boil and then simmer with a lid on for at least an hour.
Remove the vegetables by straining through a sieve or colander.

🕊 *Commercial vegetable stocks often contain monosodium glutamate and other unwanted ingredients. If you do buy instant stock, organic brands are a safe option.*

Garlic/Ginger Paste | V G Q

At Ananda, when using garlic or fresh ginger*, instead of chopping it into small pieces, we usually make a paste by blending it with oil. This is done for two reasons: one, the flavour of the garlic or ginger is diffused much better when blended with oil and, two, the paste can be stored for a few weeks in the fridge (use a glass jar with a lid), meaning that you can make it in bulk and have it ready to use whenever you need it. Approximate values are given below. ▶ *Makes about 10 Tablespoons*

Blend together in a jug using a hand blender:
   10 big cloves garlic or 75 g gingerroot, cut in pieces
   100 ml oil

The consistency should be a thick paste, not too liquid.

🜨 *Small quantities of garlic and other rajasic foods with medicinal properties can be desirable for those who have an active life. Garlic helps to prevent: high blood pressure, flu, colds, coughs, bronchitis, gastrointestinal problems and menstrual pain.*

* Ginger is mainly used in Indian cooking but also, for example, in the Carrot Puree recipe in the "Vegetables and Side Dishes" chapter of this book.

CHAPTER 2

Fruit and Vegetable Juices

Some Useful Tips for Making Juices

Gingerly Carrot

Celery Cleanse

Fennel-Carrot Mix

Vitality Drink

Zangy Zesty Apple

Summer Allotment

Carrot-Pineapple Cocktail

Beet That!

«GREAT BENEFIT MAY BE OBTAINED
by taking health cocktails made of fresh vegetable juices....
Have a health cocktail at least once a day». P.Y.

Some Useful Tips
for Making Juices

You can juice just about any fruit or vegetable, as well as sprouts, fresh ginger and herbs. Fruits and vegetables that do not juice well are: bananas, avocados, fresh figs, aubergine. Bananas and avocados, however, are delicious when blended into your juice afterwards to give a more substantial consistency, as well as added flavour and nutrition.

Try to use organic fruits and vegetables for your juices as much as possible. The peels of non-organic fruits and vegetables are covered with toxic residues from fertilisers and insecticides and should be removed. Alternatively, you can soak non-organic fruits and vegetables in water and bicarbonate of soda: a simple trick that will effectively remove most toxic residues. Because the peel contains more concentrated amounts of nutrients than the flesh does, it should be considered an important part of your juice. Some peel may alter the taste of your juice (either pleasantly or unpleasantly), whereas other peel will be unnoticeable. Experiment with quantities and find what works for you.

To make your juice you will need either a centrifuge juicer or an extractor juicer (also known as a slow juicer). Both have their advantages. Centrifuge juicers are incredibly quick at making juice and cost much less than a good extractor does. They may be the best choice if you are new to juicing and don't yet feel convinced that juices are worth a big time investment. Extractors, on the other hand, cost a lot more (a good quality one, anyway) and take a bit longer to make a juice (maybe five minutes as oppose to one minute). The advantage of extractors, however, is that they squeeze out around 30% more juice from your fruits and vegetables than a centrifuge does. Thanks to the natural *pressing* motion that is used to obtain the juice, as oppose to the more aggressive *shredding* action of the centrifuge, they also preserve the nutritional content of your juice better. Juice made in a centrifuge easily oxidises and should be drunk straight away (even before you clean the juicer), whereas juice made in an extractor is more stable and can be kept in the fridge for up to 48 hours. Extractors are also superb when it comes to juicing highly nutritious green leaves, a point on which the centrifuge is weak.

Whatever the method you use for making your juice, remember: Juices should be drunk slowly. Each mouthful should be masticated and left in the mouth for a few seconds before swallowing.

Following are some of my favourite recipes. All recipes make 350-500 ml of juice, depending on whether you use a centrifuge or an extractor.

Gingerly Carrot | V G Q

Fresh gingerroot gives a wonderful 'kick' to the sweet taste of carrots.

10 medium carrots
1 ½ cm gingerroot (you may want add less if using an extractor and
 more if using a centrifuge)

🦶 *A glass of carrot juice a day is an excellent way to alkalinise your body.*

Celery Cleanse | V G Q

A traditional combination that is sweet and delicious.

4 stalks celery
3 apples
¼ small organic lemon plus some of the rind

🦶 *100 grams of celery provides you with 37% of the RDA of Vitamin K.*

Fennel-Carrot Mix | V G Q

Delicious with a banana blended in afterwards.

½ fennel
2 carrots
2 apples
½ organic lemon plus some of the rind

🦶 *Drinking fresh juices is an easy way to help you to maintain your 60% fruit
 and vegetable target.*

Vitality Drink | V G Q

This revitalising drink is based on a recipe included in Yogananda's Nine Day Diet (found in Part Three of this book). If the taste of parsley is too strong, reduce it, or try adding a little apple. Blend half an avocado in afterwards for a delicious variation

    2 stalks celery
    4 medium carrots
    150 g chard or spinach
    40 g/one small handful of parsley

🧘 *Among all the vegetables, those with green leaves have the highest amount of Life Energy.*

Zangy Zesty Apple | V G Q

This juice will boost your energy level immediately!

3 apples
½ organic lemon plus half of the rind
1 ½ cm (7 g) fresh ginger

🧘 *Lemons give the spiritual quality of enthusiasm and hope!*

Summer Allotment | V G Q

A more savoury juice made from summer seasonal vegetables. Delicious with a splash of olive oil and a pinch of salt. Avocado can also be blended in.

    3 very big tomatoes
    5 cm cucumber
    1 stalk celery
    ⅓ large green pepper
    ¼ small red onion

🧘 *Drinking nutrient-rich vegetable and fruit juices during the summer helps us to replenish minerals we lose through perspiration.*

Carrot-Pineapple Cocktail | v g q

Want to impress your friends at dinner? Start with this cocktail!

3 carrots
4 cm slice pineapple
1 apple
5 g ginger

Carrots are at the top of the list when it comes to Vitamin A: one cup of raw carrots will provide you with over 600% of the RDA!

Beet That! | v g q

So simple, but one of my favourites.

1 medium-sized beetroot (size of a large kiwi)
2 stalks celery
3 apples

Studies show that beetroot juice significantly lowers blood pressure.

Smoothies

See also • Lassi (p. 374)

Thoughts on Smoothies

Smoothies are, I feel, one of the best inventions ever! As well as being full of nutrition, they are also quick and simple to prepare and make a delicious breakfast or evening meal.

Smoothies are a very personal taste: some people like them so thick that they have to eat them with a spoon, others like them more liquid and light. So, feel free to adjust the following recipes according to your own tastes.

A pinch of cinnamon, vanilla, cardamom or nutmeg goes down well in most smoothies, as does fresh gingerroot. A teaspoon of wheat germ, spirulina, hemp powder, or any other nutritious powder can also be added for extra nutrition.

In the winter time smoothies can be briefly heated to room temperature, or made with already warmed soya/rice milk.

All of the recipes make about 500 ml (2 portions). Just put all of the ingredients together in a blender and blend until smooth.

Nutty Smoothie | v g q

A simple trick for making your smoothies absolutely scrumptious? Nut butter!

1 ½ bananas
2 rounded Tbsp almond butter, peanut butter, or any other nut butter
2 small handfuls raisins, *soaked in boiling water for approx. 10 minutes*
250 ml unsweetened soya milk (page 182)

Eating nuts in the form of nut butters and milks is the most effective way to absorb their nutrition.

Apple Seedy Smoothie | v g q

A really healthy smoothie with a wonderful 'seedy' flavour.

1 green apple
1 ½ Tbsp sunflower seeds
1 ½ Tbsp pumpkin seeds
400 ml yoghurt (page 184) or soya yoghurt (page 183)
maple syrup to taste

The old saying "An apple a day keeps the doctor away" is a fact, not just folklore! Apples are one of the richest sources of flavonoids.

Sweet Iron Smoothie | v g q

A sweet and soft smoothie packed with iron from the spinach, pumpkin seeds and raisins.

1 banana
6-7 leaves spinach, or chard
2 Tbsp pumpkin seeds
2 Tbsp coconut
handful raisins, *soaked overnight (or for 10 minutes in boiling water if you forget)*
300 ml oat milk

The two tablespoons of pumpkin seeds in this recipe will provide you with approximately 14% of your iron RDA.

Dried Fruit Smoothie | V G Q

This smoothie will keep you feeling satisfied for hours.

1 banana
7 walnuts
3 dried figs, *soaked in boiling water for approx. 10 minutes*
3 prunes, *soaked in boiling water for approx. 10 minutes*
1 tsp cinnamon
300 ml soya milk (page 182)

A smoothie a day can help you to maintain your 60% fruit and vegetable target.

Minty Strawberry Smoothie | V G Q

A special springtime treat.

10 smallish strawberries
4 leaves mint
1 large banana
250 ml rice milk

Strawberries give the spiritual quality of dignity.

Summer Fruity Smoothie | V G Q

A refreshing summer smoothie.

1 nectarine
1 plum
1 apricot
15 almonds
2 Tbsp agave
200 ml yoghurt (page 184) or soya yoghurt (page 183)
100 ml water

Fresh fruits and vegetables have more Life Energy than any other food.

Pear, Hazelnut, Carob Smoothie | V G Q

A luxurious and rich-tasting Autumn and Winter smoothie.

1 large, ripe and juicy pear
½ banana
20 hazelnuts
200 ml soya milk (page 182)
1 ½ Tbsp carob powder
1-2 Tbsp agave

Pears are a good source of Vitamin C as well as the cholesterol-combating fibre.

Pineapple Orange Smoothie | V G Q

*Make this smoothie during the winter and early spring,
when oranges are in season and at their best.*

3 cm slice of pineapple, *without the skin*
juice of 4 oranges

Pineapples give the spiritual quality of self assurance.

CHAPTER 4

Salads

Minty Cucumber and Yoghurt Salad
208 / V G Q

Waldorf Salad
208 / V G Q

Avocado, Kiwi and Walnut Salad
209 / V G Q

Carrot and Almond Salad
210 / V G Q

German Cabbage Salad
210 / V G Q

Cabbage and Pineapple Salad
211 / V G Q

Mixed Sprouts Salad
212 / V G Q

Simple Potato Salad
213 / V G

Cooked Sprouts Salad
213 / V G Q

Creamy Yoghurt Cheese Salad
214 / V G Q

Greek-Style Tofu Salad
215 / V G Q*

See also • Guacamole (p. 227) • Quinoa Summer Salad (p. 273) • Raita (p. 304) • Seitan-Sunflower Salad (p. 323) • Mexican-Style Seitan Salad (p. 324)

Minty Cucumber
and Yoghurt Salad | V G Q

A very refreshing summer salad. When prepared a few hours before eating,
the flavours really get a chance to blend together well. ▶ *Serves 2-4*

Mix together in a bowl:
    1 tsp garlic paste (page 193)
    2 tsp dried mint or 2 Tbsp fresh mint
    2 Tbsp extra virgin olive oil
    1 tsp salt
    600 ml yoghurt (page 184) or soya yoghurt (page 183)

Add to the yoghurt mixture:
    1 ½ cucumbers, *cut in very thin half rounds*

Cucumbers contain a lot of silicon, which makes them great for maintaining
healthy and youthful skin.

Waldorf Salad | V G Q

A simple and delicious yoghurt cheese variation of the traditional English
salad combination. Traditionally, Waldorf salad is made with sour green apples,
but we have always used the sweet, red ones because their coloured skin looks
so pretty. Feel free to use whichever type of apples you prefer. ▶ *Serves 2-4*

Mix together:
    4 stalks celery, *cut in 1 cm slices*
    2 small apples, *unpeeled, cut in pieces roughly the same size as the celery*
    1-2 handfuls of walnuts, *roughly broken*
    yoghurt cheese or soya yoghurt cheese, to taste (page 187)

N.B.: If you don't serve this salad straight away, mix the apple pieces with a little
lemon juice first. This will stop them from becoming discoloured. Be careful not
to add too much lemon juice, as it will cover the sweet taste of the celery and
apples with the sour taste of lemons.

Walnuts help deep thinking and are good for brain power and concentration.

Avocado, Kiwi and Walnut Salad | V G Q

Because of the beauty of the kiwi and avocado slices laid upon a green bed of lettuce, this salad is ideal for special occasions and dinner parties. ▶ *Serves 2-4*

Arrange alternately on a bed of lettuce (the leaves can be left either whole or shredded):
   3 kiwis, *peeled and cut into thin ½ cm slices*
   1 avocado, *peeled and cut into thin ½ cm slices*

Sprinkle the kiwis and avocado with:
   20 walnuts, *broken into small pieces*

Serve with fresh cream, soya cream or simply as it is with a little salt and oil.

Walnuts are one of the best sources of omega-3 fatty acids. Just 25 grams provides 90.8% of the Recommended Dietary Allowance. Adding walnuts to your diet can be an important step in your cardiovascular health.mentazione può essere un passo importante per la tua salute cardiovascolare.

Carrot and Almond Salad | v G Q

*One of my favourite salad combinations, mixing the sweet tastes of
carrots, apples, celery and almonds, with the sour and tangy taste
of lemons. A few raisins can also be added if desired.* ▶ *Serves 2-4*

De-core and then grate:
  1 apple

Mix the apple together with:
  50 ml lemon juice

Add to the apples and mix together:
  400 g carrots, *finely grated*
  4 Tbsp parsley, *finely chopped*
  100 g almonds, *cut in half lengthways*
  1 stalk celery, *finely sliced*

🜂 *Carrots are the richest source of the pro-vitamin A carotenoids.*

German Cabbage Salad | v G Q

*The Germans are famous for their wide variety of cabbage recipes.
Here is a recipe that makes the under-loved cabbage taste great.
It's better made a few hours before serving to really allow time
for the flavours to blend together.* ▶ *Serves 2-4*

Work together with the hands until well mixed:
  400 g red or white cabbage, *finely minced*
  ½ onion, *very finely chopped*
  75 ml extra virgin olive oil
  25 ml apple vinegar
  2 tsp caraway seeds
  1 Tbsp mustard
  salt to taste

🜂 *Up to 85% of a food's nutrients can be lost by cooking: eating more raw food
is the best way to stay healthy.*

Cabbage and Pineapple Salad | v g q

Simple ingredients, but the combination is superb.
Another great way to make cabbage more exciting. ▶ *Serves 2-4*

Mix together:
  ½ of a small white cabbage, *shredded*
  250 g pineapple, *cut in 1 cm cubes*
  50 g fresh shredded coconut or dried coconut
  ¾ tsp fennel seeds
  a little extra virgin olive oil
  ½ tsp salt

Research shows that just 3-5 servings per week of cabbage or other vegetables
from the cruciferous family, is enough to lower your risk of cancer.

Mixed Sprouts Salad | V G Q

*This salad is especially for people who don't enjoy eating sprouts as they are.
With all the other ingredients added, you hardly taste the sprouts, but you
still get all of their nutritious benefits.* ▶ *Serves 2-4*

Mix together in a bowl:
  2 large handfuls of mixed sprouts (alfalfa, fenugreek, mung bean, etc.)
    (page 162)
  100 g roasted or raw sprouted peanuts
  100 g fresh coconut, *grated or minced*
  2 ½ Tbsp fresh gingerroot, *grated or minced*
  25 ml lemon juice
  salt to taste

🧍 *Sprouts are one of the best providers of Life Energy and will help you to be
willing, enthusiastic and energetic!*

Simple Potato Salad | v g

A very simple and delicious way to serve potatoes. ▶ *Serves 2-4*

Boil with their skins on, until cooked but not falling apart:
   1 kg potatoes

Let cool, remove the skins and cut the potatoes into cubes.

Mix together in a bowl:
   3 Tbsp lemon juice
   3 Tbsp extra virgin olive oil
   2 Tbsp parsley, *finely chopped*
   ½-1 tsp salt
   pinch of black pepper

Stir the cubed potatoes into the dressing and serve at room temperature.

Potatoes are a very good source of Vitamin C and a good source of Vitamin B6, potassium, manganese and fibre.

Cooked Sprouts Salad | v g q

Again, this salad is for people who have a hard time eating sprouts as they are. To start with, it is fine to sauté sprouts a little until getting used to their taste. Raisins and peanuts, if desired, can also be added to this recipe. ▶ *Serves 2-4*

Heat in a non-stick frying pan:
   1 Tbsp olive oil

Add and sauté on a high flame for 2-5 minutes:
   500 g long mung (bean) sprouts (page 162)

Then add and continue to sauté for a few more minutes:
   40 ml soya sauce

Remove from the heat and stir in:
   about 1 Tbsp lemon juice

Mung sprouts are an excellent source of protein, containing all eight essential amino acids.

Creamy Yoghurt Cheese Salad | V G Q

A delicious and deluxe salad. ▶ *Serves 2-4*

Mix together:

   400 ml yoghurt cheese or soya yoghurt cheese (page 187)
   2 tsp fresh mint, *finely chopped*
   50 ml olive oil
   1 tsp salt

Then add and mix in well:

   2 stalks celery, *very finely sliced*
   1 apple, *finely sliced*
   100 g carrots, *grated*

Just like regular yoghurt, soya yoghurt is full of friendly bacteria that have probiotic benefits.

Greek-Style Tofu Salad | v g q⁰

*This Greek-style salad uses a fantastic tofu substitute
for the usual feta cheese.* ▶ *Serves 2-4*

First make the tofu 'feta' cheese by mixing in a salad bowl:
    20 ml extra virgin olive oil
    40 ml balsamic vinegar
    1 tsp basil
    ¼ tsp oregano
    20 ml water
    pinch black pepper
    ½ tsp salt

Add: 180 g firm tofu, cut in 1 cm cubes
Mix gently and then leave to marinate for at least an hour.

Add to the tofu and dressing:
    ⅓ cucumber (10 cm), *cut in small cubes*
    15 black olives, *cut in half*
    10 cherry tomatoes, *cut in half*
    ½ red onion, *finely chopped*

Stir gently and serve.

CHAPTER 5

Salad Dressings

Tomato and Yoghurt Dressing | V G Q

This recipe combines the wonderful, refreshing taste of yoghurt and tomatoes with a little Indian spice to lift the flavour. Paprika could substitute the tandoori masala fairly well. ▶ *Makes about 600 ml*

Blend together:
> 400 ml yoghurt (page 184) or soya yoghurt (page 183)
> 200 ml tinned or fresh tomatoes
> 1 ¼ tsp tandoori masala
> 1 tsp dried basil
> ½ tsp salt

Keep refrigerated.

 *Yoghurt, because of its live bacterial cultures, is excellent for keeping your intestines healthy and for strengthening your immune system.*

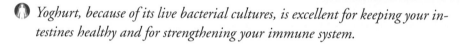

Roasted Garlic Dressing | V G

Don't be put off at the thought of a garlic-based salad dressing: roasted garlic has a completely different taste to raw garlic and makes a really flavourful salad dressing. The garlic needs to roast in the oven for a while but, after that, as with the other salad dressings, the recipe is really quick and simple. ▶ *Makes about 500 ml*

Bake in a lightly oiled, covered dish for about 30 minutes:
> 8 cloves garlic with peel left intact

When the garlic cloves are soft, remove them from the oven and peel away the skin. Then blend the garlic together with:

> 200 ml extra virgin olive oil
> 200 ml water
> 1 Tbsp mustard

> 200 ml balsamic vinegar
> ¾ tsp salt
> ½ tsp black pepper

Keep refrigerated.

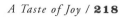 *Garlic is an excellent antioxidant and may even prevent certain cancers.*

Celery Leaf and Roasted
Peanut Dressing | V G Q

This is the salad dressing we serve every day at Ananda. It has quickly become one of the most 'asked-for' recipes. An economical and easy-to-make salad dressing and a good way to use up extra celery leaves. ▶ *Makes about 500 ml*

Blend together:
  40 g celery leaves and small stems
  115 g salted roasted peanuts
  150 ml extra virgin olive oil or sunflower oil
  150 ml water
  20 ml lemon juice
  ½ Tbsp mustard
  ½ tsp salt

Keep refrigerated.

Celery leaves are full of alkaline salts and help you to maintain the 80:20 balance.

"BECAUSE THEY CONTAIN *the largest amount of alkaline elements, the green leaves and tender stems of vegetables should make up a large part of our dietary needs. The green vegetables… are very valuable for… the minerals sodium, calcium, and iron, which are three of the most essential alkaline elements.*" **P.Y.**

Lemon and Ginger Dressing | V G Q

This is another of the most popular salad dressings we make at Ananda. The original recipe comes from The Expanding Light Cookbook, a wonderful book from the Ananda retreat centre in California, containing many excellent vegetarian recipes. We have discovered that this salad dressing is also delicious served on brown rice or with roasted seitan. ▶ *Makes about 600 ml*

Blend together until smooth:
- 250 ml sunflower oil
- 6 Tbsp soya sauce
- 100 ml lemon juice
- 100 ml water
- 50 g sunflower seeds or peanuts
- 2 Tbsp (30 g) gingerroot, *peeled and chopped*
- 1 Tbsp mustard

Keep refrigerated.

🌀 *The lemon, because of its antibiotic effects and high content of Vitamin C, is perfect for boosting your immune system and warding off colds and flu.*

"...THE LEMON, ESPECIALLY, is truly a supreme gift of the Gods, and its uses are legion. As an antiseptic it has no equal, being highly efficacious and superior to the various mixtures sold for the purpose, and certainly less expensive." **P.Y.**

Avocado and Tomato Dressing | V G Q

Avocado can be eaten in salads, but have you ever tried using it as a salad dressing? It tastes soooo good! ▶ Makes about 650 ml

Blend together:
    ½ ripe avocado
    ½ small red onion, *chopped*
    1 fresh tomato, *chopped*
    3 Tbsp balsamic vinegar
    200 ml water
    1 tsp salt

Best eaten straight away.

 *Avocados give the spiritual quality of good memory.*

CHAPTER 6

Savoury Sauces and Spreads

Béchamel Alternative

224 / V Q

Tahini Sauce

224 / V G Q

Mixed Herb and Nutritional Yeast Gravy

225 / V G* Q

Babaganoush

226 / V G

Guacamole

227 / V G Q

Peanut-Coconut Sauce

227 / V G Q

Soya Mayonnaise

228 / V G Q

Almond Butter

228 / V G Q

Peanut Butter

229 / V G Q

See also • Yoghurt / Soya Yoghurt Cheese (p. 187) • Mexican-Style
Bean Dip (p. 336) • Green Pea "Guacamole" (p. 337) • Houmous (p. 338)

Béchamel Alternative | v q

*Great for lasagnas and pastas or as a sauce served over
rice or vegetables.* ▶ *Makes 400-500 ml*

Melt in a saucepan:
   2 Tbsp vegan butter or olive oil

Add:
   6 Tbsp wholemeal wheat or spelt flour
and sauté with the vegan butter/oil for a couple of minutes.

Slowly add:
   400-500 ml oat or soya milk (page 182), or vegetable stock (page 192)
stirring continuously with a whisk.

Bring the mixture to the boil and then cook it for a few more minutes until
it thickens, all the time stirring in a clockwise direction with a whisk (stirring
in only one direction will prevent the formation of lumps). The sauce will become thicker as it cools down. Season with salt and black pepper.

🌱 *Soya milk, unlike animal sources of protein, is full of alkaline salts and helps
to keep the correct acid-alkaline balance of your body.*

Tahini Sauce | v G q

*This tahini sauce goes especially well with green leafy vegetables
and is also (surprisingly) good with sauerkraut. Made with less water
it can be served as a spread or a dip.* ▶ *Makes about 220 ml*

Blend together:
   100 ml tahini
   50-100 ml water
   3 Tbsp lemon juice
   salt
   1 small clove garlic *(less if you don't like things garlicky)*

Let it sit for about 10 minutes. The consistency will become denser.

🌱 *A balanced and varied diet of natural foods will provide you with enough nutrients to live a healthy and energetic life.*

Mixed Herb and Nutritional Yeast Gravy | V G* Q

Another wonderful sauce; based on the Béchamel Alternative given above but with lots of added herbs and ingredients for extra flavour. Great served over vegetables, wholemeal spaghetti, brown rice, spelt or roasted seitan. ▶ *Makes 1400 ml*

Heat in a large saucepan:
    4 Tbsp olive oil or vegan butter

Add to get a consistency like breadcrumbs:
    approx. 10 heaped Tbsp wholemeal wheat,
        wholemeal spelt or chickpea flour
    2 tsp sage
    1 tsp marjoram
    ½ tsp thyme
    ½ tsp rosemary
    and sauté until the flour is nicely toasted
        (3-5 minutes).

Slowly add:
    1200-1400 ml vegetable stock
stirring continuously in a clockwise direction with a whisk (stirring in one direction will prevent the formation of lumps).

Continue to cook until the mixture is thick. Then add:
    4 Tbsp nutritional yeast
    ¼ tsp black pepper
    salt, to taste

🕯 *Nutritional yeast is an excellent source of nutrition, although the nutritional content varies from brand to brand. It contains complete protein and is especially rich with the B-complex vitamins.*

Babaganoush | v g

Middle-Eastern aubergine spread, great on bruschette or crackers.
▶ *Makes about 700 ml (about 3 cups)*

Cut into 2 ½ cm cubes:
  1 kg aubergine, *peeled* (about 3 large aubergines)

Put the aubergine in an oven dish, toss with:
  3 ½ Tbsp olive oil
  1 tsp salt
and roast at about 180°C, stirring occasionally, until the aubergine is completely soft. This will take about 40 minutes.

Blend the roasted aubergine until almost smooth, together with:
  2 ½ Tbsp tahini
  1 ½ tsp lemon juice
  ½ tsp garlic paste (page 193) or about ¼ clove garlic, *crushed*
  1 Tbsp extra virgin olive oil
  salt, if necessary

Mix into the aubergine paste:
  1 ½ Tbsp fresh parsley, *finely chopped*
  1 ripe tomato, *cut in tiny cubes*

🧑 *Aubergines contain important phytonutrients, many of which have anti-oxidant properties.*

Guacamole | V G Q

This spread is not only delicious but also really nutritious. Very simple and quick to make. ▶ *Makes about 400 ml (about 1 ¾ cups)*

Blend together:
  2 ripe avocados
  1 Tbsp lemon juice
  1 ½ Tbsp onion juice *(grate an onion and squeeze out the juice through a cheesecloth)*
  4 Tbsp tomato pulp *(mash the inside part of about 1 ripe tomato with a fork)*
  ½ tsp sweet paprika
  ½ tsp salt

Other Mexican-tasting spices, such as fresh or powdered chilli, cumin and coriander, can be used instead of, or in addition to, the paprika.

🧍 *Making fruit and vegetables an important part of your diet helps to keep your body's 80:20 balance between alkalis and acids.*

Peanut-Coconut Sauce | V G Q

Delicious served with roast aubergine, carrots, cauliflower and green beans. ▶ *Enough to coat 6-8 portions of vegetables*

In a food processor, blend together until a paste:
  125 g roasted peanuts
  50 g dried coconut
  35 ml lemon juice
  piece of fresh ginger the size of half a walnut shell
  120 ml extra virgin olive oil
  75 ml water
  ¼-¾ tsp salt, *depending on how salty the peanuts are*

Toss together with 6-8 portions of cooked vegetables.

🧍 *A diet full of Life Energy foods will help to keep you positive-minded, good-humoured and cheerful!*

Soya Mayonnaise | V G Q

Even mayonnaise lovers will tell you that this egg-free soya mayonnaise tastes exactly like the real thing! Homemade soya milk will become thicker more easily than shop-bought soya milk. Simple and quick to make. ▶ *Makes about 450 ml*

In a smoothie blender, blend for a few seconds:
  200 ml cold soya milk (page 182)

Continue to blend the soya milk at the highest speed possible, adding in a continuous but very fine stream:
  any light tasting oil (I use rice oil)

Keep adding a fine stream of oil until the soya milk becomes thick and won't blend anymore (you will need around 300-400 ml). The slower you add the oil, the less you will need, but don't add it so slowly that the whole process takes more than 4 or 5 minutes.

When the milk thickens, turn off the blender and add:
  1 - 2 Tbsp apple vinegar (the acidity of different brands varies greatly)
  1 ½ - 2 Tbsp lemon juice
  2 tsp mustard
  ½ tsp salt
then blend for a few more seconds. The mayonnaise will have thickened more at this point, but put it in the fridge for a few hours to thicken it further, if desired.

🌶 *Soya is naturally low in saturated fats and, unlike eggs, can actually <u>lower</u> cholesterol, making soya mayonnaise the better choice for a healthy heart.*

Almond Butter | V G Q

Almond butter can be spread on bread or toast but, personally, I eat it straight out of the jar! ▶ *Makes about 250 ml*

Roast in the oven at 180°C for 5-10 minutes until golden brown but not dark:
  250 g almonds

Before they cool to room temperature, put in a food processor:
  the hot roasted almonds
  a pinch of salt

and blend at a high speed for up to 20 minutes until the almonds become butter (the longer you blend it, the runnier it becomes). If your food processor isn't high quality and the almonds pulverise but do not turn to butter, then simply add some light-tasting oil and continue to blend. This spread can be kept in or out of the fridge.

Almonds give the spiritual qualities of self control and moral vigour.

Peanut Butter | v g q

You'll be amazed at how good a homemade peanut butter tastes compared to a shop-bought one. I love it on toast or crackers, or in my smoothies. It's also great in cookies, giving them a unique, nutty flavour (try it in the Brownies on page 368). ▶ *Makes about 250 ml*

Put into a food processor:
  250 g roasted peanuts*
and blend at high speed until the peanuts become a smooth, buttery spread. This will take about 5-10 minutes (the longer you blend it, the creamier it becomes). If your food processor isn't high quality and the peanuts pulverise but do not turn to butter, then simply add some light-tasting oil and continue to blend. Remove the spread from the food processor with a spatula and store it in a jar. This spread can be kept in or out of the fridge.

Hydrogenated fats, conserves and sugar are often added to commercial peanut butter. Homemade peanut butter is a better choice for your health.

*Even better if you buy raw peanuts and roast them and salt them yourself.

CHAPTER 7

Soups

Spinach-Mint Soup

Italianised Leek
and Potato Soup

Curried Squash Soup

Green Pea and
Sweet Paprika Soup

Miso-Tofu Soup

Curried Lentil Soup

Gazpacho

Spinach-Mint Soup | V G

*This soup combines the wonderful flavours of spinach, mint and garlic
and can be served either hot or cold.* ▶ *Serves 4-6*

In a saucepan, sauté for a few seconds:
   1 ½ Tbsp garlic paste (page 193) or about 1 large clove crushed garlic in
   a little olive oil

Then add:
   600 g fresh spinach, including stems, or 750 g frozen spinach
   500 g potatoes, *peeled and cut into small pieces*
Sauté with the garlic for a few minutes.

Add:
   1 litre vegetable stock (page 192)
   salt, if necessary
and boil with a lid on until the potatoes are very soft. Turn off the heat and,
using a hand blender, blend the soup until smooth.

Stir in:
   2 Tbsp dried mint
   75 ml yoghurt (page 184) or soya yoghurt (page 183)
   75 ml cream or soya cream
   (or 150 ml sour cream instead of the yoghurt and cream)
Check the salt and seasonings and serve hot or cold.

🧍 *Freezing and all other methods of conservation affect the nutritional content
and even more importantly, the Life Energy of food.*

Italianised Leek and Potato Soup | v g

Fresh rosemary is the Italian twist in this classic French soup. I also substitute the traditional cream with milk or oat milk, making the soup lighter and easier to digest, as well as more alkaline. ▶ *Serves 4-6*

In a large saucepan, sauté in olive oil until soft and a little browned:
   3 large leeks, including green tops, *cut in rounds*
   pinch of salt

Add:
   1 ½ tsp rosemary, *coarsely ground*
and sauté for another minute.

Then add:
   400 g potatoes, *peeled and cut in small 2-3 cm cubes*
   1100 ml vegetable stock (page 192)
   salt, if necessary

Cover the pan, bring to the boil and then simmer for about 20 minutes until the potatoes are really soft. Turn off the heat and blend using a hand blender.

Stir in:
   about 180 ml milk or oat milk
   2 pinches black pepper

Check the salt and serve hot or cold.

🕊 *Eating vegetable soups for dinner is a good way to alkalinise your body.*

Curried Squash Soup | V G

*Squash soup and anything made with squash is always popular here at Ananda.
The key to making a good squash soup is to get a really good quality, in-season squash
(Autumn and Winter are the squash seasons). We use butternut squash. Given below
is a version we often make using Indian spices. A thick and creamy soup.* ▶ *Serves 4-6*

In a saucepan, sauté in olive oil until soft:
  1 onion, *chopped*　　　　　　　　pinch of salt

Add and fry on a low heat for 1-2 minutes:
  3 ½ tsp sweet curry powder　　　3 ½ tsp ground coriander
  1 tsp turmeric　　　　　　　　1 clove garlic, *finely chopped*

*N.B.: Make sure there is enough oil to coat the spices in. They should not be
dry-fried.*

Add to the spices and sauté for a few minutes in order to blend the flavours:
  600 g butternut squash, *peeled and cut in small chunks*
  250 g carrots, *cut in rounds*
  250 g potatoes, *peeled and cut in chunks*

Add to the squash, etc.:
  1300 ml vegetable stock (page 192)　　salt, if necessary

Cover, bring to the boil and then turn down the heat and simmer until the
squash, carrots and potatoes are completely soft. Turn off the heat and then
blend everything using a hand blender. Check the salt and then serve hot.

🌀 *Squash is an excellent source of the pro-vitamin A antioxidant, beta-carotene.*

Green Pea and Sweet Paprika Soup | v g

A highly nutritious and flavourful, thick, winter soup. ▶ *Serves 4-6*

Wash thoroughly, strain and then put in a large saucepan:
    250 g split green peas
    4 bay leaves

Cover the peas with 1300 ml of fresh, unsalted water and bring to the boil. Then turn down the heat and simmer with a lid on until the peas are completely soft and mushy and dissolve when stirred. This will take around 60 minutes. Remove any foam from the surface when the peas start to boil. If the water reduces too much, add a little more (see page 179 for more information on how to cook legumes).

When the peas are nearly ready, add:
    175 g potatoes, *peeled and chopped*
and continue to cook until the peas and potatoes are soft and mushy, as described above.

In the meantime, sauté in a smaller saucepan until soft and golden:
    1 large onion, *finely chopped*
    pinch of salt

Add to the onions:
    300 ml tinned tomatoes
and continue to cook for about 10 minutes.

When the peas are cooked remove the bay leaves.

Then add to the peas:
    the tomato sauce
    ½ tsp sweet paprika
    ⅛-¼ tsp chilli powder
    2-3 tsp salt

Cook everything together for a few minutes and then blend with hand blender, adding more water if necessary to make the right consistency. Check the salt and seasonings and serve hot.

🕭 *Split green peas are full of protein. 100 grams provide you with about 7 ½ grams of good-quality protein.*

Miso-Tofu Soup | v g q

*In true Japanese style, this soup is light and simple
but highly flavourful.* ▶ *Serves 4-6*

In a covered saucepan, bring to the boil:
   1300 ml water

Add:
   1 large onion, *cut in quarter moons*
   2 small carrots, *cut in thin half diagonals*
   1 stalk celery, *cut in thin diagonals*
   piece of fresh ginger size of 2 small walnut shells, *cut very fine*
   75 g tofu (page 190), *cut in 1 cm cubes*
   50 g rice spaghetti or Japanese-style noodles, *broken*
   1 ½ tsp salt

Re-cover and boil gently until the vegetables and spaghetti are *al dente* (about
8 minutes).

Meanwhile, mix and dissolve in a small amount of hot water:
   2 heaped Tbsp miso

When the vegetables are ready, turn off the soup and stir in the dissolved
miso.* Check the salt and serve hot.

🧍 *Miso, because of its high content of micro-organisms, is excellent for keeping
your intestines strong and healthy.*

* Miso should never be cooked but always added at the end.

Curried Lentil Soup | v g

A warming and nourishing winter soup. ▶ *Serves 4-6*

In a large saucepan, put:
    150 g brown lentils, *washed*
    1500 ml unsalted water

Cover and bring to the boil. Then lower the flame and cook until the lentils are soft, stirring occasionally. This will take 30-60 minutes.

When the lentils are half cooked, add:
    1 large carrot, *chopped into small pieces*
    2 medium potatoes, *chopped into medium-sized pieces*

In the meantime, in a smaller saucepan, sauté in olive oil until golden:
    1 large onion, *finely chopped*

Add to the onions and continue to sauté for 2 or 3 minutes, stirring regularly:
    3 cloves garlic, *finely chopped*
    piece of ginger the size of a walnut shell, *peeled and finely chopped*

Next add:
    2 tsp turmeric
    1 ¼ tsp garam masala
    ⅛ tsp chilli powder
and fry for 1 minute, stirring continuously.
N.B.: Make sure there is enough oil to coat the spices in. They should not be dry-fried.

Add:
    400 ml tinned chopped tomatoes
and cook together with the onions and spices for 5 minutes.

When the lentils are soft, add and cook together for a few minutes:
    the spiced tomato mixture
    salt, to taste

Turn off the heat and then stir in:
    ¼ tsp black pepper
    3 Tbsp extra virgin olive oil

🜂 *Although chilli tastes great, remember that it has a stimulating effect on your mind and is best eaten in small amounts.*

Gazpacho | v g q

A cold, raw Spanish soup, that is a wonderful option for summer.
Delicious served with garlic croutons. ▶ *Serves 4-6*

Blend together until smooth:
   5 large, ripe tomatoes, *cut in pieces* (put the tomatoes in the blender first)
   15 cm piece cucumber, *peeled and cut in pieces*
   ¾ large red or yellow pepper, *deseeded and cut in pieces*
   1 ½ small yellow onions, *cut in pieces*
   2 cloves garlic
   1 ½ Tbsp fruit or wine vinegar
   4 Tbsp extra virgin olive oil
   ¼ tsp cumin powder
   1 ½ tsp salt

Sift the soup through a fine mesh sieve (or leave as it is).

Refrigerate for several hours and serve cool.

🧘 *Rishis, the ancient seers of India, lived only on fruit and raw foods. In this way they purified their minds.*

CHAPTER 8

Savoury Breads, Sweet Breads and Crackers

German Farmer's Bread

South Italian Potato Focaccia

Chappatis

Cinnamon Rolls

Essene Bread (sprouted spelt bread)

Mixed Seed Crackers

See also • Healthy Cake (p. 354) • Banana Cake (p. 360)

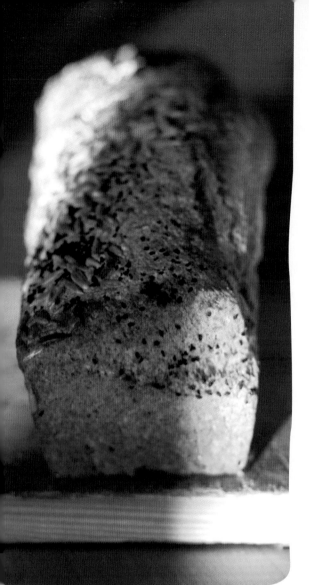

German Farmer's Bread | v

A traditional German wholemeal bread, which we serve every day here at Ananda. It's easy to make and very nutritious. ▶ *Makes one loaf*

Mix together in a large bowl:
500 g wholemeal wheat
    or spelt flour
2 ½ tsp salt

Mix together in a cup until smooth:
10 g fresh yeast
¼ tsp sugar
50 ml warm water

Make a dip in the flour and put the yeast mixture in. Cover the yeast with a thin layer of flour and then let it sit for about 15 minutes until the surface of the flour starts to crack (this means the yeast is growing).

Add to the flour and yeast:
about 350 ml cold water
3 Tbsp olive oil

Mix together to form a fairly wet and sticky dough. Remove the dough from the bowl and knead it on a floured surface for 8-10 minutes. Rub a little oil on your hands to stop the dough from sticking to you.

Towards the end of the kneading, add:
    a handful of sunflower seeds *(optional)*

Transfer the dough to an oiled bread tin (12 x 30 cm) and, with wet hands, make the surface smooth.
You can put any herbs or seeds on top of the bread at this point. We love to make it with sunflower seeds, sesame seeds, poppy seeds or caraway seeds. Push them down firmly onto the surface of the dough.

Let the bread rise for about one hour or until it doubles in size and then bake for 50-60 minutes at 180°C until the outside is golden brown and crunchy. To test if the bread is finished baking, remove it from the tin and tap the underside: if it sounds hollow then it is done (baking times and temperatures will vary according to the type of oven).

When the bread is baked, remove it from the tin immediately and let it cool upside-down before cutting.

Whole wheat grains contain impressive amounts of dietary fibre. Diets rich in fibre are thought to decrease cholesterol and high blood pressure, protect against gallstones and lower the risks of cancer.

South Italian Potato Focaccia | v

A wonderful and delicious flat potato bread from Bari.
For an alternative look, the tomatoes can be substituted with black
or green olives or pieces of garlic. ▶ *Makes a 30 cm round focaccia*

Boil until soft:

    300 g potatoes, left whole with skin intact

Leave the potatoes to cool and then remove their skins, mash them and put aside.

Mix together in a bowl:

    280 g white flour   120 g wholemeal flour
    2 tsp salt

In a separate small container, mix until dissolved:

    16 g fresh yeast   ½ tsp sugar
    80 ml lukewarm water

Now add to the flour mixture:

    the dissolved yeast   2 Tbsp extra virgin olive oil
    the mashed potatoes   approx. 200 ml warm milk, vegan milk or water

and mix together to form a dough. The consistency should be fairly sticky; adjust the amount of milk/water accordingly.

Transfer the dough to a surface and knead for 8-10 minutes. Because this dough is sticky, it is easier to knead using only your fingers and not your whole hand. Put a little oil on your fingers, if needed, to stop the dough from sticking.

In a round 30 cm diameter tin, pour a thin layer of extra virgin olive oil. Spread the dough out on top, wetting your hands beforehand to make it easier.

Leave the dough to rise in a warm place for about 1 hour or until you see that it has doubled in size (a warm oven is the best, as long as it is turned off and no warmer than 50°C).

While the bread is rising, take:
    15-20 cherry tomatoes or the ends of 8-10 tinned plum tomatoes
and squeeze the juice and seeds out.

When the dough has risen, place the tomatoes on top and press them down very gently (you don't want them to sink to the bottom).

Then sprinkle on top:
large granule salt	black pepper
lots of oregano	a little more olive oil

Bake for about 25 minutes at 180°C until the focaccia is completely cooked inside (cooking times and temperatures will vary according to the type of oven).

In order to have a restful sleep, remember to avoid eating carbohydrates late at night.

Chappatis | v

Given below is a simple version as well as a more traditional version. The difference lies in the cooking. With the simple version, the chappati is cooked all the way in a flat pan; with the traditional version the chappati begins cooking in the pan but is then transferred directly onto the flame, making it inflate with air. Start with the simple version, and then have a go at the traditional version. ▶ *Makes 10 chappatis*

Simple version

In a bowl, mix together:
> 200 g wholemeal flour
> 200 g durum flour
> 2 tsp salt

Add to the flour:
> 200-300 ml warm water

and knead to make a smooth dough. The consistency should be soft, like the lobe of an ear, but not sticky.

Optional: Put the dough in a bowl, cover with a damp cloth, and leave to sit for at least 20 minutes. This rest allows certain enzymes to develop that help with digestion.

Form the dough into 10 little balls, each weighing 80 g. Try to make each ball smooth with no cracks in the surface.

Take a ball and, on a lightly floured surface, press it down flat. Roll the flattened ball out into a fairly thin circle, with a diameter of about 18 cm. This is the hardest part and takes patience and practice. The trick to rolling the chappati into a perfectly round circle is this: Always roll from the centre of the chappati diagonally to the right. After each roll, rotate the chappati 45° in a clockwise direction. Repeat these two steps until the chappati is the right thickness.

When rolling the chappati, try to use as little flour as possible. It is better to have a pile of flour that you can dip the chappati dough into between rolls than to roll out on a heavily floured surface.

Heat up a non-stick frying pan or skillet. When it is hot, put your first chappati in and cook on a medium heat. When the underside is lightly browned, flip it over and cook the other side. Do not turn the chappati over more than once or it will become hard.

Pile the cooked chappatis one on top of the other on a plate and cover with a cloth to keep them soft and warm while you cook the remaining chappatis. Eat them straight away, when they are at their best!

Traditional version

This is the way they do it in India! Follow the instructions given above for the simple version until the chappati is in the frying pan.

Instead of cooking the first side until lightly browned, heat it only until you see small bubbles start to appear on the surface. This may take about 60 seconds (the first one always takes longer). Turn the chappati over immediately and do the same on the other side. Heat it only until bubbles start to appear on the surface. The second side is much quicker than the first side and may only take 20-30 seconds.

Using flat wooden or stainless steel tongs, gently remove the chappati from the pan and hold it directly over the flame of your gas ring. When it inflates, turn it over and do the other side. Leave it over the flame until both sides are nicely browned. This gives a much lighter, much more authentic-tasting chappati.

Chappatis can also be made with spelt flour. Herbs, seeds, spices or fresh green chillies can be added to the dough.

Whole grains, as opposed to refined grains, provide you with a long-lasting and steady energy.

Cinnamon Rolls | v

*One of the favourite Ananda breakfasts; a recipe passed down
from "generation to generation".* ▶ *Makes about 20 rolls*

In a large bowl, mix together:
    400 g wholemeal flour
    400 g durum flour
    50 g raw cane sugar
    1 tsp cinnamon
    1 tsp salt

In a small container, mix together until dissolved:
    16 g fresh yeast
    ½ tsp sugar
    about 50 ml warm water
and then add to the flour mixture.

Next add:
    50 ml sunflower oil
    approximately 380 ml warm water
and mix together with your hands to form a dough. The consistency should
be neither sticky nor dry, but soft and elastic, similar to an earlobe.

Turn the dough out onto a floured surface and knead for 8-10 minutes. Put the dough in a bowl, cover with a damp cloth and leave it to rise in a warm place for about an hour or until it doubles in size (a warm oven is the best, as long as it is turned off and no warmer than 50°C).

In the meantime, in a small pan, melt:
    100 g butter or vegan butter

Stir into the butter:
    200 g raw cane sugar
    1 ½ tsp cinnamon
and then set aside.

On a floured surface, roll out the dough until it is about 40 cm x 40 cm.

Spread the melted butter/margarine and sugar mixture on top of the dough, leaving a gap of about 2 cm along the top length. Brush a little water along this 2 cm gap. This will help to seal the roll.

Next, roll up the dough into a type of Swiss roll. Start from the lower border and roll tightly towards the upper border.

Cut the roll into 1 ½ cm slices and lay each slice down on baking trays lined with baking paper. Allow plenty of space for each roll to grow.

Let the rolls rise for another 20-30 minutes.

Bake at 180°C for about 20 minutes until the rolls are golden brown and completely cooked (cooking times and temperatures will vary according to the type of oven).

Best eaten while still warm!

Limiting carbohydrates to only 20% of your diet helps to keep the correct balance of acid and alkali in your body.

Essene Bread | v
(sprouted spelt bread)

This is an adaptation of the traditional bread made by the Essenes, a group of yogi-like mystics who lived around the time of Christ. Recommended for people who don't eat wheat and very quick and easy to make. A simplified version can be made without the sunflower seeds and soya sauce. ▶ *Makes one 30 x 30 cm tray*

In a food processor, roughly grind:
>   150 g sunflower seeds

Remove the seeds from the food processor and put aside.

Next, blend in the food processor until a paste is formed (it doesn't have to be smooth):
>   400 g wholegrain spelt, *sprouted* (page 162)

Then add and blend a few seconds until mixed:
>   100 ml water
>   75 ml soya sauce
>   3 Tbsp extra virgin olive oil
>   the roughly ground sunflower seeds

Spread the mixture on a 30 cm x 30 cm baking tray, lined with baking paper.

Sprinkle and drizzle on top:
>   fresh or dried rosemary
>   a little extra virgin olive oil

Cook for 20-40 minutes at 175°C until you see that the surface is firm and crispy (cooking times and temperatures will vary according to the type of oven). Leave to cool down before eating.

🌰 *Sprouts are little miracle foods. During the process of sprouting, the vitamin, mineral and protein contents of the seed multiply significantly.*

Mixed Seed Crackers | v

A quick and simple alternative to bread. Delicious served with yoghurt cheese (page 187) spread on top. ▶ *Makes a 30 cm x 30 cm tray*

In a bowl, mix together:
- 125 g rolled oats
- 125 g wholemeal wheat or wholemeal spelt flour
- 120 g mixed seeds, such as sunflower seeds *(slightly ground)*, sesame seeds, pumpkin seeds *(slightly ground)* and linseeds *(slightly ground)*
- a few aniseeds, fennel seeds, caraway seeds or cumin seeds for flavour (caraway seeds taste great)
- any spices or herbs you like, such as coriander or rosemary
- ½ tsp turmeric
- 4 Tbsp extra virgin olive oil
- 400 ml cold water
- 1 tsp salt

Let the mixture rest for one hour and then spread it out on a 30 cm x 30 cm baking tray, lined with baking paper.

Cook the cracker at about 175°C for 20 minutes. Remove the cracker from the oven and, using a sharp knife, cut it into square portions. Put the crackers back in the oven and continue to cook for a further 40 minutes or until crunchy (cooking times and temperatures will vary according to the type of oven).

When the crackers are cooked, leave them to cool and then break them into pieces.

🜂 *Commercial crackers often contain monosodium glutamate. These homemade seed crackers are not only nutritious and delicious but are also a safer option for your health.*

CHAPTER 9

Pasta

Tagliatelle with Seitan Ragù | v

Traditionally served with tagliatelle but can also be served with spaghetti, fusilli, penne, farfalle, etc. ▶ Serves 4-6

Sauté in oil in a large and deep frying pan (preferably non-stick):
    1 onion, *minced*
    2 carrots, *minced*
    1 courgette, *minced*
    few sprigs parsley, *minced*
    pinch salt

When the vegetables are soft, add and then continue to sauté, stirring all the time:

    300 g seitan, minced (page 191)
    2 Tbsp soya sauce
    2 tsp garlic paste

After about 10 minutes, add:

    600 ml tomato passata
    small sprig fresh rosemary
    2 cloves, *whole*
    ½ tsp salt

Cover and cook on a low heat for 30-40 minutes, stirring regularly and adding a little water if the ragù starts to dry up. The more the sauce cooks, the better it will be.

Either mix the sauce together with, or pour it over the top of:

    400 g tagliatelle

Serve with a little parmesan cheese or nutritional yeast on top (*optional*).

🐄 *Seitan is a much healthier alternative to meat. A 100 gram serving contains less than 1% saturated fat.*

Pappardelle in Creamy Tomato Sauce | v g*

A luxurious version of the more simple tomato sauce.
Can also be served with any other long pasta. ▶ *Serves 4-6*

In a saucepan, sauté for about 10 minutes:
  1 onion, *very finely chopped*
  1 carrot, *minced*
  1 stalk celery, *minced*
  pinch salt

Add to the vegetables:
  700 ml tinned chopped tomatoes
  1 tsp oregano
  1 ½ tsp salt

Cook on a low heat for about 25 minutes, stirring occasionally.

Turn off the heat and, using a hand blender, blend until smooth.

Once the sauce is blended, stir in:
  150 ml cooking cream or soya cooking cream
  ⅛ tsp chilli powder

Either mix the sauce together with or pour it over the top of:
  400 g pappardelle

Serve with a little parmesan cheese or nutritional yeast on top (*optional*).

🧘 *According to Yogananda, tomatoes are one of the few vegetables that maintain their nutritional properties even when tinned.*

Deluxe Pasta Salad | V G* Q

The artichoke-basil pesto and the walnuts, turn this recipe into a luxurious version of a traditional pasta salad. We sometimes make this salad with trophy pasta (shown in the photo), but because this shape is hard to find outside of Italy, fusilli can be used instead. ▶ *Serves 4-6*

Blend together:

165 g artichoke hearts   8 leaves basil
½ small clove garlic   ⅛ tsp salt

and set aside.

Cook in salted water until *al dente*:

400 g fusilli

When the fusilli is cooked, strain it and run it under cold water to stop the cooking process and cool it down. Add the artichoke-basil pesto to the fusilli and stir gently to coat the pasta.

Then add:

15 walnuts, *broken in pieces*   8 sun-dried tomatoes, *cut in thin strips*
20 black olives, *cut in halves*   1 large handful rocket (30 g), *roughly cut*
4 leaves basil, *torn in small pieces*

Serve at room temperature.

🕴 *Adding walnuts to your diet can be an important step for cardiovascular health.*

Buckwheat Pasta with Tofu, Potatoes and Chard | v g*

This is an Ananda alternative to a traditional Italian dish. It's usually made with a special type of buckwheat pasta (pizzoccheri), but any kind of buckwheat pasta will work (alternatively, normal wholemeal pasta). Tagliatelle, fusilli or penne are all ideal choices. ▶ *Serves 4-6*

Cut into 1 cm cubes:
  200 g tofu (page 190)

Put the tofu in an oven dish and add:
  2 Tbsp soya sauce   1 Tbsp extra virgin olive oil

Peel and cut into 1 cm cubes:
  300 g potatoes

Put the potatoes in a separate oven dish and toss with:
  2 Tbsp extra virgin olive oil   a little salt

Roast the tofu and the potatoes in the oven at 180°C until crispy on the outside.

Cook in a covered saucepan with a small amount of water and a little salt:
  500 g chard, *coarsely chopped*

In a frying pan, fry in ghee (page 188) or vegan butter for 1-2 minutes:
  2 Tbsp sage

Add the cooked chard and sauté for another 5 minutes.

When all of your ingredients are ready, cook until *al dente* in salted water:
  500 g wholemeal penne

Mix together:
  the penne   the roasted tofu
  the roasted potatoes   the chard sautéed in ghee/vegan butter and sage
  1 ½ Tbsp soya sauce   2-3 Tbsp extra ghee or vegan butter
  ½ tsp black pepper   1 ½ Tbsp nutritional yeast
  salt, if necessary
Serve immediately.

🌙 *Because nothing is removed during processing, whole-grain pastas contain more natural fibre and nutrients than refined white pasta.*

Bucatini with Cabbage Pesto | v g* q

*You may be slightly suspicious of a pesto made with cabbage,
but every person I have made it for so far has loved it. If possible,
leave the pesto to sit for a few hours to allow the flavours to
blend together. A winter alternative to basil pesto.* ▶ Serves 4-6

Put in a large saucepan:
   200 g savoy cabbage, *excluding the hard stalk, roughly chopped*
   pinch of salt
   small amount of water
then cover and cook for about 5 minutes.

Using a hand blender, blend the steamed cabbage together with:
   100 ml extra virgin olive oil
   50-100 ml warm water
   100 g roasted peanuts, *finely ground*
   1 clove garlic
   2 tsp dried basil or 2 Tbsp fresh basil
   pinch ground cloves
   salt, as needed

Mix the pesto together with:
   400 g bucatini

Serve with parmesan cheese or nutritional yeast (*optional*).

🧍 *Cabbage is an excellent source of Vitamin K. Just 150 grams of boiled cabbage
will provide you with 91.7% of the recommended dietary allowance.*

Chinese-Style Wholemeal Spaghetti | v g* q

A true blend of cultures! We originally came up with the spaghetti idea
because Chinese noodles are hard to find in Italy (at least in the large
quantities that we would need of them). Although the concept may sound
a little strange, it's surprisingly good! Try it and see if it works for you!
When you are pushed for time, you can simplify the recipe and make it
with three or four vegetables only. Other vegetables that work well
with this dish are mushrooms, peppers and broccoli. It's important that
the vegetables are cut thinly to ensure they cook properly. ▶ *Serves 4-6*

Cook in salted water until *al dente*:
  400 g wholemeal spaghetti (or normal noodles)
Strain and put aside.

Heat in a Chinese wok:*
  a little sunflower oil

When the wok is hot, add:
  300 g tofu (page 190), *cut in 4 cm strips*
  4 Tbsp soya sauce

* If you don't have a wok, you can use a large, non-stick frying pan.

and sauté until the tofu is nicely crisped on the outside, turning it over gently with a spatula when necessary.

Remove the tofu from the wok and set aside.

Heat another small amount of oil in the wok and then add:
    2 cloves garlic, *chopped finely*
    2 pieces of gingerroot the size of a walnut shell, *chopped finely*
    2 onions, *cut in thin half moons*
    2 medium-sized carrots, *cut in very thin half diagonals*
    2 stalks celery, *cut in very thin diagonals*
    200 g savoy cabbage, *cut in thin strips, the same length as the carrot and celery slices*
    1 tsp salt

and fry on a high flame, stirring continuously, until the vegetables are a little softer but still crunchy. Every so often add a splash of water. The water will evaporate immediately as steam, helping the vegetables to cook but leaving them crunchy.

After about 5 minutes, add:
    2 very large handfuls of long mung (bean) sprouts (page 162)

Once the vegetables are nearly ready, add:
    100 ml soya sauce
and stir-fry for another minute.

Now add to the vegetables:
    the cooked spaghetti
    the sautéed tofu
Turn up the heat and stir-fry everything together for a minute or so.

Turn off the heat and stir in:
    3 Tbsp sesame seeds, *toasted*
    2 Tbsp fresh parsley, *roughly chopped*
    extra soya sauce to taste

Soya sauce has antioxidant properties.

Garlic-Chilli Spaghetti | v g* q

One of the quickest and most simple traditional
Italian pasta dishes. ▶ *Serves 4-6*

Boil in salted water until *al dente*:
    400 g spaghetti

In the meantime, in a large (28 cm), deep frying pan, heat using a low flame:
    90 ml olive oil

When the oil is hot, add:
    2 large cloves garlic, *minced*
    1-2 red chillies, *deseeded and cut in small pieces*
and fry on a low heat until the garlic turns golden brown.

Turn up the heat and add:
    50 g (5 Tbsp) breadcrumbs
and fry for a couple of minutes.

When the spaghetti is cooked, strain and then mix together with the garlic-chilli breadcrumb mixture in the frying pan, along with:
    2 Tbsp extra virgin olive oil
    2 Tbsp parsley, *chopped*

🐾 *Although moderate amounts of refined pasta are fine, try to balance this by eating more wholegrain pasta, such as wholemeal spelt pasta, wholemeal wheat pasta and buckwheat pasta.*

Orecchiette and Chickpeas | v g*

This is a typical dish from Puglia, in southeast Italy. When made with a little more liquid, it also makes a good soup. ▶ *Serves 4-6*

Soak for 6-8 hours in plenty of water:
   350 g chickpeas

Strain the soaked chickpeas, rinse and then cook in plenty of fresh, unsalted water until they are completely soft. This will take about 90 minutes.

Remove the cooked chickpeas from the water (do not throw the water away) and put ⅓ of them aside. Blend the remaining ⅔ together with:
   about 500 ml of their cooking water

In a large saucepan, sauté in olive oil until soft:
   1 ½ leeks, including the green tops, *cut in half rounds*
   pinch of salt

Add to the leeks and sauté for a minute:
   2 tsp rosemary, *coarsely ground*

Then add:
   the blended chickpeas
   the remaining whole chickpeas

Check the salt and then cook the mixture on a medium flame for about 10 minutes, stirring often.

While the chickpea mixture is cooking, boil in salted water until *al dente*:
   400 g orecchiette

N.B.: If you have enough water left over from cooking the chickpeas, cook the pasta in this.

When the pasta is cooked, mix it together with the chickpea sauce. Then stir in:
   1 Tbsp fresh parsley, *finely chopped*
   3 Tbsp extra virgin olive oil

Check the salt and serve immediately.

🜂 *Eating fibre-providing legumes with refined grains helps to slow down the rate at which glucose from the refined grain is released into your bloodstream.*

CHAPTER 10

Rice and Other Grains

Brown Rice with Squash and Tomato Stew
268 / V G

Basmati Rice with Curried Roast Pepper and Carrot Sauce
269 / V G

Chinese-Style Basmati Rice
270 / V G Q

Quinoa and Spinach with Tahini Sauce
272 / V G Q

Quinoa Summer Salad
273 / V G Q

**Couscous with Moroccan-Style Chickpea
and Vegetable Stew**
274 / V G*

Spelt with Italian Green Pea and Tomato Sauce
276 / V G*

"Spelt-otto" with Butternut Squash
277 / V G*

Roast Polenta and Red Cabbage with Chunky Tomato Sauce
279 / V G

Spelt with Roasted Cherry Tomatoes and Pesto Sauce
280 / V G*

Baked Millet and Cauliflower Squares
281 / V G

See also • Essene Bread (p. 250) • Basmati Rice with Cabbage
and Coconut (p. 300) • Basmati Rice with Raisins and Toasted
Almonds (p. 302) • Coconut Rice (p. 303) • Yoghurt Rice (p. 301)

Brown Rice with Squash and Tomato Stew | V G

Squash and tomatoes combine extremely well together; with the leeks and sweet paprika, the taste is even more delicious. Good quality, in-season squash is essential (squash season is autumn and winter). We usually use butternut squash. ▶ *Serves 4-6*

In a fairly large saucepan, sauté in ghee (page 188) or oil until soft and a little browned:
    1 leek, including green top, *cut in half rounds*
    ¼ tsp salt

While the leeks are sautéing, boil or steam until soft:
    1 kg butternut squash, *cut in small 1 cm cubes*

When the leeks are nearly ready, add and sauté for another minute:
    1 tsp garlic paste (page 193) or about ½ clove crushed garlic

Add to the leeks:
    the cooked squash cubes
    500 ml tinned chopped tomatoes
    2 bay leaves
    2 tsp salt
    a little water

Mix well and then cover with a lid. Cook on a medium flame for about 10 minutes, stirring occasionally. Add a little more water if necessary.

When the stew is almost cooked, add:
    2 tsp sweet paprika

Turn off the heat, remove the bay leaves and then stir in:
    1 ½ Tbsp ghee *(optional)*

Check the salt and flavourings and serve over brown rice (see chart on page 176 for cooking instructions). Alternatively, mix the stew and rice together to make a risotto-like dish.

🌀 *Whole grains are much more nutritious than refined grains: up to 80% of a grain's nutrients are contained in the bran and the germ.*

Basmati Rice with Curried
Roast Pepper and Carrot Sauce | V G

*The roast peppers and sweet curry give a special taste
to this delicious sauce.* ▶ *Serves 4-6*

Roast in the oven at 200°C:
   3 large yellow peppers, *whole*
until their skin is dark, almost burnt. This will take 30-50 minutes, depending on your oven.

When the peppers are ready, put them in a bowl sealed tight with cling film or covered with a plate and leave them to steam for ten minutes. This will allow you to remove their skins easily.

While the peppers are roasting, sauté in a saucepan until golden:
   1 onion, *finely cut*
   pinch of salt

Add to the onion:
   2 tsp sweet curry powder
and sauté for another couple of minutes to blend the flavours.

Add to the curried onions:
   650 g carrots, *cut in thin rounds*
   about 400 ml water
   1 ½ tsp salt
Put a lid on and cook on a medium flame until the carrots are very soft.

Remove the peppers from the bag or bowl and split them open. Remove the seeds and the burnt skin. Add the peppers to the carrots and onions and then, using a hand blender, blend everything together. If the consistency is too thick, add a little water.

Finally, stir in:
   some fresh or dried dill *(optional)*
   a little cream or soya cream

Adjust the salt and then serve over freshly made basmati rice (see chart on page 176 for cooking instructions).

🜨 *Grains give the spiritual quality of strength of character.*

Chinese-Style Basmati Rice | v g q

*The distinct taste of Chinese food comes from the stir-frying of the
finely cut vegetables. However, for those who like to avoid frying food,
a healthier version can be made by steaming, instead of frying them.
When you are pushed for time, you can simplify the recipe and
make it with three or four vegetables only.* ▶ *Serves 4-6*

Cook according to the instructions given in the "Basic Recipes" chapter
(page 176):
    2 cups (250 ml cups) basmati rice
*N.B.: If you start cooking the rice about the same time as you start to stir-fry
the vegetables, they should be ready at the same time.*

Heat up in a non-stick wok*:
    a little sunflower or sesame oil

When the wok is really hot, add:
    300 g tofu (page 190), *cut in 4 cm thin strips*
    4 Tbsp soya sauce
and sauté until nicely crisped on the outside, turning over gently with a
spatula when necessary. Remove the tofu from the wok and set aside.

Heat another small amount of oil in the wok and then add:
    2 cloves garlic, *finely chopped*
    piece of gingerroot, size of 2 walnut shells, *cut finely*
    2 onions, *cut in thin half moons*
    2 medium-sized carrots, *cut in very thin, half diagonal slices*
    2 stalks celery, *cut in very thin diagonals*
    200 g savoy cabbage, *cut in thin strips, the same length as the carrot and
      celery slices*
    1 tsp salt

Stir-fry the vegetables on a high flame, stirring continuously, until they are a
little softer but still crunchy. Every so often add a small splash of water. The
water will evaporate immediately as steam, helping the vegetables to cook
but leaving them crunchy.

After about 5 minutes, add:
    2 very large handfuls of long mung (bean) sprouts (page 162)

* If you don't have a wok, you can use a large frying pan.

Once the vegetables are nearly ready, add:
    100 ml soya sauce
and fry for another minute.

Now add to the vegetables:
    the cooked rice
    the sautéed tofu
Turn up the heat and stir-fry everything together for a minute or so.

Turn off the heat and stir in:
    3 Tbsp sesame seeds, *toasted*
    2 Tbsp fresh parsley, *roughly chopped*
    extra soya sauce to taste

Mung sprouts are very rich in vitamins and the minerals calcium, potassium, iron, phosphorus and zinc.

Quinoa and Spinach with Tahini Sauce | v g q

This is one of my favourite lunch recipes and, so far, everyone that I've made it for has loved it. A quick, simple and nutritious recipe. ▶ *Serves 4-6*

Wash and then cook according to the instructions given in the "Basic Recipes" chapter (page 176):

    1 ½ cups (250 ml cup) quinoa

While the quinoa is cooking, wash and then put in a saucepan:

    450 g fresh spinach, including stems
    pinch salt

and cook, covered, until tender (no need to add water).

When tender, strain and then roughly cut the spinach with a knife.

Mix the spinach and the cooked quinoa together and adjust the salt.

Serve the quinoa and spinach onto plates. Pour over the top of each portion:

    2-3 Tbsp tahini sauce (page 224)

Serve with a fresh tomato salad.

Quinoa is a very good source of magnesium, the mineral that relaxes blood vessels, making quinoa a good grain for cardiovascular health.

Quinoa Summer Salad | v g q

*A very quick, delicious and especially nutritious recipe.
Good for packed lunches and picnics.* ▶ *Serves 4-6*

Cook in salted water or vegetable stock, according to the instructions given
in the "Basic Recipes" chapter (page 176):

    1 cup (250 ml cup) quinoa

and then leave to cool.

Blend together:

    a large handful fresh basil leaves, *washed and well dried*
    130 ml olive oil
    2 Tbsp lemon juice
    ½ tsp black pepper
    ¼ tsp salt

and then mix into the cooled quinoa.

Then mix in:

    20 cherry tomatoes, *cut in quarters*
    30 black olives, *cut in halves*
    180 g sweet corn
    2 small handfuls sunflower baby greens (page 172)
    6 lettuce leaves, *cut in very thin strips*

Check the salt and seasonings and serve at room temperature.

Quinoa is a good source of protein, supplying all eight essential amino acids.

Couscous with Moroccan-Style Chickpea and Vegetable Stew | v g*

This recipe is always a success when we serve it at Ananda. ▶ *Serves 4-6*

Soak for 6-8 hours in plenty of water:
150 g dried chickpeas

Strain the chickpeas, rinse them well and then boil in plenty of water (no salt) until they are soft. This will take about an hour (see page 179 for more information on how to cook legumes). Then, put the chickpeas aside.

In a large, heavy-based saucepan, sauté until soft and slightly golden:
1 large onion, *cut into half moons*

Add to the onion and continue to sauté for another 1 or 2 minutes:
½ tsp turmeric
½ tsp garam masala
½ tsp cinnamon
¼ tsp curry powder
¼ tsp cumin powder
pinch chilli powder

Next add:

    300 g potatoes, *peeled and cut into 2 cm cubes*

    2 medium-sized carrots, *cut into 1 cm half rounds*

    70 g raisins

    600 ml water

    300 ml tinned chopped tomatoes

    1 tsp salt

Cover and bring to the boil and then simmer until the potatoes are soft (about 15 minutes).

Then add:

    1 large courgette, *cut into 1 cm half rounds*

    100 g aubergine, with or without skin, *cut into 2 cm cubes*

    ½ red or yellow bell pepper, *deseeded and cut into 2 cm cubes*

    the cooked chickpeas

and continue to cook on a low flame until the potatoes are starting to dissolve around the surface and the peppers are tender, about 25 minutes.

When cooked, check the seasoning and then serve on top of couscous (see page 177 for cooking instructions).

Balancing your grains with lots of vegetables helps you to maintain the correct acid-alkaline balance of your organism.

Spelt with Italian Green Pea and Tomato Sauce | v g*

An easy and uncomplicated recipe. This sauce is also delicious served over any other grain or brown pasta. ▶ *Serves 4-6*

Cook according to the instructions given in the "Basic Recipes" chapter (page 176):
  1 ½ cups (250 ml cups) spelt

In a separate saucepan, sauté until golden:
  1 medium onion, *finely chopped*
  pinch salt

Add to the onion:
  1 medium-sized carrot, *minced*
  1 stalk celery, *minced*
  2 ½ -3 tsp garlic paste (page 193)
    or about 1 large clove crushed garlic
  1 ½ tsp thyme
  1 ½ tsp basil
  1 ½ tsp marjoram
and sauté for about five more minutes.

Then add:
  300 ml tinned chopped tomatoes
  400 g frozen green peas
  pinch of chilli powder
  300 ml water
  1 ½ tsp salt

Cover, bring to the boil and then cook on a medium flame until the peas are completely cooked. This will take about 30 minutes.

Check the salt and seasonings and then serve the tomatoey green pea sauce over the cooked spelt.

Spelt is an excellent source of riboflavin and a good source of thiamine and niacin.

"Spelt-otto" with
Butternut Squash | v g*

*The name of this recipe is a play on the word risotto, because instead of rice
in this recipe, you use spelt. This version is made with squash, which gives
a wonderful, warming, wintery texture. Good quality butternut squash is
essential (squash seasons are autumn and winter). The more orange
the flesh of the squash, the more intense its flavour will be.* ▶ *Serves 4-6*

Cook according to the instructions given in the "Basic Recipes" chapter (page 176):
  1 ½ cups (250 ml cups) spelt

In a separate saucepan, sauté in a little olive oil until golden:
  1 ½ onions, *finely chopped*
  pinch of salt

Add to the onions:
  2 cloves garlic, *very finely chopped*
  1 ½ stalks celery, *cut in thin slices*
  1 tsp thyme
and continue to sauté for another 5 minutes.

Next add:
  1 kg butternut squash, *cut in ½ cm cubes*
  2 bay leaves
  approx. 250 ml vegetable stock
  salt

Cover and cook on a medium-low flame, stirring occasionally, until the squash
is soft. Add a little vegetable stock if necessary.

Add to the squash mixture:
  the cooked spelt
  250 ml vegetable stock
and continue to cook for about 20 minutes, adding a little vegetable stock when
necessary, stirring often, until the consistency is similar to risotto.

Check the salt and seasonings and serve hot.

🌢 *A diet rich in fibre is thought to lower high cholesterol levels and high blood
pressure and protect against cardiovascular diseases.*

Roast Polenta and Red Cabbage with Chunky Tomato Sauce | v g

This is a tasty and unique polenta-cabbage combination. Cooking time is around 1 hour, plus another 15 minutes for the polenta to set. ▶ *Serves 4-6*

Put in a saucepan:

    300 g red cabbage, *cut into 2 cm long strips*   3 Tbsp water
    ½ tsp salt

Cover and cook on a low flame, stirring occasionally, until *al dente*. This will take about 10 minutes. Add a touch more water if necessary.

In a separate saucepan put:

    200 g polenta (coarsely ground type)   1½ tsp salt
    3 Tbsp ghee (page 188) or vegan butter

and cook according to the instructions given on the packet, stirring frequently.

While the polenta is cooking, make the tomato sauce. Sauté in oil for about 10 minutes:

    1 onion, *chopped in cubes*   1 ½ tsp salt
    500 g mixed vegetables, *cut in small pieces* (carrots, courgettes, yellow
        peppers, celery and squash are all good)

Add to the sautéed vegetables:

    700 ml tinned chopped tomatoes
    ½ tsp sugar *(optional, but it helps balance the sourness of the tomatoes)*

Cover and simmer for about 30 minutes, until the vegetables are soft and the sauce has thickened.

When the polenta is cooked, turn off the heat then stir in:

    2 Tbsp nutritional yeast   pinch black pepper

Then stir in:

    the cooked red cabbage

taking care to stir as little as possible so that the polenta and cabbage retain their separate colours.

Transfer the polenta and cabbage into an oven dish and leave to cool down and set (around 15 minutes). Cut the polenta into square slices and serve with the chunky tomato sauce on top.

🜨 *Corn (polenta) gives the spiritual quality of mental vitality.*

Spelt with Roasted Cherry Tomatoes and Pesto Sauce | v g*

*Could anything be more simple? Or more tasty?! The pesto sauce
in this recipe is a slight adaptation of traditional Italian pesto. A very
simple, quick and nutritious summertime recipe.* ▶ *Serves 4-6*

Cook according to the instructions given in the "Basic Recipes" chapter
(page 176):
    2 cups (250 ml cups) spelt

Roast in the oven with a little olive oil (no salt) for about 20 minutes:
    30-40 cherry tomatoes, *cut in halves*

In the meantime, blend together:
    30 g fresh basil leaves
    50 g walnuts
    50 g almonds
    1-1 ½ cloves garlic
    150 ml olive oil
    ½ tsp salt

Mix together:
    the cooked spelt
    the roasted cherry tomatoes
    the pesto

Serve at room temperature.

Spelt offers a broader spectrum of nutrients compared to many of its more in-bred cousins in the wheat family.

Baked Millet and Cauliflower Squares | v g*

These millet and cauliflower squares are delicious served with Béchamel Alternative or Mixed Herb and Nutritional Yeast Gravy. Both recipes are found in the "Savoury Sauces and Spreads" chapter. ▶ *Serves 4-6*

In a saucepan, sauté in olive oil until soft:
    1 red onion, *finely chopped*
    pinch of salt

Add to the onion:
    1 stalk celery, *cut in small cubes*
    2 tsp thyme
    1 bay leaf
    1 clove garlic, *finely chopped*
and sauté for another five minutes.

Now add:
    ½ small cauliflower, *cut into tiny florets*
    1 cup (250 ml cup) millet, *washed and dry-roasted (optional)*
    3 cups (250 ml cups) water
    4 Tbsp soya sauce

Bring to the boil then lower the temperature and cook, covered, until all the water has been absorbed. This will take about 25 minutes.

When the millet is cooked, stir in:
    2-3 Tbsp fresh parsley, *chopped*

Spread the mixture onto a baking tray lined with greaseproof paper until it is about 1 cm thick. Bake at 180°C until crispy on top. This will take 20-30 minutes (cooking times and temperatures vary according to the type of oven used).

Millet is a good source of some very important nutrients, including manganese, phosphorus and magnesium.

Other Main Meals

Lentil Duchess | v g

A vegetarian version of the traditional English "Shepherd's Pie": tomatoey lentils covered with a layer of creamy mashed potatoes. ▶ *Serves 4-6*

Sauté in a little olive oil until golden:
   1 small onion, *finely chopped*
   ½ leek, *finely sliced in ¼ rounds*

Add to the onion and leek:
   2 medium-sized carrots, *minced*
   1 stalk celery, *minced (not too much or it becomes wet)*
and sauté for about 10 more minutes, stirring when needed.

Then add:
   200 g brown lentils, *washed thoroughly*
   200 ml tinned chopped tomatoes
   2 bay leaves
   any herbs, such as rosemary, thyme, oregano, marjoram *(optional)*

Cover the lentil mixture with water (unsalted) and bring to the boil. Then turn the heat down to a simmer.

Cook the lentils until they are really mushy, adding hot water when necessary. The water level should remain about ½ cm above the lentils; no more. When the lentils are cooked, all of the excess water should be absorbed. If you do get stuck with unwanted water, you can evaporate it using a high heat or remove it with a ladle.

When the lentils are soft but not yet mushy add:
   2 tsp salt

While the lentils are cooking, peel and cut into chunks:
   1300 g potatoes

Boil the potatoes until very soft, almost falling apart. Then mash them together with:
   200 ml milk or any vegan milk
   50 g butter, ghee (page 188) or vegan butter
   1 ½ tsp salt
   2-3 pinches black pepper

Pour the cooked lentils into an oven dish and, using a spatula, spread the mashed potatoes over the top. Use a fork to make a pattern on the surface.

Bake in the oven or put under the grill until golden brown on top.

Lentils have an impressive nutritional profile; they provide excellent amounts of six important minerals, two B-vitamins and protein - all with virtually no fat.

Savoury Strudels with Various Fillings | v

*There are so many fillings that can be put in a strudel. Follow the basic
instructions given below, and then choose one of the fillings to put inside or
make up your own. The fillings should be cooled a little before putting them
on the rolled out dough (otherwise they melt it). Therefore, depending on
the filling you choose, you may want to make the filling before you make the
dough, to give it time to cool down. The recipe may seem complicated but,
with a little practice, it's not as difficult as it first appears. Good for dinner
parties and special occasions.* ▶ *Makes a large strudel (12 slices)*

To make the dough:

Knead together until well mixed and then for about another 5 minutes:
    200 g durum flour
    ½ tsp salt
    40 ml olive oil
    splash of apple or fruit vinegar
    about 80 ml warm water

The dough should be very soft and elastic, like an earlobe, but not sticky. Put
the dough in a bowl, cover with a damp cloth and put in the fridge for about
30 minutes.

Take the dough out of the fridge and roll out on a floured surface until it is approximately 45 cm high and 70 cm wide.* Yes, it will become that big! Don't worry if it tears a little - the holes will not be visible when everything is rolled together.

Transfer the rolled-out dough onto a large cloth using the length of your arms. (It's not as hard as it sounds.)

Spread the filling of your choice out onto the dough, leaving a 2 cm border all around. Tuck the empty borders of the top, bottom and left-hand sides over, onto the filling.

Now, using the cloth to help you, roll the dough and filling tightly, starting from the left and going towards the right, making a strudel.

Again, using the cloth, transfer the rolled strudel onto a baking tray lined with grease-proof paper. The fold should be hidden underneath.

Next, use a knife to make small cuts on top of the strudel, approximately 3 cm apart. These cuts mark where you will cut the slices, after the strudel is baked.

Bake at 180°C for 30-40 minutes, until you see that the outside is golden brown. (Cooking times and temperatures will vary according to the type of oven.)

Let cool a little before cutting.

Creamy Cabbage Filling | V G Q

Put in a large saucepan:
> 1300 g white cabbage (about one large cabbage), *de-cored and cut in ½ cm strips*
> 150 ml salted vegetable stock (page 192)
> ½ tsp salt

*If you want to make a smaller strudel, lets say half the size, divide the height by half (which would be 22 ½ cm), but always leave the width at 70 cm. This will make your strudel the same thickness but give only 6 slices.

Put a lid on and let cook on a medium flame until the cabbage is soft. Add a little more water if necessary. When the cabbage is cooked, all the water should be completely absorbed. If you see any liquid remaining, take off the lid and cook for a few minutes on a high flame, allowing the water to evaporate.

Once cooked, turn off the heat and then stir into the cabbage:
    250 ml cooking cream or soya cooking cream
    1 ½ Tbsp mustard
    ½ tsp black pepper

Leave the filling to cool down a little before putting it on the dough.

Roast Squash Filling | V G

This is such a simple filling, but people love it! The more orange the flesh of the squash, the less watery, and therefore the more flavourful, it will be. We use butternut squash.

Put on a large baking tray:
    2400 g squash, *cut in 2½ cm cubes*

Toss the squash with:
    4 ½ Tbsp olive oil
    1 ½ tsp salt

Bake at about 200°C until soft on the inside and brown and crunchy on the outside (if there is too much steam created in your oven the squash won't become crunchy. Either change the setting or open your oven door occasionally to let the steam out).

Put the baked squash in a bowl and, using a hand blender, roughly blend it. You don't want to blend it into a smooth paste; it just needs to get a little mushy so that it spreads out easily onto the strudel dough.

Let the squash cool down.

Tomatoey Tofu-Spinach Filling | V G Q

In a largish frying pan sauté until soft:
    1 onion, *finely cut*
Add and sauté for another minute:
    ½ tsp garlic paste
    ¾ tsp thyme

Next add and sauté for a few minutes:
    300 g tofu, *crumbled*
    200 ml tomato passata (blended tomatoes)
    1 tsp salt

Finely add:
    450 g fresh spinach, *finely cut (bunch it together to cut- no need to be precise)*

Cover and cook until the spinach is wilted. Then remove the cover, turn up the heat and allow the excess liquid to evaporate.

Including more vegetables in your diet helps you to alkalinise your body.

Sunburgers | v g

*These really nutritious and quick-to-make sunflower seed burgers
can be served on their own or in a bun with lettuce and tomato slices.
An adaptation of the recipe from the American Ananda cookbook,
"Simply Vegetarian". This is a version without eggs.* ▸ *Makes 8-10 burgers*

Put into a food processor:
- 1 small onion
- 2 medium-sized carrots
- 2 stalks celery

and mince until fine. Put the vegetables in a large bowl.

Next, put into the food processor:
- 225 g sunflower seeds

and grind until they are in small pieces but not powder; it's nice to crunch on
something when you eat a burger! Remove from the food processor and add
to the large bowl in which you have the minced onion, celery and carrots.

In a small bowl, mix together to obtain a thick paste:

    8 Tbsp (70 g) chickpea flour

    water, as needed

and then add the paste to the minced vegetables and sunflower seeds.

Finally add:

    2 Tbsp soya sauce

    2 tsp dried oregano or basil

    2 Tbsp fresh parsley, *finely chopped (optional)*

and use your hands to mix the ingredients together well.

Form the mixture into burger shapes and place on a baking tray lined with baking paper (the mixture may seem a little wet and to not want to hold together, but once the chickpea paste starts baking, it will solidify and hold everything together- so if you can get them on to the baking tray in burger shapes, the oven will do the rest!)

Cook in the oven at 180°C for 25-35 minutes or until the burgers are nicely crisped on the outside (cooking times and temperatures will vary according to the type of oven used).

Serve with soya mayonnaise (page 228).

A handful of sunflower seeds will enhance your health by supplying significant amounts of vitamin E, magnesium and selenium.

Eggless Wholemeal Crêpes
with Various Fillings | v q

*Eggless crêpes are so straightforward and quick to prepare and, with a
filling, make an excellent and nutritious dinner. You can fill crêpes with just
about anything. Many ideas are given below, or you can just make one up!
They can also be filled with sweet things, like bananas and honey,
and eaten for breakfast — yummy!* ▶ *Makes 4-6 crêpes*

To make the batter, mix together with a whisk:
    175 g wholemeal wheat, spelt or buckwheat flour
    400 ml water, or any vegan milk
    2 tsp baking powder
    1 Tbsp olive oil
    ¾ tsp salt

Now you will need a non-stick frying pan and a ladle.* Apply a tiny amount
of oil to the pan with a tissue (this will be enough to do all the crêpes). Next,
get the pan really hot. Test to see if it is hot enough by splashing water in the
pan: If tiny bubbles form on the surface, the pan is hot enough.

Carefully pour one small ladleful of the batter into the centre of the pan. Use
the rounded edge of the ladle to smooth the batter out evenly, starting from
the central point and working out towards the edge in a clockwise spiral. Try
to get the batter more or less evenly distributed. The crêpes should be thin.
Cook the crêpes on a medium-high flame until they are light brown underneath and then turn them over and do the other side (the first crêpe will be
the slowest to cook).
Put the ready crêpes one on top of the other on a plate and cover with a cloth
to keep them warm. That's it!

*If you want to be quicker, then you can use two pans at the same time.

Mediterranean Vegetables | V G Q

Sauté an onion. Add some courgette and aubergine cut in 1 cm cubes. Sauté until they start to soften and then cover and cook until completely soft. Add some fresh chopped tomatoes and cook until slightly softened. Season.

Leeks, Squash and Peas with Nutritional Yeast | V G Q

Sauté a leek. Add some frozen peas, some squash cut in 1 cm cubes and a little water. Cover and cook until the squash and peas are soft. Roughly mash the vegetables with a potato masher. Stir in some nutritional yeast and season to taste. For a richer version add some cream or yoghurt.

Curried Yoghurt and Pepper | V G Q

Sauté some onions cut in half moons. Add some peppers cut in strips and sauté until soft (or use roast peppers for an even tastier version). Turn off the heat and stir in some yoghurt or soya yoghurt flavoured with sweet curry powder and some fresh coriander. Season.

Garlic Chicory and Fresh Tomatoes | V G Q

Boil some finely cut chicory and then strain it well. Sauté the chicory in a little garlic paste. Add some fresh tomatoes and cook until the tomatoes slightly soften. Turn off the heat, add some olive oil and season.

Avocado, Tomato, Red Onion and Sweetcorn | V G Q

Mash some avocado. Add some finely cubed fresh tomatoes, some finely cubed red onions and some sweetcorn. Season.

Iranian Spinach | V G Q

See the recipe on page 344.

Whole grains give the spiritual quality of strength of character.

Curried Stuffed Potato Halves | v g

Very worthwhile for special occasions and dinner parties.

Makes 8 potato halves

Wash thoroughly:
  4 large thick-skinned potatoes

Cut each potato in half lengthways and place face down on an oiled baking tray. Brush the skin of the potatoes with olive oil.

Bake the potatoes in the oven at 180°C until they are completely soft. This will take about 40-60 minutes.

In the meantime, prepare the other ingredients:

Boil in salted water or steam until tender:
  500 g squash, *chopped into pieces* *
Put aside.

Sauté until golden:
  1 onion, *finely chopped*

Add to the onion:
  3 cloves garlic, *finely chopped*
  piece of fresh ginger, size of a walnut shell, *peeled and finely chopped*
and sauté for a few minutes, stirring continuously.

Next, add to the onion mixture:
  ½ tsp each: coriander powder, turmeric, ground cumin, curry powder,
    garam masala
and fry for a further minute or two *(make sure there is enough oil to coat the spices in. They should not be dry-fried).*

When the potatoes are cooked, remove them from the oven and leave to cool down. Once they are cool, scoop out most of the inside, leaving about ¼ cm attached to the skin, and put in a bowl.

*Squash can be replaced with carrots or any leftover cooked vegetable.

Put the empty potato skins face-up on a baking tray. Brush the inside with a little olive oil and sprinkle with a little salt. Return to the oven and bake for 5-10 minutes until crispy.

While the skins are baking, mash together in a bowl:
    the inside of the potatoes
    the boiled squash pieces
    the onions and Indian spices
    salt, as needed

Heap the mashed potato mixture back into the crispy skins and bake in the oven until browned on top.

As well as tasting wonderful, Indian spices, such as coriander, turmeric, cumin, cardamom and fennel, have many medicinal and healing properties.

CHAPTER 12

Indian Cuisine

About Indian Cooking

All the recipes contained in this chapter are authentic Indian dishes, although soya yoghurt and coconut oil are often given as vegan options, even though these are not traditionally used in India. Our Indian food is always well-received by our Indian friends and guests.

Authentic Indian cuisine is very different from the 'curries' you find in the European curry houses, which are actually often Pakistani-owned establishments. Not all Indian food is hot, as many are led to believe; it is creative, colourful and delicately flavoured with diverse combinations of the traditional Indian spices.

All of the ingredients called for in these recipes can be found in Indian shops or in the international section of most large supermarkets. Ghee (see below) can easily and simply be made at home (see recipe page 188).

Most Indian spices, as well as garlic and gingerroot, are always fried in oil or ghee before adding them to the main dish. This enhances, and slightly changes, their flavour. For proper frying of spices, the amount of oil is important; it should be just enough to saturate all the spices, but not so much that the dish tastes oily and heavy. Try to use a non-stick frying pan to fry the spices, as ginger, especially, has a tendency to stick.

Some Common Indian Ingredients

Rice is the most common ingredient in Indian cooking, usually served with

every meal. In India, many different types of rice are available (all low starch types), but the only rice to be exported to the West is **basmati** rice. Basmati rice has a wonderful fragrance and nutty flavour and is considered the world's best long grain rice.

Although the brown, unrefined basmati rice is more nutritious than its refined counterpart, Indian cooking uses only white basmati. Basic cooking instructions for basmati rice can be found in the "Basic Recipes" chapter (page 176).

Dhal, a curried legume, soup-like dish, is usually served with every meal. Dhal is made with split, dehulled legumes: about 60 different types are used! Some of the most common dhals are *channa dhal* (split chickpeas), *mung dhal* (split soya beans) and *toor dhal* (split yellow pigeon peas), but split red lentils and split green peas are also commonly used. Dhal is always served with basmati rice or chappatis.

Chappatis, traditional Indian flatbreads, are fun and quick to make; the recipe is given in the "Savoury Breads, Sweet Breads and Crackers" chapter (page 246).

Ghee (clarified butter) is often used in Indian cooking instead of oil. It has a rich, sweet flavour, which adds an extra delightful taste to any dish. The recipe for ghee can be found in the "Basic Recipes" chapter (page 188).

Paneer, a fresh Indian cheese, is often added to vegetable and rice dishes. Paneer is very simple and quick to make; the recipe is given in the "Basic Recipes" chapter (page 189).

Indian spices include: cumin, coriander, turmeric, fresh chillies, chilli powder, cardamom, black pepper, aniseed, fenugreek, fennel, paprika and cloves. Whole cumin seeds and black mustard seeds (popped) are also used.

Garam masala and tandoori masala are two of the most common spice mixes used in Indian cooking (masala means 'mix'). Curry powder is more of a Western commodity than a traditional Indian ingredient.

Garlic and **fresh gingerroot** are two of the main ingredients used to flavour Indian food and are used in almost every dish. We usually blend the garlic and ginger together with sunflower oil to create a paste, allowing the flavour to be distributed evenly throughout the dish. The approximate proportions for making these pastes are given in the "Basic Recipes" chapter (page 193).

For those who don't eat garlic, a powdered root called asafoetida is often used in its place. Asafoetida is always used in tiny quantities and fried for 1-2 seconds in oil.

Fresh coriander and **mint** are very often added at the end of cooking.

Basmati Rice with Cabbage
and Coconut | v g

A special combination of flavours. With practice, this dish can be made in about 35-40 minutes. ▶ *Serves 4-6*

Cook:
> 2 cups (250 ml cups) basmati rice (see chart on page 176 for cooking instructions)

When the rice is ready, fluff it with a fork and put it aside.

While the rice is cooking, sauté in oil in a non-stick pan until soft:
> 1 onion, *cut in half moons*
> pinch of salt

Add to the onions and fry for about 1 more minute, making sure there is enough oil to coat the spices:
> 2 tsp ginger paste
> 1 tsp garlic paste
> 1 tsp fennel seeds
> ½ tsp turmeric

Then add and fry for 2-3 more minutes until browned:
> 80 g dried coconut

Lastly, add to the spices and coconut:
> 200 g white cabbage, *shredded*
> 100 ml water
> ½ tsp salt

Cover and cook on a low flame, stirring occasionally, until the cabbage is soft. Add a touch of water if necessary.

When the cabbage is soft, mix it into the cooked basmati rice along with:
> ½ Tbsp mustard seeds, *popped**
> 2 Tbsp fresh parsley/coriander, *chopped*

🜛 *Fibre-related components in steamed cabbage, bind readily together with bile acids in your digestive tract, giving cholesterol-lowering benefits.*

---

*Heat the mustard seeds in a small frying pan covered with a lid. When you hear them begin to pop (like popcorn), leave them for about 10 seconds, then remove from the heat.

Yoghurt Rice | V G Q

The hot taste of this rice is balanced by the cooling taste of yoghurt.
Very straight-forward and quick to make. ▶ *Serves 4-6*

Cook:

    2 cups (250 ml cups) basmati rice (see chart on page 176 for cooking instructions)

Turn off and then stir into the rice:

    500 ml yoghurt (page 184) or soya yoghurt (page 183)
    enough water to make a risotto-like consistency (about 100 ml)

Then add:

    3 Tbsp fresh gingerroot, *finely chopped*
    1 Tbsp black mustard seeds, *popped**
    2 Tbsp fresh coriander or mint, *finely chopped*
    fresh chilli, *finely chopped (optional)*
    salt to taste

Serve with any Indian vegetable dish (pages 297-313), chutney (pages 313) or on its own.

🧍 *Yoghurt, because of the live cultures it contains, is excellent for balancing your digestive system.*

*Heat the mustard seeds in a small frying pan, covered with a lid. When you hear them begin to pop (like popcorn), leave them for about 10 seconds, then remove from the heat.

Basmati Rice with Raisins and Toasted Almonds | v g q

Another very simple-to-make basmati rice dish, flavoured with ghee (page 188) o coconut oil, raisins and toasted almonds. ▶ *Serves 4-6*

Cook:
> 2 cups (250 ml cups) basmati rice (see chart on page 176 for cooking instructions)

While the rice is cooking, fry in plenty of ghee (vegans can use coconut oil) until light golden brown:
> 125 g almonds, *slivered*

Remove the almonds from the ghee and then strain the ghee through a sieve so that it can be reused.

Soak in boiling water for 5-10 minutes:
> 100 g raisins

Stir into the cooked basmati rice:
> 100 ml ghee (you can use the ghee you used to fry the almonds in)
> /coconut oil
> the fried almonds
> the soaked raisins
> salt, if necessary

Serve with any Indian vegetable (pages 308-311) or dhal (pages 305 and 306).

🌿 *Raisins are an anti-oxidant rich fruit.*

Coconut Rice | V G Q

A delicious South Indian rice dish, combining fresh coconut with many other typical Indian ingredients. Very simple and quick to make. ▶ *Serves 4-6*

Cook:

> 2 cups (250 ml cups) basmati rice (see chart on page 176 for cooking instructions)

Heat in a frying pan, covered with a lid:

> 1 Tbsp black mustard seeds

When you hear the mustard seeds start to pop (like popcorn), remove the pan from the heat immediately.

Add to the mustard seeds:

> 2 Tbsp ghee (page 188) or coconut oil
> 300 g fresh coconut, *grated** (or half the amount of dried coconut)
> 1 Tbsp fresh gingerroot, *very finely cut*

Return to the heat and fry together for about 10 minutes.

Mix together:

> the cooked rice
> the fried coconut mixture
> 5 Tbsp ghee or coconut oil
> 2 tsp dried mint or more fresh mint if in season
> 2 Tbsp lemon juice

Check the salt and flavourings and then serve with any Indian vegetable dish.

🕉 *The coconut is a sattwic food; it gives the qualities of spiritual upliftment and awareness.*

---

*Open the coconut in the following way: Outside, bounce the coconut on the ground several times to dislodge the inner flesh from the outer shell. Next, using a cork screw, pierce at least two of the 'eyes' of the coconut (small indentations found at one of the ends) and empty the liquid into a glass. Now break the coconut open by either throwing it energetically on the ground or by using a hammer. Remove the coconut flesh from the hard outer shell with the help of a knife.

Raita | v g q

(yoghurt salad)

Indian salads are usually dressed in yoghurt and are called 'raita'. Many raita recipes exist, but the concept is always the same: vegetables cut in small cubes or pieces, yoghurt and a little fresh coriander or spice. ▶ *Serves 4-6*

Mix together:

    250 g fresh tomatoes, *cut into tiny ½ cm cubes*
    250 g cucumber, *peeled and cut into tiny ½ cm cubes*
    ½ medium red onion, *very finely cut*

Stir in:

    250 ml yoghurt (page 184) or soya yoghurt (page 183)
    2 Tbsp fresh coriander or mint, *finely chopped*
    ¾ tsp salt

Serve at room temperature.

Soya yoghurt and, according to some, regular yoghurt, both have an alkalinising effect on the body.

Red Lentil and Tomato Dhal | v g

A North Indian Dhal. ▶ *Serves 4-6*

Wash thoroughly, strain and then put in a large saucepan:
    400 g split red lentils

Cover the lentils with water (no salt), bring to the boil and then turn down the flame and simmer with a lid on until they are completely soft and mushy. This will take about 30 minutes (see page 179 for more information on how to cook legumes).

Add hot water whenever necessary, keeping the water level no more than ½ cm above the lentils. There should be no excess water once the lentils are soft.

In another, smaller saucepan, sauté in a little ghee (page 188) or oil until soft:
    1 medium onion, *finely chopped*

Add to the onion:
    750 ml tinned chopped tomatoes or fresh tomatoes, *cut in 1 cm cubes*
    3 tsp salt
and cook covered on a low flame for about 15 minutes. Then, using a hand blender, blend the tomato sauce (*optional*).

In a small, non-stick frying pan, fry in ghee or oil for about 2 minutes:
    4 tsp cumin seeds

Then add and fry for another 1-2 minutes:
    4 tsp ginger paste (page 193)
    2 tsp garlic paste (page 193) or about 1 clove crushed garlic
    2 tsp turmeric

N.B.: Make sure there is enough ghee/oil to coat the spices in. They should not be dry-fried.

When the lentils are cooked, add the tomato sauce and fried spices. Cook everything together for about 10 minutes, in order to blend the flavours.

Adjust the salt and then serve over basmati rice (see chart on page 176 for cooking instructions).

🝚 *Eating meals that combine grains and legumes provides you with complete protein.*

Carrot and Coconut Dhal | v g

*This dish combines the much-loved channa dhal (broken chickpeas)
with coconut, carrots and sweet Indian spices.* ▶ *Serves 4-6*

Soak for 6-8 hours in plenty of water:*
  400 g channa dhal

Strain the dhal, wash thoroughly and then put in a large saucepan, with:
  ½ handful dried curry leaves

Cover the dhal with fresh, unsalted water, bring to the boil and then turn
down the flame. Simmer with a lid on until the broken chickpea pieces are
completely soft and mushy and dissolve when stirred. This will take about
an hour (see page 179). Add a little hot water, whenever necessary, keeping
the water level no more than ½ cm above the chickpeas. If the dhal starts to
foam, remove the foam with a tea strainer.

When the split chickpeas are soft, add:
  2 tsp salt

In a non-stick frying pan, sauté in ghee (page 188) or oil until soft:
  1 medium onion, *finely chopped*
  ½ tsp salt

Add and fry for a further 1-2 minutes:
  2 ½ Tbsp ginger paste (page 193)
  1 ½ Tbsp garlic paste (page 193) *or about 1 ½ cloves crushed garlic*
  1 tsp turmeric powder
  1 pinch asafoetida

Then add and fry for a further 5-7 minutes until soft:
  50 g dried coconut
  100 g carrots, *minced*

Add the carrot and coconut mixture to the cooked channa dhal. If the consistency is too thick, add a little water. If necessary, adjust the salt and spices
and then serve on top of basmati rice (see chart on page 176).

🜂 *Chickpeas are an excellent source of manganese, folate, phosphorus and iron.*

*Soaking the channa dhal beforehand is optional but will speed up the cooking process. If you for-
get or don't have time, soak the channa dhal in hot water while you prepare the other ingredients.

Squash, Cauliflower and Cabbage Curry | v g

Another sweet-tasting dish from South India. ▶ *Serves 4-6*

In a non-stick frying pan, fry in ghee (page 188) or oil for about 2 minutes:
  1 Tbsp ginger paste (page 193)
  1 Tbsp garlic paste (page 193) or about 1 large clove crushed garlic
  ½ tsp turmeric
  tsp ground coriander
  ½ tsp fennel seeds, *ground*
  ¼ tsp aniseeds, *ground*
N.B.: Make sure there is enough ghee/oil to coat the spices in. They should not be dry-fried.

Add and sauté until soft:
  1 medium onion, *finely chopped*
  pinch of salt

Next, add to the onion and spice mixture:
  1 kg squash, *cut into cubes the same size as the cauliflower*
  ½ small cauliflower (200 g), *cut into bite size florets*
  ¼ small white cabbage (about 200 g), *cut in thin strips*
  10 dried curry leaves
  40 g dried coconut
  1 Tbsp salt
and sauté together for 5 minutes in order to blend the flavours.

Then add:
  200 ml water
Cover and cook until the vegetables are soft, stirring occasionally, and adding a little hot water when needed.

When the vegetables are well cooked and soft, stir in:
  1 tsp dried mint (fresh is better, if in season)
  40 ml ghee *(optional)*
  100 ml yoghurt (page 184) or soya yoghurt (page 183) *(optional)*

Serve with basmati rice (see chart on page 176 for cooking instructions) or chappatis (page 246).

🕉 *Eating sweet curries like this one, is an excellent way to enjoy Indian cooking without getting the rajasic effects of hot spices like chilli.*

Smoked Aubergine Curry | V G

This is one of my all-time favourites. Gas rings are an essential part of this dish to give the smoked flavour to the aubergine. ▶ *Serves 4-6*

Let sit in boiling water until defrosted:
　　180 g frozen peas
Strain and put aside.

Turn on 3 gas rings and balance on top:
　　3 medium-sized aubergines
Roast the aubergines on the open flame, turning frequently, until the skin is burnt all over and the aubergine is soft. This will take about 10 minutes. Then, under cold running water, remove the burnt skin. Roughly cut the aubergines into small pieces.

Sauté until soft:
　　3 onions, *finely chopped*

When nearly soft add:
　　3 cloves garlic, *finely minced*
　　3 Tbsp (30 g) fresh ginger, *finely minced*

When the onions are soft, add:
　　1 ½ tsp garam masala
　　¾ tsp turmeric
and fry with the onions for around 2 minutes, making sure there is enough oil to coat the spices in (they should not be dry-fried).

Then add and cook for another 10 minutes:
　　the smoked, chopped aubergine
　　450 ml tinned chopped tomatoes
　　the defrosted peas
　　2 tsp salt

Garnish with:
　　fresh coriander, chopped
Serve with basmati rice or chappatis (page 246).

Aubergine is a very good source of fibre, vitamin B1 and copper, as well as a good source of manganese, vitamin B6, niacin, potassium, folate and vitamin K.

Curried Mashed Potatoes | V G

One of the Ananda all-time favourites! These curried potatoes can also be used as a filling for strudels (page 286) and puff pastries. ▶ *Serves 4-6*

Scrub until clean and then boil whole, with skin left on, in salted water until very soft:
   2 kg potatoes
N.B.: Do not throw away the cooking water!

In a non-stick frying pan, sauté in ghee (page 188) or vegan butter until golden:
   3 medium-sized onions, *cut in half moons*
   pinch of salt

Add and continue to sauté for about 2 minutes, stirring continuously:
   2 ½ Tbsp cumin powder
   2 ½ Tbsp spicy curry powder
   1 ½ Tbsp coriander powder
   1 Tbsp garlic paste (page 193) or about 1 large clove crushed garlic
   2 tsp ginger paste (page 193)
   1 ½ tsp turmeric
   pinch ground fenugreek
N.B.: Make sure there is enough ghee/vegan butter to coat the spices in. They should not be dry-fried.

In a small frying pan, heat with a lid on:
   1 Tbsp black mustard seeds
When you hear the mustard seeds start to pop (like popcorn), remove them from the heat immediately.

When the potatoes are cooked, remove their skin and mash coarsely, together with:
   200 ml of the potato water
   4 Tbsp ghee or vegan butter
   salt, to taste

Then mix in:
   the spiced onions
   the popped mustard seeds
Put the curried potatoes in an oven dish and bake in the oven until crispy on top. Alternatively, make little patties and, in a frying pan, fry on both sides.

 Potatoes have an extremely alkalinising effect on the body.

Chutneys

A chutney usually combines the tastes of hot, sweet and sour. Chutneys, having intense flavours, are eaten in very small quantities, usually with popadoms, pakoras (deep-fried vegetable fritters) or rice. Three different recipes are given below.

Raisin Chutney | V G Q

Ginger gives the spicy kick in this chutney, while lemon juice and raisins provide the contrasting sweet and sour. An ideal chutney for those who don't eat sugar. ▶ *Serves 4-8*

Soak in boiling water for half an hour:
 300 g raisins

Strain the raisins, and then blend until smooth, together with:
 60 ml lemon juice
 piece of fresh ginger, size of 1 ½ walnut shells
 1 ½ cloves garlic
 pinch of salt

Raisins are high-energy foods that contain fructose and glucose, which are much better for your health than the sucrose found in sugar.

Coconut Chutney | V G Q

This chutney is also wonderful served with boiled potatoes. ▶ *Serves 4-8*

Blend together until smooth:
 ½ fresh coconut (200 g), *cut into small pieces**
 piece of fresh ginger, size of a walnut shell
 1 large clove garlic
 ¾ tsp dried mint
 250 ml yoghurt (page 184) or soya yoghurt (page 183)
 ½ tsp salt

*Open the coconut in the following way: Outside, bounce the coconut on the ground several times to dislodge the inner flesh from the outer shell. Next, using a cork screw, pierce at least two of the 'eyes' of the coconut (small indentations found at one of the ends) and empty the liquid into a glass. Now break the coconut open by either throwing it energetically on the ground or by using a hammer. Remove the coconut flesh from the hard outer shell with the help of a knife.

Stir into the dhal:

    1 ½ tsp black mustard seeds, *popped**

 *Coconut is an alkaline food. Eating a diet rich with alkaline foods ensures that the enzymes in your body can function efficiently.*

Pineapple Chutney | v g

This is my favourite chutney: succulent and sweet, with a little spice. The sour taste is not as prominent as it is with the other chutneys. ▶ *Serves 4-8*

In a medium-sized frying pan, fry for 2 minutes in 2 Tbsp ghee (page 188) or oil:

    1 ½ tsp cumin seeds

    ½ tsp turmeric

Add:

    1 medium pineapple, *de-cored and cut into ½ cm cubes*

and continue to fry on a high flame for about 4 or 5 minutes.

Add to the pineapple:

    ¼ tsp chilli powder

    5 Tbsp water

    ¼ tsp salt

Cover and cook on a low flame, stirring occasionally, for about 15 minutes. If any excess water remains after 15 minutes, remove the lid and continue cooking until all the liquid evaporates.

Stir into the cooked pineapple:

    100-200 g raw cane sugar (depending on how sweet the pineapple is)

and continue to cook for about 10 minutes on a low flame, stirring often, until the chutney becomes dense.

Remove the chutney from the pan and then coarsely blend, leaving lots of lumps. Serve at room temperature.

 *Pineapples are an excellent source of the antioxidant Vitamin C.*

*Heat the mustard seeds, covered, in a small frying pan. When you hear them start to pop (like popcorn), leave them for about 10 seconds, and then remove from the heat.

CHAPTER 13

Tofu and Seitan

Creamy Mushroom, Leek and Tofu Pastries | v

Great for special occasions and dinner parties. These pastries are not as complicated as they seem. The preparation process is very simple and can be completed in about 45 minutes. Sometimes, for an extra special version, I prepare them with puff pastry instead of the wholemeal pastry. ▶ *Makes 9 pastries*

First start by making the pastry:
Knead together:
    200 g wholemeal flour
    1 ½ tsp salt
    2 Tbsp olive oil
    splash of apple or fruit vinegar
    approximately 100 ml warm water (add slowly as it may need less)

Wrap the dough in cling film and then leave in the fridge while you prepare the other ingredients.

Make a half quantity of the "Alternative Béchamel" recipe (page 223). Use soya or oat milk as the base.

Now for the mushrooms and leeks:
Sauté in olive oil until soft:
    ½ leek, *cut in half rounds*
    3 mushrooms, *cut in thin slices*
    pinch salt

Add to the leek and mushrooms and fry for a minute:
    1 ½ tsp garlic paste (page 193) or about ¾ clove crushed garlic

Then add:
    200 g tofu (page 190), *crumbled*
    ½ tsp sage
    ½ tsp thyme
    1 tsp salt
and continue to sauté for another few minutes.

Mix the béchamel together with the mushrooms, leeks and tofu. Adjust the seasoning as needed and then leave to cool (if the mixture is hot it will melt the rolled dough).

Remove the dough from the fridge and roll out on a floured surface until it is approximately 40 x 40 cm. Trim the edges and then cut the dough into 9 even squares.

On each square place about a tablespoon of the filling, leaving the borders empty. Fold the square in half to make a triangle and seal the edges by pressing the two folds together with a fork.

Place the triangles on a baking tray lined with baking paper. Brush the triangles with a little oil or (vegan) milk, prick them with a fork (this lets the air out while baking) and then bake at about 180°C until they are golden brown. This will take about 20-30 minutes. (Cooking times and temperatures will vary according to the type of oven used.)

Tofu is a very good source of iron and copper, essential minerals for the transporting and releasing of oxygen throughout your body.

Curried Tofu and Spinach | v ɢ ǫ

Made with a beautiful blend of sweet Indian spices. Serve as a side dish or with basmati rice or chappatis (page 246). ▶ *Serves 4-6*

In a saucepan, cover and steam until tender:
 700 g fresh spinach, including stems (the water left on them after washing will be sufficient to steam them)
 pinch salt
When the spinach is cooked, drain off the excess water and chop coarsely.

In the meantime, in a non-stick frying pan, sauté in oil until golden:
 1 onion, *finely chopped*
 pinch of salt

Add to the onion and fry for 1-2 minutes:
 3 tsp garlic paste (page 193) or about 1 large clove crushed garlic
 3 tsp ground coriander
 1 tsp ground cardamom
 1 tsp cumin seeds
 1 tsp turmeric
 enough oil to coat the spices

Next add:
 300 g tofu (page 190), *cut into 1 cm cubes*
 ½ tsp salt
and fry together with the spices for 5 minutes, stirring gently so as not to
break the tofu.

Add:
 the cooked spinach
and fry for another few minutes, continuing to stir.

Turn off the heat and stir in:
 200 ml cream or soya cream

🌀 *Regular intake of soya can help you to lower your LDL (bad cholesterol) levels.*

Green Pea, Tofu and Leek Quiche | v

A delicious and easy dish that's regularly featured in my menus. ▶ *Serves 4-6*

Start by making the crust. Knead together:
    200 g wholemeal wheat or spelt flour
    1 tsp salt
    75 g butter or vegan butter, room temperature
    approximately 100 ml warm water
Push the dough into a 20 x 25 cm rectangular oven dish, covering the sides as
well as the base. Bake the crust at 180°C for about 10 minutes, until it is cooked,
but not over-cooked.

*N.B.: A trick is to fill the empty crust with dried beans to prevent it from inflating
while it is cooking. The dried beans can easily be removed and then reused for the
same purpose for future occasions.*

Sauté in oil until soft:
    1 ½ large leeks (including green top), cut in rounds
    pinch of salt

When the leeks are soft, add and sauté for a couple more minutes:
    1 ½ tsp garlic paste (page 193) or about ¾ clove crushed garlic
    2 ¼ tsp sage

Add to the leeks and cover and cook until tender:
    225 g frozen peas
    a little water

Mix together in a bowl:
    450 g tofu (page 190), *blended in a food processor until smooth*
    the leeks and peas
    a fresh tomato, *cut in cubes*
    1 ½ Tbsp nutritional yeast
    2 Tbsp lemon juice
    pinch black pepper
    about 1 tsp salt

Fill the crust with the tofu mixture and then bake at 180°C for about half an
hour until set and lightly browned.

🌀 *Unless your tofu is organic, it is likely that the soya has been genetically modified.
Genetic modification is prohibited in the production of any certified organic food.*

Roast Vegetable Tofu "Sandwich" | V G

Roast pepper, aubergine and courgette make up the filling, while tofu is the 'bread' for this alternative, sophisticated sandwich. This recipe can be made in about 45 minutes. Good for party food! ▶ *Makes 4 sandwiches*

Cut into 1 ½ cm round slices:
   ½ aubergine

Slice lengthways into 1 cm slices:
   2 courgettes

Cut into 8 cm squares:
   1-2 yellow peppers

Place the vegetables on an oiled baking tray, brush with olive oil and sprinkle with a little salt (you can also dress them with balsamic vinegar).
Bake the vegetables at 180°C until soft and nicely browned, but not burnt and crispy. This will take 20-40 minutes.

In the meantime, slice into 8 even slices:
    approx. 800 g firm tofu (page 190)

Fry the tofu slices on both sides, together with a mixture of:
    7 Tbsp soya sauce
    4 Tbsp water
    1 Tbsp olive oil

Assemble the sandwiches by taking 2 slices of tofu and filling with layers of the following:
    the roast pepper
    the roast aubergine
    the roast courgettes
    a fresh lettuce leaf (the lettuce looks nice if it sticks out of the sides)
    a slice of fresh tomato

Hold everything in place with a tooth pick (*optional*) and serve hot or at room temperature with tahini sauce (page 224).

Soya's high content of phytoestrogens could be beneficial for menopausal symptoms, such as hot flushes.

Tofu Burgers with Lemon-Parsley Sauce | v g

This is a basic recipe for tofu burgers. You can substitute the given vegetables with any others and change the spices as you like. ▶ *Makes 4-6 burgers*

Dry-roast (separately) until lightly browned:
    25 g sesame seeds
    25 g sunflower seeds

Using a spice grinder or food processor, finely grind the seeds and then put them in a large bowl.

Next, in the food processor, mince:
    1 stalk celery
    ¼ onion
    ½ small red pepper

Using a cheese cloth, squeeze out the excess water from the minced vegetables and then put them in the bowl with the roasted seeds.

Again, in the food processor, blend until smooth:
    225 g tofu (page 190)

Add to the bowl with the seeds and vegetables:
    the blended tofu
    1 Tbsp parsley, *finely chopped*
    2 Tbsp soya sauce
    1 Tbsp extra virgin olive oil
    ½ tsp turmeric
and mix together.

When you have a firm consistency, make balls the size of a tangerine and then form into burger shapes. Put on a baking tray lined with baking paper and bake at 180°C for 20-30 minutes until browned.

Lemon-Parsley Sauce

Blend together until smooth:
    40 g parsley leaves and small stems
    50 g sunflower seeds
    1 Tbsp lemon juice
    100 ml olive oil
    100 ml water
    ½ tsp salt

 *Tofu is virtually free of saturated fats, with less than 1 gram in a 100 gram serving.*

Seitan-Sunflower Salad | v ℚ

An attractive, summery salad. ▶ *Serves 4-6*

Cut into 5 cm long strips:
    600 g seitan (page 191)

Toss the seitan together with:
    3 Tbsp soy sauce
    1 ½ Tbsp olive oil
    2 ½ tsp garlic paste (page 193)
and then sauté in a non-stick frying pan for about 10 minutes, or roast in the oven for about 25 minutes until slightly crispy on the outside.

Blend together:
    one large handful of fresh basil leaves
    100 ml extra virgin olive oil

When the seitan is ready, toss it together with the basil paste.

Finally, mix the seitan together with:
    2 large handfuls of sunflower greens (page 172), *well washed (black hulls removed)*
    15-20 cherry tomatoes, *cut in halves*
    30 good quality black olives, *cut in halves*
    salt to taste

 *Seitan is a healthy and safe way to get high-quality protein.*

Mexican-Style Seitan Salad | v

A very quick recipe if you prepare the seitan and cook the beans beforehand. The fresh salad vegetables, combined with the seitan, make this dish balanced and nutritious. Because the salad looks so pretty, it is also perfect for party food. ▶ *Serves 4-6*

Soak for 6-8 hours and then gently boil in fresh, unsalted water until soft:
    50 g kidney beans

When the beans are very nearly soft, add a little salt to the cooking water (see page 179 for more information on how to cook legumes).

Roughly cut into thin bite-size slices:
    300 g seitan (page 191)

Toss the seitan together with:
    2 Tbsp soya sauce
    1 Tbsp olive oil
    1 ½ tsp garlic paste (page 193)
    1 ½ tsp oregano
    1 tsp sweet paprika
    1 tsp cumin powder
and then sauté in a non-stick frying pan for about 10 minutes, or roast in the oven for about 25 minutes until slightly crispy on the outside.

When the seitan is ready, let it cool a little and then toss together with:
    the cooked kidney beans
    ¼ red onion, *very finely chopped*
    10 cherry tomatoes, *cut in halves or quarters*
    100 g tinned sweet corn
    ½ red pepper, *very finely chopped or minced*
      head butternut lettuce, *cut in thin strips*
    a little fresh chilli, *finely cut* or chilli powder *(optional)*
    2 Tbsp extra virgin olive oil
    salt, to taste

Serve at room temperature.

Seitan is low in saturated fats and cholesterol. A 100 gram serving contains less than 1 gram of saturated fat.

Seitan Steaks | v ℚ

This is the simplest seitan recipe given in this chapter.
▶ *Makes about 6 large steaks or 12 smaller ones*

Cut into 1 ½ cm slices:

   400 g seitan (page 191)

Place in an oiled frying pan or in an oiled oven dish that is no bigger than the laid out steaks.

Blend together:

   100 ml water
   60 ml (4 Tbsp) soya sauce
   1 ½ Tbsp olive oil
   1 ½ cloves garlic
   3 tsp rosemary

and pour evenly over the steaks.

Fry or bake the steaks until all the liquid has been absorbed.

Seitan contains seven of the eight essential amino acids: adding kombu to the cooking water, or soya sauce once it is cooked, makes it a source of complete protein.

〰 〰 〰

Seitan and Mushrooms in Nutritional Yeast Gravy | v

A popular Sunday lunch dish at Ananda. ▶ *Serves 4-6*

Sauté in a little olive oil until soft:

   7 medium mushrooms (300 g), *thinly sliced*

Remove the mushrooms from the pan and put aside.

Cut into rough bite-size slices:

   600 g seitan (page 191)

Using the same pan as the mushrooms, sauté the seitan together with:

   3 Tbsp soya sauce
   2 ½ Tbsp olive oil
   2 ½ tsp garlic paste (page 193)

Add the cooked mushrooms to the seitan and sauté together for a minute.

Make one quantity of the Mixed Herb and Nutritional Yeast Gravy, found in the "Savoury Sauces and Spreads" chapter (page 225).

Serve the mushrooms and roasted seitan with the gravy over the top.

Protein should be limited to 20% of your overall food intake.

Seitan with Pizza-Style Sauce | v ℚ

A traditional Italian-style recipe. Simple and quick to make,
and a good way to serve seitan to kids. ▶ *Serves 4-6*

Heat some olive oil in a non-stick frying pan then add and fry for a few seconds:
    3 tsp garlic paste (page 193)

Add to the frying pan:
    400 g seitan, *cut in 1 cm slices*
    2 Tbsp soya sauce
and fry the seitan for a few minutes. Then turn the slices over and fry the other side.

In a separate, smaller frying pan, fry for a few seconds:
    1 tsp garlic paste

Then add:
    400 ml tinned chopped tomatoes
    20 black olives, *de-stoned and cut in slices*
    ½ tsp oregano
    ½ tsp salt
and cook for 5 minutes.

Add a splash of extra virgin olive oil to the tomato sauce, and then pour it over the cooked seitan slices.

A 100 gram serving of seitan contains 18 grams of protein: that's even more than tofu and many kinds of meat!

Seitan and Roast Pepper Kebabs with Tahini Sauce | v

Great for special occasion and party food. You can make kebabs with anything you like. ▶ *Makes about 6 kebabs*

Roast in the oven at 180°C:
    2 yellow peppers, *whole*
    2 red peppers, *whole*
until their skin is dark, almost burnt. This will take 30-50 minutes, depending on your oven.

When the peppers are ready, remove them from the oven, put them in a bowl sealed tight with cling film and leave them to steam for ten minutes. This will allow you to remove their skins easily. Remove the peppers from the bowl and split them open. Remove the seeds and burnt skin. Cut the peppers into 3 cm squares.

While the peppers are roasting, toss together in an oiled oven dish:
    250 g seitan (page 191), *cut into 2 cm cubes*
    1 Tbsp olive oil
    2 tsp garlic paste (page 193)
    2 ½ Tbsp soya sauce

Bake the seitan for about 25 minutes, stirring occasionally, until nicely roasted.

Assemble your kebabs by placing the following ingredients on kebab sticks in any order you like:
    seitan
    yellow pepper
    red pepper
    fresh spinach or basil leaves
    black olives

Serve the kebabs with tahini sauce (page 224) poured over the top.

🕊 *A diet low in saturated fats reduces the risks of heart disease and stroke.*

Seitan with Houmous and Capers | v

Prepare the seitan and boil the chickpeas ahead of time, and this recipe becomes really quick. An adaptation of a traditional Italian dish – very nutritious and satisfying. ▶ *Serves 4- 6*

Soak for 6-8 hours:
 190 g dried chickpeas

Strain the chickpeas, rinse thoroughly and then boil in unsalted water until they are soft. This will take about an hour. Remove any foam that appears on the surface (see page 179 for more information on how to cook legumes). *N.B.: Do not throw away the cooking water.*

Cut into ½ cm slices:
 500 g seitan (page 191)

Place in an oiled frying pan or in an oiled oven dish that is no bigger than the laid out slices.

Then pour over the seitan a mixture of:
>   2 ½ Tbsp soya sauce
>   1 ½ Tbsp olive oil
>   2 tsp garlic paste (page 193)

Either fry or bake the seitan until all the liquid has been absorbed (turn the seitan over half way through if you do it in the frying pan).

While the seitan is frying/roasting, blend together until smooth:
>   the cooked chickpeas
>   200 ml cooking water from chickpeas
>   3 Tbsp tahini
>   3-4 Tbsp lemon juice
>   1 ½ Tbsp extra virgin olive oil
>   1 tsp garlic paste or about ½ clove
>   about 1 ½ tsp salt

When the seitan is ready, spread the houmous evenly on top of each slice.

Lastly, sprinkle the houmous with:
>   2 handfuls of whole capers (well washed)

Serve warm or at room temperature.

Protein intake should be limited to 20% of your diet: Too much protein in your diet can cause problems for your kidneys.

CHAPTER 14

Legumes

Italian Lentils

334 / V G

Borlotti Beans with Rosemary
and Balsamic Vinegar

335 / V G

Mexican-Style Bean Dip

336 / V G

Green Pea "Guacamole"

337 / V G Q

Houmous

338 / V G

Black-Eyed Beans
and Spinach

339 / V G

See also • Green Pea and Sweet Paprika Soup (p. 235)
• Curried Lentil Soup (p. 238) • Orecchiette and Chickpeas (p. 265)
• Moroccan-Style Chickpea and Vegetable Stew (p. 274)
• Lentil Duchess (p. 284) • Red Lentil and Tomato Dhal (p. 305)
• Carrot and Coconut Dhal (p. 306) • Tofu Recipes in General
(p. 316-322) • Seitan with Houmous and Capers (p. 330)

Italian Lentils | v g

A very simple and classic way to serve lentils in Italy. ▶ *Serves 4-6*

In a saucepan, sauté in a little olive oil until golden:
    1 small onion, *finely chopped*
    ½ leek, *finely sliced in ½ or ¼ rounds*

Add to the onion and leek:
    2 medium-sized carrots, *minced*
    1 stalk celery, *minced (not too finely or it becomes mushy)*
and sauté for about 10 minutes until nicely browned.

Add:
    200 ml tinned chopped tomatoes
    2 bay leaves
    200 g brown lentils, *washed thoroughly*

Add just enough water to cover the lentils and bring to the boil. Then, turn down the heat to a simmer and cook the lentils until they are completely soft, adding a little hot water when necessary. When the lentils are cooked, there should be no excess liquid. If there is, you can evaporate it or remove it with a ladle (see page 179 for more information on how to cook legumes).

Once the lentils are soft, add:
    2 tsp salt
    any Italian herbs you like, such as rosemary, thyme, oregano *(optional)*
and cook for another 5 or 10 minutes.

Just before serving stir in:
    some fresh parsley, *coarsely chopped*

Lentils provide good amounts of six important minerals, two B-vitamins and protein – all with virtually no fat.

Borlotti Beans with Rosemary
and Balsamic Vinegar | V G

A delicious, moist and wintery bean dish. ▶ *Serves 4-6*

Soak for 6-8 hours in plenty of water:
   400 g borlotti beans

Strain the beans and rinse them well. Then put the beans in a saucepan with plenty of fresh, unsalted water. Bring to the boil and then turn down the heat and simmer until they are completely soft and tender. This will take about an hour (see page 179 for more information on how to cook legumes).

N.B.: Do not throw away the cooking water.

In a separate saucepan, sauté in a little olive oil until golden:
   1 medium onion, *finely chopped*

When the onion is nearly golden, add:
   1 ½ tsp rosemary
and sauté for about 1 minute.

Next add:
   the cooked beans
   800 ml cooking water from beans
   2 tsp salt

Cook on a medium flame until all the water has been absorbed and a thick cream is formed (about 30 minutes).

Turn off the heat and then stir in:
   2 Tbsp balsamic vinegar

Adjust the salt if necessary.

Let the beans cool a little before serving. The sauce will become thicker.

All beans are high in dietary fibre, which can lower your cholesterol and help to prevent digestive disorders.

Mexican-Style Bean Dip | V G

This bean dip can be eaten as a spread on crackers or
as part of a full Mexican meal. ▶ *Serves 4-6*

Soak for 6-8 hours in plenty of water:
   400 g kidney beans

Strain the soaked beans, rinse and then cook in fresh, unsalted water until completely soft. This will take about an hour (see page 179 for more information on how to cook legumes).
N.B.: Do not throw away the cooking water.

Remove the kidney beans from the water, put them in a bowl and, using a hand blender, blend together with:
   100 ml of kidney bean cooking water
   2 tsp garlic paste (page 193) or about 1 clove crushed garlic
   2 tsp oregano
   1 tsp cumin powder
   1 small fresh red chilli, including seeds, *finely chopped* or ½ tsp chilli powder (or more, to taste)
   2 ¼ tsp mustard
   3 Tbsp extra virgin olive oil
   ¼ tsp black pepper
   salt to taste

🌢 *Kidney beans, when combined with whole grains such as rice, provide virtually fat-free, high quality protein.*

Green Pea "Guacamole" | v G Q

*A surprisingly good and tasty imitation of authentic
Guacamole (page 227).* ▶ *Serves 4-6*

Boil in salted water until soft:
   600 g frozen green peas

At the same time, in a separate pan, boil in salted water until soft:
   300 g potatoes, *peeled and cut into small pieces*

In a large bowl, using a hand blender, blend together:
   the cooked peas
   the cooked potatoes
   1 Tbsp mustard
   4 Tbsp lemon juice
   3 Tbsp extra virgin olive oil

Then stir in:
   ¾ red onion, *very finely minced* (spring onion is also good)
   2 small handfuls tinned sweet corn
   2 Tbsp fresh coriander or parsley, *finely chopped*

Check the salt and seasonings and then serve with tortilla chips.

🌰 *Green peas are bursting with nutrients. They provide good amounts
of 8 vitamins, 7 minerals, dietary fibre and protein.*

Houmous | V G

*We all know houmous... but did you ever try making your
own at home? As a super-healthy alternative, chickpea sprouts
can be used instead of boiled chickpeas.* ▶ *Serves 4-6*

Soak for 6-8 hours in plenty of water:
    375 g chickpeas

Strain the soaked chickpeas, rinse and then cook in fresh, unsalted water
until they are completely soft. This will take about 90 minutes (see page 179
for more information on how to cook legumes).
N.B.: Do not throw away the cooking water.

Remove the chickpeas from the water, put them in a bowl and, using a hand
blender, blend together with:
    6 Tbsp tahini
    6 Tbsp lemon juice
    1 tsp garlic paste (page 193) or about ½ large clove crushed garlic
    200 ml cooking water from chickpeas
    3 Tbsp extra virgin olive oil
    about 2 ½ tsp salt

Check the taste and adjust accordingly. You might like to add more lemon
juice or garlic.

For colour (and nutrition), you can add some chopped fresh parsley to the
houmous.

Serve at room temperature.

Chickpeas, like other beans, are rich in both soluble and insoluble dietary fibre.

Black-Eyed Beans and Spinach | v g

A very simple-to-make, slightly Indian tasting dish. ▶ *Serves 4-6*

Soak for 6-8 hours in plenty of water:
270 g black-eyed beans

Strain the soaked beans, rinse and then cook in fresh, unsalted water until completely soft. When the beans are soft, strain and set aside (see page 179 for more information on how to cook legumes).

Sauté in a little olive oil for a couple of minutes:
3 large cloves garlic, *finely chopped*

Add:
1 ½ tsp ground coriander
1 ½ tsp cumin powder
and fry with the garlic for one minute.

Add to the garlic and spices:
750 g fresh spinach, including stems
a little salt

Cover and cook until the spinach is soft.

When cooked, blend the spinach using a hand blender.

Add to the spinach:
the cooked beans
3-4 Tbsp lemon juice or to taste

Mix well, check the salt and seasonings and adjust to suit your taste.

When combined with a whole grain, such as wholemeal pasta or brown rice, beans provide protein comparable to that of meat or dairy, without the high calories or saturated fat.

CHAPTER 15

Vegetables and Side Dishes

Olive and Caper
Stuffed Tomatoes

342 / V

Vegetable Stuffed Courgettes

343 / V

Iranian Spinach

344 / V G Q

Cauliflower Puree

345 / V G

Carrot Puree

346 / V G

Open Jacket Potatoes
with Yoghurt Cheese

347 / V G

See also • Simple Potato Salad (p. 215)

Olive and Caper Stuffed Tomatoes | v

The key to success with this recipe is good quality, in-season tomatoes.
Actually, you can stuff tomatoes with just about anything.
A more substantial dish can be made by scooping out
the insides of the tomatoes and filling them with a rice salad,
made using the same ingredients given below. Great for
buffets and party food. ▶ *Makes 6 stuffed tomatoes*

Wash and then cut into 2 even halves (horizontally, not vertically):
   3 very large, ripe tomatoes

Place the tomatoes on a baking tray lined with baking paper and sprinkle
with enough salt to flavour each half.

Blend together:
   270 g black olives, *well rinsed* (choose good quality ones—they will make
      the difference in taste)
   3 Tbsp capers, *well rinsed*
   1 ½ small cloves garlic
   1 ½ tsp oregano
   6 Tbsp olive oil
   salt to taste (careful! Olives and capers are salty!)

Mix into the mixture:
   7-9 Tbsp fresh breadcrumbs (white or brown)
and make a fairly firm mixture. Readjust the salt if necessary.

Using your hands, cover the top of each tomato half with a mound of the
stuffing and press it down firmly so that it will not fall off.

Bake the tomato halves in the oven until they are soft but still firm enough
to hold their shape. This will take about 25 minutes.

When the tomatoes are cooked, decorate each half with:
   fresh rocket, *roughly chopped*

🜚 *Olives are a good source of vitamin E.*

Vegetable Stuffed Courgettes | v

Very simple and relatively quick to make.
Great for kids and adults alike. ▶ Serves 4-6

Cut in half lengthwise:
    2 large or 3 medium courgettes

Boil the courgette halves in salted water until *al dente* (you will cook them further in the oven). Using a teaspoon, scoop out the seedy pulp of the courgettes, leaving a border of about ½ cm at each end.

While the courgettes are boiling, sauté until soft:
    1 large onion, *minced*
    1 large carrot, *minced*
    1 stalk celery, *minced*

When the vegetables are soft, add:
    the courgette pulp, *blended*
    100 ml tinned tomatoes
    ½ tsp oregano
    ½ tsp salt
and cook for a further 5 minutes.

Turn off the heat and stir in:
    40 g (4 Tbsp) breadcrumbs

Oil the whole surface of the emptied courgettes (outer and inner) and sprinkle the inside with salt. Fill the courgettes with the stuffing and then bake in the oven for about 20 minutes, or until the courgettes are soft and the stuffing is browned on top.

🌱 *The alkalinizing effect of vegetables, such as courgettes, helps to balance the acidic effect of carbohydrates and proteins.*

Iranian Spinach | V G Q

A creamy spinach, combining the
complimentary flavours of mint and garlic.
As always, fresh spinach will give you
better results than frozen spinach.
This recipe goes wonderfully with rice
and also with chappatis (page 246)
and crêpes (page 292). ▶ *Serves 4-6*

Boil in salted water until soft:
400 g potatoes, *peeled and cut in 1 ½ cm cubes*

Cook in a covered pan with a small amount of
water and salt:
600 g fresh spinach (or 750 g frozen spinach)

N.B.: If you use fresh spinach, the water
remaining on them after washing will be
sufficient to cook them in.

Strain the spinach well and then chop coarsely
or blend.

Fry with a little olive oil for 15-30 seconds:
    3 tsp garlic paste (page 193) or about 1 large clove crushed garlic

Add the spinach and sauté on a medium-high flame for a couple of minutes
and then turn off the heat.

Add to the garlicky spinach and mix in well:
    2 tsp dried mint
    3 heaped Tbsp cream or soya cream
    3 heaped Tbsp yoghurt (page 184) or soya yoghurt (page 183)

Then stir in:
    the cooked potatoes

Check the salt and seasonings and serve hot.

Spinach is one of the most concentrated sources of chlorophyll, containing
about 300-600 milligrams in every 30 grams.

Cauliflower Puree | V G

A clever way to include cruciferous vegetables in the diet.
It's great served over brown rice or on its own as a side dish.
Made a bit thinner, it's nice as a soup. ▶ *Serves 4-6*

Sauté in vegan butter until soft:
  1 small onion, *finely chopped*
  ¼ tsp salt

Add and sauté for another 5 minutes:
  1 small clove garlic, *finely chopped*
  1 stalk celery, *finely cut (do not discard the leaves)*
  1 small bay leaf

Add:
  650 g cauliflower, *cut into small florets*
  300 g potatoes, *cut in small pieces*
  300 ml water
  1 ½ tsp salt
Cover and cook until the vegetables are soft (about 15-20 minutes).

Remove the bay leaf and then blend until smooth.

Stir in:
  1 ½ Tbsp celery leaves, *finely chopped*
  ¼ tsp black pepper

🌱 *Cauliflower is rich in nutrients and, like other cruciferous vegetables, provides health-promoting compounds not found in many other vegetables.*

Carrot Puree | v g

Kids love this creamy carrot puree, especially if you substitute the ginger with rosemary. It's great served with basmati rice or on its own as a side dish. ▶ *Serves 4-6*

In a fairly large saucepan, sauté in a little olive oil until golden:
  1 ½ onions, *finely chopped*
  pinch of salt

Add to the onions:
  2 Tbsp ginger paste (page 193)
and continue to sauté for a couple of minutes, stirring continuously to prevent the ginger paste from sticking.

Then add:
  700 g carrots, *cut in thin rounds*
  450 g potatoes, *peeled and cut in cubes or slices*
  300 ml water
  2 tsp salt

Mix everything together well, then cover and cook on a low flame until the carrots and potatoes are completely soft, adding a little more water if necessary.

Turn off the heat, then add:
  300 ml yoghurt (page 184) or soya yogurt (page 183) *(optional)*
and blend everything together with a hand blender until smooth.

Finally, stir in:
  1-2 Tbsp fresh coriander or parsley, *chopped (optional)*

Check the salt and adjust the taste if necessary (you might like it a little more gingery, in which case you can add a touch of raw ginger paste).

🍃 *Carrots are an excellent source of antioxidant compounds and the richest vegetable source of the pro-vitamin A carotenoids.*

Open Jacket Potatoes
with Yoghurt Cheese | V G

The skin is where most of the potato's nutrients are to be found.
Because you're eating the skin, however, it is recommended to use
organic potatoes for this recipe. Simple and quick to make, as well
as highly nutritious and tasty. ▶ Makes 12 mini potato halves

Scrub thoroughly:
   6 potatoes, weighing about 250 g each (you can use larger potatoes, but
   they will take longer to cook)

Cut each potato in half, lengthways, and then lay face up on an oiled baking
tray. Brush the skin and flat side of each potato with olive oil, sprinkle with a
little salt (this will make them become really crispy) and then bake in the oven
at about 180°C until they are completely soft inside and a little bit crunchy
on the outside. This will take about 30 minutes.

Remove the potatoes from the oven and serve with generous helpings of
Yoghurt Cheese or Soya Yoghurt Cheese (page 187) flavoured with garlic and
mint or other fresh herbs.

As well as genetic modification, chemical fertilisers and pesticides are also
banned in organically-certified foods.

Desserts and Sweet Snacks

*Sugar-free desserts.

Apple Strudel | v

A traditional German-style strudel. Lovely served with vanilla ice cream, whipped cream or custard (see recipe on page 360). ▶ *Makes one strudel (12 slices)*

For photos illustrating the procedure used to make a strudel, see page 286.

To make the dough:
Knead together until well mixed and then for about another 5 minutes:
    200 g durum flour
    splash of apple or fruit vinegar
    40 ml sunflower oil
    about 80 ml warm water
    ½ tsp salt

The dough should be very soft, like an earlobe, but not sticky. Put the dough in a bowl, cover with a damp cloth and put in the fridge for about 30 minutes.

In the meantime, make the apple filling:
Soak in hot water for about 30 minutes:
    275 g sultanas
and then strain them.

While the sultanas are soaking, peel, de-core and then cut into very thin slices:
    1 kg apples (about 7 apples)

Mix the apples together with:
    juice of 1 ½ small lemons

Bake the apples in a covered dish at 180°C for about 15 minutes. Then let cool.

Blend together:
    the soaked raisins
    vanilla, to taste
    1 ½ tsp cinnamon
    pinch of cloves
Mix the raisin mixture together with the baked apples.

Now you are ready to make the strudel.
Take the dough out of the fridge and roll out on a floured surface until it is aproximately 45 cm (height) x 70 cm (width). Yes, it will become that big! Don't worry if it tears a little — the holes will not be visible when everything is rolled together.

Transfer the rolled-out dough onto a large cloth using the length of your arms. (It's not as hard as it sounds.)

Sprinkle the dough with:
    a little melted butter, ghee (page 188) or vegan butter *(optional)*

Spread the apple filling out onto the dough, leaving a 2 cm border all around.
N.B.: The filling must be cool.

Tuck the empty borders of the top, bottom and left-hand sides over, onto the filling.

Now, using the cloth to help you, roll the dough and filling tightly, starting from the left and going towards the right, making a strudel.
Again, using the cloth, transfer the rolled strudel onto a baking tray lined with grease-proof paper. The fold should be hidden underneath.

Next, use a knife to make small cuts on top of the strudel, approximately 3 cm apart. These cuts mark where you will cut the slices after the strudel is cooked.

Bake at 180°C for 30-45 minutes until you see that the outside is golden brown. (Cooking times and temperatures will vary according to the type of oven.)

Remove the strudel from the oven and pour over the top:
    melted honey
    almonds, *toasted*

Let the strudel cool a little before cutting.

Apples give the spiritual quality of peaceful clarity.

Homemade Berry Ice Cream | V G Q

A wonderful and refreshing, sugar-free alternative to the ice cream you usually find in the shops. Any frozen fruit can substitute the berries (the bananas, however, are fundamental): just put the fresh fruit (chopped) in a Tupperware container and leave in the freezer for several hours. ▶ Makes 2 portions

Blend together (but not for too long or it becomes too liquid):
  200 g frozen berries
  ½ frozen banana, *in pieces (cut into pieces before freezing)*
  75 ml yoghurt (page 184) or soya yoghurt (page 183)
  75 ml maple syrup (or other sweetener)
Serve immediately.

Blackberries give the spiritual quality of purity of thought.

Carob-Hazelnut Spread | V G Q

A deliciously rich, yet healthy spread. ▶ Makes one medium jar full

Grind until fine in a food processor:
  250 g toasted hazelnuts

Add:
  100 ml sunflower oil
  4-5 Tbsp honey or other sweetener, such as malt or agave
  3-5 Tbsp carob powder*
  approximately 100 ml water

and continue to blend until the mixture becomes a smooth paste. Remove from the food processor and transfer to a jar.

This carob-hazelnut spread will spread better if stored at room temperature. However, you can also put it in the fridge until it is solid and then make little balls that you can roll in coconut or ground hazelnuts.

Carob powder has an excellent nutritional value: along with up to 80% protein, it contains magnesium, calcium, iron, phosphorus, potassium manganese, barium, copper, nickel and the vitamins A, B1, B2, B3 and D.

*Toasted carob powder was used for this recipe. Non-toasted carob powder will give a lighter taste.

Chocolate Cake | v

This has to be the best chocolate cake recipe in the world!
Moist, light, chocolaty... and dairy free. For a more 'special occasion' cake,
you can cover it with whipped cream, flavoured with cocoa powder
and icing sugar. This recipe also works wonderfully with
carob powder instead of cocoa. ▶ *Makes one large ring cake*

In a small bowl, mix together:
   75 g unsweetened cocoa powder
   675 ml very hot water

In a separate bowl, mix together:
   600 g white flour
   400 g raw cane sugar
   1 Tbsp bicarbonate of soda, *sieved*
   1 ½ tsp cinnamon
   ¾ tsp salt

In a third, larger bowl, mix together:
   225 ml sunflower oil
   3 Tbsp apple vinegar
   a little vanilla essence

Add the dissolved cocoa to the oil and vinegar mixture and then slowly add and stir in the dry ingredients until well mixed.

Pour into a buttered and floured 25 cm ring mould and bake for 40-50 minutes at 180°C until the cake is completely cooked. (Cooking times and temperatures will vary according to the type of oven.) You will know the cake is ready when an inserted tooth pick comes out clean.

Leave the cake in the tin until it has cooled down.

ⓝ *No dairy means that this cake is virtually free of saturated fats.*

Healthy Cake! | v

This is a long-time breakfast favourite amongst many of the Ananda community members. It's a perfect treat for those who don't eat sugar, eggs or dairy. ▶ *Makes 1 medium loaf*

In a bowl, mix together:
300 g wholemeal flour
2 ½ tsp baking powder
45 g bran flakes (or cornflakes)
300 g sultanas
75 g dried coconut
100 g sesame seeds, *toasted*

In a separate container, blend together:
3 ripe bananas
500 ml vegan milk

Using your hands, mix the banana mixture with the dry ingredients. Then pour into a well-oiled 12 x 30 cm bread pan.

Bake at 180°C for about 60 minutes. (Cooking times and temperatures will vary according to the type of oven.) You will know the cake is ready when an inserted knife comes out sticky but not wet.

This cake keeps for over a week in an airtight container or in the fridge. Warming it up a little before you eat it helps to keep it moist-tasting.

Raisins, especially raisins without preservatives, are a healthier option to white sugar, which has undergone an unnatural chemical refining process that strips the sugar cane of its natural nutrients.

Lemony Fruit and Nut Balls | V Q

These balls are made with raw ingredients only. They make an energetic and nutritious breakfast or snack. ▶ *Makes about 25 balls*

Put in a food processor and blend until one sticky clump:
    500 g mixed dried fruit (sultanas and raisins cost the least)

Remove the fruit from the food processor, put in a bowl and then knead together with:
    75 g toasted hazelnuts, *coarsely chopped*
    75 g sunflower seeds, *coarsely chopped*
    100 g rolled oats
    rind of 2 organic lemons (inorganic lemons are covered with wax)

Shape the mixture into bite size balls. Serve raw.

These balls preserve very well in the fridge.

🙏 *Organic dried fruit is more nutritious. Check that it has not been sulphured or preserved with chemical additives.*

Almond-Cardamom Balls | V G Q

Quick to make and a delicious between-meals snack. An equally delicious alternative can be made by substituting the almonds with toasted sesame seeds and the ginger with cinnamon. ▶ *Makes 20-25 small balls*

Grind in a food processor until a fine powder:
    300 g almonds

Add to the almonds:
    5 Tbsp honey
    2 tsp ground cardamom or some orange essence or orange zest
and continue to blend until the mixture holds together.

Make balls the size of a walnut shell. Roll the balls in dried coconut.

🙏 *Almonds give the spiritual quality of self control and moral vigour.*

Yoghurt Mousse with Berry Sauce | V G Q*

A luxury dessert, great for dinner parties. ▶ *Serves 4*

Hang in a cheese cloth for about 9 hours:
    1 litre yoghurt (page 184) or soya yoghurt *(shop bought)*
(see the "Yoghurt Cheese" recipe on page 187)

Mix the yoghurt cheese together with:
    150 ml cream or soya cream, *whipped*

To make the berry sauce, mix together:
    75 ml berry flavoured ice cream topping
    50 ml water
(You could also blend fruits of the forest or strawberry jam with a little water if you don't have the ice-cream topping.)

Add:
    150 g fresh or defrosted frozen mixed berries

Using an ice cream scoop, serve the yoghurt mousse onto individual plates. Pour the berry sauce over the top.

Berries are packed with antioxidant phyto-nutrients that neutralise free-radical damage to cells and tissues.

Apple Crumble | v

Admittedly, this recipe was included more with the Italian audience in mind… but, I thought, maybe there actually are English-speaking people who have never made an apple crumble. If this is you, then now is a good time to start! The apples can be substituted with any other fruit. Softer fruits, such as berries, peaches and bananas, do not need to be pre-cooked before baking. ▶ *Serves 6-8*

Peel, de-core and then cut into 1 cm chunks:
   1500 g apples (about 10 small apples)

Put the apples in a saucepan with 2 Tbsp water. Cover and cook for about 5 minutes, stirring occasionally, until they become slightly soft but not mushy. Add some sugar if you like things a little sweeter.

Transfer the soft apples into an oven dish.

Next, make the crumble by rubbing together with your fingertips:
   250 g wholemeal wheat or wholemeal spelt flour
   120 g butter or vegan butter, *diced*, at room temperature
   75 g raw cane sugar
until the mixture resembles bread crumbs.

Cover the apples with the crumble mixture and bake in the oven for approximately 25 minutes at 180°C until the surface is golden brown. (Cooking times and temperatures will vary according to the type of oven.)

Serve hot or cold with custard poured over the top (see next recipe).

🌰 *The nutritional stars of apples are fibre, flavonoids and fructose.*

Custard | v g q

Feel free to put it on all your desserts! ▶ *Makes one litre*

Mix together with a whisk:
  1 litre milk or vegan milk
  70 g corn flour (cornstarch)

Then mix in:
  100 g raw cane sugar
  vanilla to taste

Bring the milk to the boil, stirring continuously with a whisk. When the custard becomes a thick, sauce-like consistency, remove from the heat. Serve hot or cold.

🕉 *Soya milk has a very alkalinising effect on the body.*

Banana Cake | v

This banana cake is so light and fluffy that it seems impossible that it has no eggs, but it is completely vegan and incredibly delicious. ▶ *Makes one 20 x 25 cm cake*

In a bowl, mix together:
  300 g wholemeal flour
  2 tsp baking soda

In a separate, bigger bowl, mix together:
  2-3 ripe bananas, mashed
  250 ml maple syrup (or other liquid sweetener)
  150 ml any vegan milk
  175 ml sunflower oil
  vanilla to taste

Add the dry ingredients to the wet ingredients and, using your hands, mix well.

Stir in:
  75 g walnuts, *chopped*

Put the mixture in an oiled 20 x 25 cm oven dish and bake at 180°C for approximately 30 minutes. When the cake is cooked, an inserted knife will come out clean.

🕉 *Bananas give the spiritual quality of humility rooted in kindness.*

Sweet Rice Pudding | v g

*Thanks to Helmut and Mayadevi for sharing the secret
of their fabulous rice pudding with us. This has been an
Ananda favourite breakfast dish for years.* ▶ *Serves 4-6*

Wash:
> 1 cup (250 ml cup) basmati rice

Put the rice in a medium-sized saucepan, together with:
> 90 g raw cane sugar
> 50 g raisins
> pinch ginger powder or ½ tsp fresh ginger, *cut in very small pieces*
> ¾ tsp cardamom
> pinch nutmeg
> ½ tsp cinnamon
> pinch salt

Cover with just enough water to cover the rice (the main liquid will be milk or any vegan milk), bring to the boil and then turn down the heat a little.

After a few minutes, add:
> 200 ml milk or any vegan milk

At this point you will need to start stirring fairly often.

Wait until all the milk has been absorbed and then add:
> another 200 ml of milk or vegan milk

Keep adding milk, 200 ml at a time, waiting until the previous amount has been absorbed. Do this until the rice is cooked and has a consistency similar to risotto. You will probably add about 1 litre of milk in total. The cooking will take 30-40 minutes.

Turn off the heat and stir in:
> 1 ½ tsp lemon zest (*use organic lemons*)

🜃 *Lemon peel, as well as containing 5-10 times the amount of vitamins as lemon juice, contains important compounds that combat cancer, regulate blood pressure and help maintain bone strength.*

Lemon Pie | v

This pie makes a special summertime treat but is scrumptious
any time of the year. ▶ *Makes one 22 cm pie*

First make the crust:

Knead together to make a dough:
    300 g white flour
    100 g raw cane sugar
    150-200 g butter or vegan butter *(use the least amount possible)*
    pinch of salt

Press the dough into the base and sides of a greased and floured 22 cm cake tin (the type where the sides can be separated from the base).

Using a fork, prick the crust in several places and then bake at 180°C for approximately 20 minutes until light brown. (Cooking times and temperatures will vary according to the type of oven.)

In the meantime, make the filling. In a saucepan, mix together:
    800 ml vegan cream* (unheated)
    80 g corn flour

Gently bring the cream to a boil, stirring continuously. When it boils, add:
    100 g raw cane sugar
    200 ml lemon juice
and continue to stir.

Bring the cream back to the boil, let it re-thicken and then turn off the heat.

Pour the filling into the cooled pie crust and then leave it to set. This will take between 1 and 2 hours.

Once the filling has set, top the pie with:
    200 ml whipped cream or soya cream

Sugary desserts should be eaten in small quantities: big portions can leave you feeling sluggish, mentally as well as physically.

---

*Dairy cream tastes too rich in this dessert.

Choc-Chip and Orange Cookies | v Q*

A healthy and vegan version of the much-loved, traditional American Cookies.
▶ *Makes about 18 big cookies*

In a bowl, mix together:
    350 g wholemeal flour   3 tsp baking powder
    ½ tsp salt

In a larger bowl, mix together:
    200 g raw cane sugar   200 ml sunflower oil
    rind of 2 organic oranges   about 100 ml water
    (or orange essence)

Add the dry ingredients to the sugar and oil etc and mix well to make a cookie dough.

Add to the cookie dough:
    200 g dark chocolate chips (or chocolate broken into small chunks)
    and mix in well.

Make balls the size of a small tangerine and place at least 4 cm apart on an oven tray lined with baking paper (they grow!). Flatten the balls with the palm of your hand.

Bake at 180°C for about 15 minutes until the cookies are light golden. (Cooking times and temperatures will vary according to the type of oven.) The cookies should be soft and chewy, but if you prefer them to be crunchy, you can leave them in the oven longer.

Let the cookies cool before eating.

🕉 *Refined carbohydrates and sugar are both acidic and should be kept for special treats!*

Choc-Chip and Coconut Cookies | v Q*

One of my favourite variations of these vegan Chocolate Chip Cookies.
▶ *Makes about 18 big cookies*

Toast in a frying pan, stirring continuously, until every piece is browned (but not burnt!):
   60 g dried coconut

Put the toasted coconut in a bowl and mix together with:
   300 g wholemeal flour
   3 tsp baking powder
   ½ tsp salt

In a larger bowl, mix together:
   200 g raw cane sugar
   200 ml sunflower oil
   about 120 ml water

Add the dry ingredients to the sugar and oil etc and mix well to make a cookie dough.

Add to the cookie dough:
   200 g dark chocolate chips (or chocolate broken into small chunks)
and mix in well.

Make balls the size of a small tangerine and place at least 4 cm apart on an oven tray lined with baking paper (they grow!). Flatten the balls with the palm of your hand.

Bake at 180°C for about 15 minutes until the cookies are light golden. (Cooking times and temperatures will vary according to the type of oven.) The cookies should be soft and chewy but, if you prefer them to be crunchy, you can leave them in the oven longer.

Let the cookies cool before eating.

🌀 *To avoid an overflow of glucose in your blood, sugary desserts should be limited to small quantities. quantità limitate di dessert molto zuccherati.*

Spicy Oatmeal Breakfast Cookies | v ℚ*

These delicious cookies are so good that it's hard to stop eating them!
Really easy and quick to make. ▶ *Makes 12 large cookies or 24 smaller ones*

In a bowl, mix together:
  270 g rolled oats
  150 g wholemeal flour
  190 g raw cane sugar
  1 tsp baking powder
  100 g sultanas
  75 g dried coconut
  3 Tbsp fresh ginger, *grated or very finely chopped*
  2 ¼ tsp cinnamon
  pinch of salt

Add to the dry ingredients:
  100 ml sunflower oil
  190 ml water (approximately)
and knead together with your hands until the mixture sticks together.

For larger, softer cookies, make balls the size of tangerines; for smaller, crispier cookies, make balls the size of golf balls. Put the balls on a baking tray lined with baking paper, and then press down slightly with the palm of your hand.

Bake at 180°C for about 15 or 20 minutes until the outside of the cookies are golden brown. (Cooking times and temperatures will vary according to the type of oven.)

Let cool before eating.

Oats are a good source of dietary fibre, helping to lower high cholesterol.

Brownies | v

An incredibly chocolaty Brownies recipe, easily made vegan. Peanut butter (page 229) swirls or chunks of white chocolate can be added to make delicious variations. ▶ *Makes 15 large brownies or 60 bite-size ones*

Melt in a double boiler:
    400 g very chocolaty dark chocolate
    150 g butter or vegan butter
    50 g unsweetened cocoa powder
Put aside and let cool to room temperature.

N.B.: Do not let the mixture re-solidify.

In a small saucepan, cook until completely thick, stirring continuously with a whisk:
    50 g white flour
    235 ml water
Put aside and let cool to room temperature.

Using an electric whisk, beat together in a large bowl:
    the cooled flour and water mixture
    300 g raw cane sugar
    ¼ tsp salt
    vanilla to taste

Add and mix well:
    the cooled chocolate and butter/vegan butter

Lastly, mix in:
    225 g white flour
    ¾ tsp baking powder

Put the brownie dough into a 20 x 30 cm buttered oven dish and spread out
evenly with wet hands. Bake at 175°C for about 25 minutes until the surface
of the brownies is slightly firm. (Cooking times and temperatures will vary according to the type of oven.) The consistency should remain soft and gooey on
the inside and slightly crunchy on the outside.

Allow to cool completely before cutting into
squares (better still, leave to solidify in the
fridge for a couple of hours).

Even rajasic foods, when cooked with love,
become sattwic.

CHAPTER 17

Drinks

See also • "Fruit and Vegetable Juices" chapter (p. 195–199)
• "Smoothies" chapter (p. 201–205)

Masala Chai | v g q

A popular sweet and milky Indian spiced tea. ▶ *Makes 2 mugs*

Firstly, prepare the spices. In a spice grinder, or with a mortar and pestle, roughly grind:

12 cardamom pods	piece of fresh ginger, the size of a
4 cm stick cinnamon	walnut shell (12-15 g)
4 cloves	1 black pepper granule

Pull out all the other ingredients you will need (the timings are quick so you will need to have everything at hand).

In a saucepan, bring to the boil:
    300 ml water
When the water boils, add the spices and let the spices boil for about 30 seconds.

Then add:
    the contents of one black teabag (don't just put the
        teabag in)
    4 tsp brown sugar, or to taste
and boil for a few more seconds.

Lastly, add:
    300 ml milk or oat milk (if using oat milk then it should
    be a brand that contains sunflower oil, otherwise it will
    separate when it boils)
and bring to the boil. When it boils, turn it off immediately.

Filter the chai through a tea strainer and enjoy hot (although the flavours blend together better if you let it sit for around 10 minutes before drinking).

🜁 *The spices in this masala chai are all traditionally used in Indian ayurvedic medicine for their powerful digestive benefits, as well as their many other healing properties.*

Ginger Tea | V G Q

*Because of ginger's heating action, ginger tea is excellent for
digestion and for throwing off unwanted colds and mucus.
Can be served plain or with a little honey and lemon (to be added
at the end – honey becomes toxic when heated).* ▶ *Makes 2 mugs*

Blend together:
    200 ml water
    piece of fresh gingerroot, size of a walnut shell (no need to peel)

Add another:
    650 ml water

Put in a saucepan, cover and then boil for 5-10 minutes.

Strain and serve hot.

*Taken on a daily basis, ginger serves as a mild appetite stimulant and digestive
toner to keep your digestive system working well. Recent studies suggest that fresh
gingerroot may slow or prevent the growth of tumours.*

Banana Lassi | V G Q

Lassi is a classic Indian drink, usually served with meals to aid digestion. You can make lassi with just about any fruit – banana and mango, however, are the most delicious. Sugar-free versions can be made by adding figs (soaked), dates (soaked) or maple syrup. ▶ *Makes 2 tall glasses full*

Blend together:
    250 ml yoghurt (page 184) or soya yoghurt (page 183)
    350 ml water
    1 ½ large ripe bananas
    50 g sugar
    ¼ tsp cardamom*

Serve at room temperature, with or without an Indian meal!

🌀 *Bananas are one of the best sources of potassium, an essential mineral for maintaining normal blood pressure and heart function.*

Almond Milk | V G Q*

This almond milk is so thick and tasty and is a wonderful alternative to regular cow's milk. It tastes great in smoothies or on your breakfast cereal. Keeps for about two days in the fridge. ▶ *Makes 750 ml*

Leave to soak overnight:
    200 g almonds

Blend the soaked almonds with:
    250 ml water
to make a thick paste.

Gradually add:
    500 ml water
and blend again until completely smooth (it will take just a couple of minutes).

*We grind the whole pod of cardamom. If you grind only the seeds, then your cardamom powder will be much stronger, and you will need to add less.

Now squeeze the almond mixture through a thin cheese cloth and catch the milk in a bowl. Leave plain like this or add any sweetener you like (maple syrup is delicious).

 *Almonds give the spiritual qualities of self control and moral vigour.*

Coconut Milk | v g q

As with almond milk, coconut milk is a wonderful alternative to cow's milk. To make sure the coconut that you buy is fresh, shake it close to your ear. If you hear the liquid inside, it's fresh; if you hear nothing, it's not. Keeps for about two days in the fridge. ▶ *Makes 750 ml*

Blend together:
    250 g coconut flesh,* *cut into small pieces*
    250 ml water
to make a thick paste.

Gradually add:
    500 ml water
and blend again until smooth (it will take just a couple of minutes).

Now squeeze the coconut mixture through a thin cheese cloth and catch the milk in a bowl.

Leave plain like this or add any sweetener you like (maple syrup is delicious). Another delicious way to drink it is to add honey, cardamom, saffron and ground pistachios.

 *A diet full of Life Energy foods will help to keep your body strong and healthy.*

*To open the coconut, see the instructions given in the footnote on page 303.

Recipe Index

V VEGAN: Vegan recipe or vegan version given in the recipe (without dairy and eggs but may include honey).

G GLUTEN FREE: Gluten-free recipe or gluten-free version given in the recipe.

G* These recipes easily become gluten-free by substituting the wheat pasta with rice, corn or buckwheat pasta; or the grain with rice, quinoa, buckwheat or any other gluten-free grain.

Q QUICK: Quick recipe that can be made in 30 minutes or under or a quick version given in the recipe. The time given is for an average-speed person. Bear in mind that the first time you make a recipe you'll be a bit slower, but the more you make it, the quicker you'll become.

Q* Quick recipes to carry out but require periods of waiting or soaking; or that the oven is already pre-heated.

Appendices

APPENDIX I

Some of the Best Sources of Various Nutrients

APPENDIX II

Seasons of Fruit and Vegetables

APPENDIX III

White Sugar Refining-Process Chart

APPENDIX IV

Protein Contents Chart

APPENDIX V

Soya compared to Meat and Eggs

APPENDIX VI

Nutrition of Different Types of Sprouts

APPENDIX VII

**Comparison of Physical Traits of Carnivores,
Frugivores and Human Beings**

APPENDIX VIII

The Birth of Factory Farms

APPENDIX IX

Extraordinary Encounters

Some of the Best Sources of Various Nutrients

IRON

Food	Quantity	RDA%*
Soya beans, cooked	1 cup / 172 g	49.1%
Lentils, cooked	1 cup / 198 g	36.6%
Spinach, boiled	1 cup / 180 g	35.7%
Tofu	113 g	33.8%
Sesame seeds	0.25 cup / 36 g	29.1%
Pumpkin seeds	0.25 cup / 34.4 g	28.7%
Chickpeas, cooked	1 cup / 164 g	26.3%
Olives, raw	1 cup / 134 g	24.7%
Chard, boiled	1 cup / 175 g	22%
Quinoa, raw	0.25 cup / 42.5 g	21.8%

CALCIUM

Food	Quantity	RDA%*
Yoghurt, low fat	1 cup / 235 ml	44%
Sesame seeds	0.25 cup / 36 g	35.1%
Goat's milk	1 cup / 235 ml	32.6%
Cow's milk, 2% fat	1 cup / 235 ml	29.7%
Mozzarella cheese	28.35 g	28.35 g
Spinach, boiled	1 cup / 180 g	24.5%
Chard, boiled	1 cup / 180 g	10.2 %
Tofu	113 g	10%
Broccoli, steamed	1 cup / 156 g	7.5%
Green beans, boiled	1 cup / 125 g	5.8%

PHOSPHORUS

Food	Quantity	RDA%*
Soya beans, cooked	1 cup / 172 g	42%
Pumpkin seeds	0.25 cup / 34.4 g	40.5%
Lentils, cooked	1 cup / 198 g	35.6%
Yoghurt, low fat	1 cup / 235 ml	35.2%
Tempeh	113.4 g	28.7%
Beans, cooked	1 cup / about 170 g	24-28%

*Recommended Daily Allowance

Goat's milk	1 cup / 235 ml	27%
Sunflower seeds	0.25 cup / 36 g	25.4%
Millet, cooked	1 cup / 240 g	24%
Barley, cooked	1 cup / 200 g	23%

IODINE

Sea Kelp	0.25 cups / 20 g	276.7%
Yoghurt	1 cup / 235 ml	58.1%
Milk, 2%	1 cup / 235 ml	39%
Eggs	1 egg	15.8%
Strawberries	1 cup / 144 g	8.6%
Mozzarella cheese	28.35 g	6.7%

POTASSIUM

Chard, boiled	1 cup / 175 g	27.4%
Legumes, cooked	1 cup / about 170 g	20-27%
Avocado, raw	1 cup / 146 g	25%
Spinach, boiled	1 cup / 180 g	24%
Mushrooms, raw	141.75 g	18.1 g
Yoghurt, low fat	1 cup / 235 ml	16.4 %
Beetroot, boiled	1 cup / 170 g	14.8%
Broccoli, steamed	1 cup / 156 g	14.4%
Goat's milk	1 cup / 235 ml	14.2%
Bananas	1 banana / 118 g	13.4%

MAGNESIUM

Pumpkin seeds	0.25 cups / 34.5 g	46.1%
Spinach, boiled	1 cup / 180 g	39.1%
Chard, boiled	1 cup / 175 g	37.6%
Soya beans, cooked	1 cup / 172 g	37%
Sunflower seeds	0.25 cup / 36 g	31.9%
Sesame seeds	0.25 cup / 36 g	31%
Beans, cooked	1 cup / about 170 g	20-30%
Millet, cooked	1 cup / 240 g	26.4 %
Almonds	0.25 cup / 34.50 g	24.7%
Quinoa, uncooked	0.25 cup / 42.50 g	22.3%

MANGANESE

Brown rice, cooked	1 cup / 195 g	88%
Spinach, boiled	1 cup / 180 g	84%
Rye, uncooked	0.33 cup / 56.33 g	75.5%
Tempeh	113 g	72.5%
Soya beans, cooked	1 cup / 172 g	71%
Oats, cooked	1 cup / 234 g	68.5%
Bulgur, cooked (whole wheat)	1 cup / 182 g	55.5%
Pumpkin seeds	0.25 cup / 34.4 g	52%
Quinoa, uncooked	0.25 cup / 42.50 g	48%
Pinto beans, cooked	1 cup / 171 g	47.5%

VITAMIN A

Carrots, raw	1 cup / 122 g	683.3%
Spinach, boiled	1 cup / 180 g	294.8%
Kale, boiled	1 cup / 130 g	192.4%
Squash, baked	1 cup / 205 g	145.8%
Chard, boiled	1 cup / 175 g	109.9%
Peppers, raw	1 cup / 92 g	104.9%
Cantaloupe	1 cup / 160 g	103.2%
Romaine lettuce	2 cups / 112 g	58.2%
Broccoli, steamed	1 cup / 156 g	45.6%
Asparagus, boiled	1 cup / 180 g	19.4%

VITAMIN B1 (THIAMINE)

Sunflower seeds	0.25 cup / 36 g	54.7%
Black beans, cooked	1 cup/ 172 g	28%
Green peas, boiled	1 cup / 160 g	27.3%
Navy beans, cooked	1 cup / 182 g	24.7%
Dried peas, cooked	1 cup / 196 g	24.7%
Spelt flour	56.7 g	24.7%
Corn, cooked	1 cup / 164 g	24%
Lentils, cooked	1 cup / 198 g	22%
Pinto beans, cooked	1 cup / 171 g	21.3%
Lima beans, cooked	1 cup / 188 g	20%

VITAMIN B2 (RIBOFLAVIN)

Spelt flour	56.7 g	76.5%
Mushrooms, raw	141.75 g	40.6%
Yoghurt, low fat	1 cup / 235 ml	30.6%
Soya beans, cooked	1 cup / 172 g	28.8%
Spinach, boiled	1 cup / 180 g	24.7%
Tempeh	113 g	23.5%
Milk, 2%	1 cup / 235 ml	23.5%
Goat's milk	1 cup / 235 ml	20%
Almonds	0.25 cup / 34.50 g	17.6%
Green beans	1 cup / 125 g	14.1%

VITAMIN B3 (NIACIN)

Mushrooms, raw	141.75 g	26%
Spelt flour	56.7 g	24%
Peanuts, raw	0.25 cup / 36.50 g	22%
Green peas, boiled	1 cup / 160 g	16.1%
Asparagus, boiled	1 cup / 180 g	9.8%
Squash, baked	1 cup / 205 g	7.2%
Carrots, raw	1 cup / 122 g	5.6%
Tomatoes, ripe	1 cup / 180 g	5.6%
Raspberries	1 cup / 123 g	5.5%
Broccoli, steamed	1 cup / 156 g	4.7%

VITAMIN B5 (PANOTHENIC ACID)

Sunflower seeds	0.25 cup / 36 g	24.3%
Mushrooms, raw	141.75 g	21.3%
Yoghurt, low fat	1 cup / 235 ml	14.5%
Corn, boiled	1 cup / 164 g	14.4%
Broccoli, steamed	1 cup / 156 g	7.9%
Squash, baked	1 cup / 205 g	7.2%
Cauliflower, boiled	1 cup / 124 g	6.3%
Eggs	1 egg / 44 g	6.2%
Strawberries	1 cup / 144 g	4.9%
Tomatoes, ripe	1 cup / 180 g	4.4%

VITAMIN B6 (PYRIDOXINE)

Bananas	1 banana / 118 g	34%
Spinach, boiled	1 cup / 180 g	22%
Garlic, raw	1 head (about 30 g)	17.5%
Brussels sprouts, boiled	1 cup / 156 g	14%
Peppers, raw	1 cup / 92 g	11.5%
Asparagus, boiled	1 cup / 180 g	11%
Broccoli, steamed	1 cup / 156 g	11%
Watermelon	1 cup / 152 g	11%
Cauliflower, boiled	1 cup / 124 g	10.5%
Kale, boiled	1 cup / 130 g	9%

VITAMIN B9 (FOLIC ACID)

Lentils, cooked	1 cup / 198 g	89.5%
Pinto beans, cooked	1 cup / 171 g	73%
Chickpeas, cooked	1 cup / 164 g	70%
Asparagus, boiled	1 cup / 180 g	65.7%
Spinach, boiled	1 cup / 180 g	65%
Black beans, cooked	1 cup / 172 g	64%
Navy beans, cooked	1 cup / 182 g	63.7%
Kidney beans, cooked	1 cup / 177 g	57.3%
Romaine lettuce	2 cups / 112 g	38%
Beetroot, boiled	1 cup / 170 g	34%

VITAMIN B12 (COBALAMIN)

Yoghurt, low fat	1 cup / 235 ml	23%
Milk, 2%	1 cup / 235 ml	14.8%
Eggs	1 egg / 44 g	8.2%

VITAMIN C (ASCORBIC ACID)

Papaya	1 papaya / 304 g	313%
Peppers, raw	1 cup / 92 g	291%
Broccoli, steamed	1 cup / 156 g	205%
Brussels sprouts, boiled	1 cup / 156 g	161%
Oranges	1 orange / 131 g	116%
Cantaloupe	1 cup / 160 g	112%

Kiwi	1 kiwi / 76 g	95%
Cauliflower, boiled	1 cup / 124 g	91.5%
Kale, boiled	1 cup / 130 g	88.8%
Grapefruit	0.5 grapefruit / 123 g	78.1%

VITAMIN D

| Milk, 2% | 1 cup / 235 ml | 24.4% |
| Eggs | 1 egg / 44 g | 8.2% |

VITAMIN E

Sunflower seeds	0.25 cup / 36 g	90.5%
Almonds	0.25 cup / 34.50 g	44.9%
Chard, boiled	1 cup / 175 g	16.6%
Spinach, boiled	1 cup / 180 g	8.6%

VITAMIN K

Kale, boiled	1 cup / 130 g	1327.6%
Chard, boiled	1 cup / 175 g	716%
Spinach, boiled	1 cup / 180 g	482.9%
Brussels sprouts, boiled	1 cup / 156 g	273.5%
Broccoli, steamed	1 cup / 156 g	194%
Parsley, fresh	2 Tbsp / 7.50 g	153%
Romaine lettuce	2 cups / 122 g	143%
Asparagus, boiled	1 cup / 180 g	114%
Cabbage, boiled	1 cup / 150 g	91.7%
Celery, raw	1 cup / 128 g	44.1%

N.B.: Where food is indicated as being cooked, the nutrient content increases if that food is consumed raw or sprouted.

The data in this appendix was taken from the George Mateljan Foundation website: http://www.whfoods.com

Seasons of Vegetables

	January	February	March	April	May	June	July	August	September	October	November	December
Artichoke							■	■	■	■	■	
Asparagus					■	■						
Aubergine						■	■	■	■	■		
Basil							■	■				
Beetroot	■	■	■				■	■	■	■	■	■
Broad beans					■	■	■	■	■			
Broccoli							■	■	■			
Brussels sprouts	■	■	■							■	■	■
Butternut squash									■	■	■	■
Cabbage		■	■	■								
Carrots						■	■	■	■	■		
Cauliflower	■	■	■	■	■							
Celeriac	■	■	■				■	■	■	■	■	■
Celery										■	■	■
Chestnuts	■								■	■	■	■
Chicory										■		
Courgettes						■	■	■	■			
Cucumber						■	■					
Fennel							■	■				
Garlic						■	■	■	■			
Jersey royals			■	■	■	■						
Jerusalem artichoke	■	■	■							■	■	■

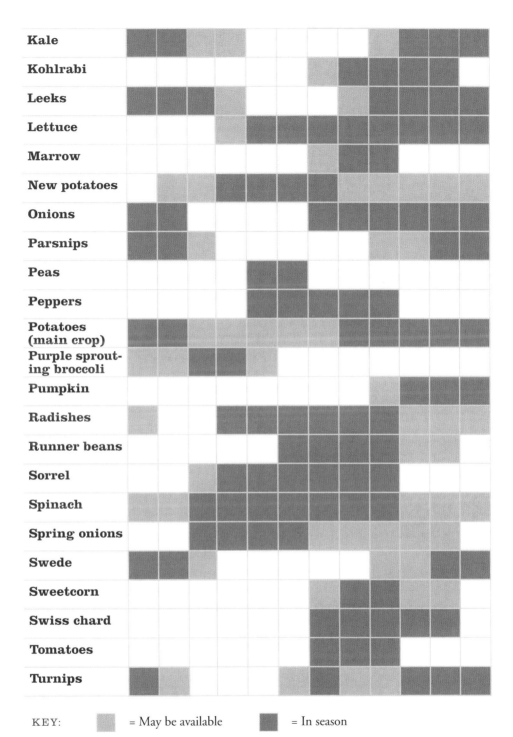

KEY: = May be available = In season

N.B.: The growing seasons indicated in this table correspond to UK produce where applicable. For foods not originating in the UK, the seasons indicated correspond to produce from Europe rather than farther afield. The indications given may vary depending on the elevation, latitude, etc. of your locality, as well as climatic changes, so use this table as a rough guide, but then go and see what's there.

Seasons of Fruit

	January	February	March	April	May	June	July	August	September	October	November	December
Apples	●	●						●	●	●	●	●
Apricots					●	●	●	●	●			
Bananas	●	●	●	●	●	●	●	●	●	●	●	●
Blackberries								●	●	●		
Blackcurrants						●	●	●				
Blueberries							●	●				
Cherries						●	●					
Chestnuts	●								●	●	●	●
Clementines	●	●									●	●
Cranberries										●	●	●
Damsons								●	●			
Elderflowers					●	●						
Figs							●	●	●	●		
Gooseberries						●	●	●				
Grapefruits	●	●	●	●	●						●	●
Grapes									●	●		
Kiwi fruit	●	●	●	●	●	●	●					
Lemons	●	●	●									
Loganberries						●						
Melons						●	●	●	●	●		

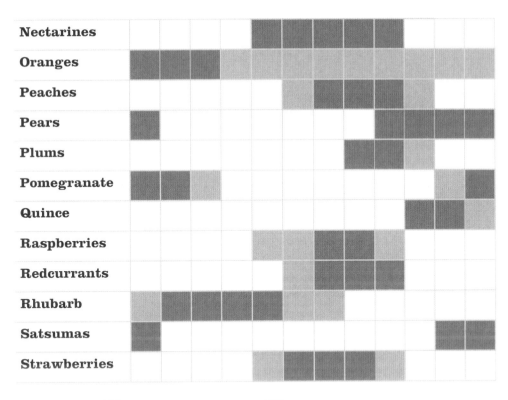

Nectarines
Oranges
Peaches
Pears
Plums
Pomegranate
Quince
Raspberries
Redcurrants
Rhubarb
Satsumas
Strawberries

KEY: ▢ = May be available ▪ = In season

N.B.: The growing seasons indicated in this table correspond to UK produce where applicable. For foods not originating in the UK the seasons indicated correspond to produce from Europe, and not farther afield. The indications given may vary depending on the elevation, latitude, etc. of your locality, as well as climatic changes, so use this table as a rough guide but then go and see what's there.

White Sugar Refining-Process Chart

Sugar Cane

↓

Pressing

↓

Sugar Liquor

Sugar Beet

↓

Slicing

↓

Diffusion
(extraction with hot water)

↓

Sugar Liquor

⋈   ⋈

Purification With Lime Milk
(organic substances, proteins
and colourings are removed)

↓

Carbonation
(excess lime milk is removed
with carbon dioxide)

↓

Sulphur Dioxide Treatment
(with sulphur, to decolourise the syrup)

↓

Filtering

↓

Concentration And Crystallisation

↓

Filtering And Decolourisation
(with animal bone charcoal)

↓

Colouring
(with ultramarine blue, to eliminate
the yellowish reflections)

↓

Crystallisation

↓

Refined White Sugar

Source: Il Nuovo Cucchiaio Verde, ("The New, Green Spoon") edited by Paolo Pigozzi
and Walter Pedrotti, Demetra, 1996.

Protein Contents Chart

Food	Quantity	Protein
LEGUMES		
Black beans, cooked	(1 cup /172 g)	15.24 g
Chickpeas, cooked	(1 cup / 164 g)	14.43 g
Dried peas, cooked	(1 cup / 196 g)	16.35 g
Kidney beans, cooked	(1 cup / 177 g)	15.35 g
Lentils, cooked	(1 cup / 198 g)	17.86 g
Lima beans, cooked	(1 cup / 188 g)	14.66 g
Navy beans, cooked	(1 cup / 182 g)	15.83 g
Pinto beans, cooked	(1 cup / 171 g)	14.04 g
SOYA BEANS AND SOYA FOODS		
Soya beans, cooked	(1 cup / 172 g)	28.62 g
Tempeh, cooked	(100 g)	17.50 g
Tofu, raw	(100 g)	11.50 g
Soya milk	250 ml	10.00 g
Soya yoghurt	250 ml	10.50 g
Miso	(34.38 g)	4.06 g
NUTS		
Almonds, dry roasted	(0.25 cup / 34.5 g)	7.62 g
Cashews, raw	(0.25 cup / 34.25 g)	5.24 g
Peanuts, raw	(0.25 / 36.50 g)	9.42 g
Walnuts, raw	(0.25 g / 25 g)	3.81 g
SEEDS		
Linseeds	(2 Tbsp / 19.38 g)	3.78 g
Pumpkin seeds, raw	(0.25 cup / 34.50 g)	8.47 g
Sesame seeds	(0.25 cup / 36 g)	6.40 g
Sunflower seeds	(0.25 cup / 36 g)	8.20 g

Food	Quantity	Protein
GRAINS		
Barley, cooked	(1 cup / 200 g)	7.42 g
Brown rice, cooked	(1 cup / 195 g)	5.03 g
Buckwheat, cooked	(1 cup / 168 g)	5.68 g
Bulgur, cooked	(1 cup / 182 g)	5.61 g
Corn, cooked	(1 cup / 164 g)	5.44 g
Millet, cooked	(1 cup / 240 g)	8.42 g
Oats, wholegrain, cooked	(1 cup / 234 g)	6.08 g
Quinoa, uncooked	(0.25 cup / 42.50 g)	5.57 g
Rye, wholegrain, uncooked	(0.33 cup /56.33 g)	8.31 g
Spelt flour	(56.70 g)	7.56 g
EGGS AND DAIRY		
Egg, whole, boiled	(44 g)	5.54 g
Milk, cows, 2 %	(1 cup / 235 ml)	8.13 g
Milk, goats	(1 cup / 235 ml)	8.69 g
Mozzarella, low fat	(28.35 g)	6.88 g
Yoghurt, low fat	(1 cup / 235 ml)	12.86 g
VEGETABLES		
Avocados, sliced	(1 cup / 146 g)	2.89 g
Broccoli, steamed	(1 cup / 146 g)	4.66 g
Chard, boiled	(1 cup / 175 g)	3.29 g
Green beans, boiled	(1 cup / 125 g)	2.36 g
Green peas, boiled	(1 cup / 160 g)	8.58 g
Spinach, boiled	(1 cup / 180 g)	5.35 g
OTHER		
Seitan	100 g	25 g

The data in this appendix was mainly taken from the George Mateljan Foundation website: http://www.whfoods.com

Soya Compared to Meat and Eggs

	Soya Beans cooked 172 g	**Beef lean** grilled 113.40 g	**Chicken** roasted 113.40 g	**Egg** whole boiled 44 g
ESSENTIAL AMINO ACIDS				
Tryptophan	0.37 g	0.36 g	0.39 g	0.07 g
Threonine	1.18 g	1.40 g	1.41 g	0.27 g
Isoleucine	1.31 g	1.44 g	1.73 g	0.30 g
Leucine	2.21 g	2.53 g	2.49 g	0.47 g
Lysine	1.80 g	2.67 g	2.80 g	0.40 g
Methionine	0.36 g	0.81 g	0.92 g	0.17 g
Phenylalaine	1.41 g	1.25 g	1.33 g	0.29 g
Valine	1.35 g	1.56 g	1.66 g	0.34 g
Total protein	28.62 g	32.04 g	33.79 g	5.54 g
MINERALS				
Calcium	175.44 mg	7.93 mg	15.88 mg	22 mg
Copper	0.70 mg	0.20 mg	0.06 mg	–
Iron	8.84 mg	4.05 mg	1.21 mg	0.52 mg
Magnesium	147.92 mg	34.03 mg	30.62 mg	4.40 mg
Manganese	1.42 mg	–	0.02 mg	–
Phosphorus	421.40 mg	269.89 mg	242.68 mg	75.68 mg
Selenium	12.56 µg	27.67 µg	28.01 µg	13.55 µg
Zinco	1.98 mg	6.33 mg	1.16 mg	0.46 mg
VITAMINS				
Vitamin B2 (riboflavin)	0.49 mg	0.35 mg	0.13 mg	0.23 mg
Vitamin K	33.02 µg	–	–	–
OTHER				
Fibre	10.32 g	–	–	–
Omega 3	1.03 g	0.04 g	0.11 g	0.03 g
Cholesterol	–	95.25 mg	95.26 mg	186.56 mg

The data in this appendix was taken from the George Mateljan Foundation website: http://www.whfoods.com (well worth a visit).

Nutrition of Different Types of Sprouts

Seed (100 g)	Properties	Protein	Carbohydrates
	LEAFY SPROUTS		
Alfalfa	regulates cholesterol, against arthritis, rheumatism and diabetes	35%	3%
Broccoli	diuretic, antioxidant, improves bodily defences	4 %	3%
Buckwheat	lowers cholesterol, detoxifies	12%	73%
Cress	detoxifies, balances sugar levels		
Fennel	diuretic, detoxifies	1%	1%
Garlic	antioxidant, anti-inflammatory, antibiotic	6%	20%
Leek	antioxidant, protects against cardiovascular diseases	1%	5%
Linseed	antioxidant, protects against cardiovascular diseases	25%	34%
Millet	energiser, antioxidant	10%	73%
Mustard	liver cleanser, strengthens immune system, decongestive, stimulates circulation	27%	28%
Onion	antioxidant, anti-inflammatory, antibiotic	1%	4%
Pumpkin		50%	2%
Quinoa	energiser, antioxidant	20%	64%
Radish	improves bodily defences	4%	3%
Red cabbage	improves bodily defences	2%	3%
Red clover	blood depurative, healthy nervous system	39%	6%
Sesame	improves bodily defences	40%	
Sunflower	healthy nervous and muscular tissues	30%	19%

Vitamins	Mineral salts	Other
A, B, C, D, E, K	calcium, magnesium, potassium, manganese, iron, zinc, selenium, sodium, phosphorous	chlorophyll
A, B, C, E	potassium, phosphorus, iron, sulphur, calcium	chlorophyll, fibre
B	potassium, phosphorus, calcium	chlorophyll, lecithin, rutin
A, B, C, D	calcium, potassium, iodine, phosphorous	chlorophyll
	potassium	chlorophyll
B, C	calcium, phosphorous, iron	chlorophyll
A, C	calcium, phosphorous, iron	chlorophyll
E, F, K	calcium, iron, magnesium, phosphorous, potassium	chlorophyll, omega 3, fibre
B, E	phosphorous, selenium	chlorophyll
A, B, C	calcium, magnesium, potassium, iron, selenium, phosphorous, sulphur	chlorophyll
A, B, C	calcium, phosphorous, iron	chlorophyll
A, B, C, E	phosphorous, iron, zinc, magnesium	
A, C, E	magnesium, phosphorous, calcium	chlorophyll, lecithin, rutin
A, C	potassium, phosphorous, calcium, magnesium, sulphur	chlorophyll
A, B, C	sulphur, potassium, calcium	chlorophyll, fibre
A, B, C, E	calcium, magnesium, phosphorous, potassium	chlorophyll, flavonoids
B, E	calcium, magnesium, potassium, iron, phosphorous	
A, B, C, D, E	phosphorous, potassium, calcium, magnesium, iron	chlorophyll, Selenium

Seed (100 g)	Properties	Protein	Carbohydrates
LEGUMES			
Chickpea	regulates cholesterol, regulates insulin	20%	50%
Fenugreek	blood, liver and kidney depurative, disinfectant	23%	55%
Green Pea	stimulates metabolism	20%	53%
Lentil	lowers cholesterol, regulates insulin	25%	22%
Mung bean	lowers cholesterol, regulates insulin, anti-rheumatic	20%	6%
Red adzuki	lowers cholesterol, regulates insulin, anti-cancer	25%	6%
Soya bean	prevent high blood pressure, lower cholesterol	40%	20%
CEREALS			
Barley	energiser, antioxidant	9%	79%
Kamut	energiser	17%	68%
Oat	energiser, antioxidant	13%	66%
Rye	energiser, antioxidant	15%	78%
Wheat	energiser, antioxidant	26%	69%

Data adapted from: Bavicchi, Dario; Mantellini, Roberta. Sprouts for Health. Bavicchi S.p.a. 2002.

Vitamine	Sali minerali	Altro
A, C, E	iron, calcium, magnesium, potassium	
A, B, D, E	phosphorous, magnesium, zinc, iron, potassium, calcium	
A, B, C, D, E	Calcium, iron, magnesium, phosphorus, potassium	chlorophyll, fibre
A, B, C, E	iron, calcium, magnesium, potassium, selenium, zinc, sodium	
A, B, C, E	calcium, potassium, iron, phosphorous, zinc	fibre
A, C, E	calcium, potassium, magnesium, iron, zinc, selenium, phosphorous	
A, B, C, E, K	potassium, phosphorous, calcium	

B, E	phosphorous, potassium, magnesium, calcium	
B, E	potassium, magnesium, calcium, zinc	
B, E	phosphorous, potassium, magnesium, iron, zinc	
B, C, E	magnesium, phosphorous, potassium	
B, C, E	magnesium, phosphorous, potassium, calcium	beta-carotene

Comparison of Physical Traits of Carnivores, Frugivores and Human Beings

CARNIVORES	FRUGIVORES	HUMANS
Have claws.	Have no claws	Have no claws
Don't have pores in the skin but sweat through tongue to cool the body down	Sweat through pores in skin	Sweat through pores in skin.
Canines long, smooth and pointed; molars pointed; incisors little developed	All teeth of nearly the same height; canines little projected, conical and blunt; molars broad-topped to chew up food	All teeth of nearly the same height; canines little projected, conical and blunt; molars broad-topped to chew up food
Small salivary glands in mouth (not necessary to pre-digest grains and fruit)	Salivary glands well developed, necessary to predigest grains and fruit	Salivary glands well developed necessary to predigest grains and fruit
Acidic saliva; lack of ptyalin to predigest grains	Alkaline saliva; lots of ptyalin to digest grains	Alkaline saliva; lots of ptyalin to digest grains
Large amounts of strong chloric acid in stomach to digest the hard muscles of animals, bones etc.	Gastric juices 10 times less acidic than those of the carnivore	Gastric juices 10 times less acidic than those of the carnivore
Stomach almost spherical	Stomach broader than carnivorous animals, with continuation in duodenum serving purpose of second stomach	Stomach broader than carnivorous animals, with continuation in duodenum serving purpose of second stomach
Intestines only 3-5 times the length of body* so that putrefying meat can be expelled quickly	Intestines 10-12 times length of body*	Intestines 10-12 times length of body*

*Measuring from mouth to anus

Sources: The Holy Science. Swami Sri Yukteswar Giri. Yogoda Satsanga Society of India, 1990; Cibo per la Pace, ("Food for Peace"). Coop. C.D.B., Ragusa, 2005.

APPENDIX VIII

The Birth of Factory Farms

What you are about to read may shock you; it is, however, purely the description of some facts about which very few people are aware. Everyone, in my opinion, has the right to be informed about these facts so that, having a more complete picture of the situation, they are then able to make a conscious choice regarding their dietary habits.

At one time, animals were raised on small farms, treated humanely and lived a good and natural life, before being killed to be eaten as meat. These days, the situation is very different. The demand for meat and the industry's ever-increasing objective to produce more profit quickly, and with as little cost as possible, has led to the birth of what are known as, 'Factory Farms'. Thousands of animals, bred to be slaughtered, are crammed into tiny spaces, never seeing the light of day, suffering intensely from the inhumane treatment, living one miserable moment after the next, while they await their death. Factory farms are also known as Confined Animal Feeding Operations or Conventional Farms. This type of farming has become the new way of producing meat for the meat industry and the method is quickly being adopted all over the world.

Life in a Factory Farm as Meat Cattle

Calves are taken from their mothers immediately after birth. They are crammed together, often 8,000 at a time, in dark and enclosed factory farm buildings. Usually, there are no windows, and the floor is concrete, not straw, causing many calves to suffer from lameness. Here the calves spend the rest of their miserable lives, day-in, day-out, until they are fat enough to be slaughtered at the young age of 11 or 12 months.

Many calves die from stress and disease; their dead corpses get left for days amongst the other calves. The floors are covered with excrement. As well as causing an unbearable stench, the large amounts of manure which are produced and left to collect in the enclosed buildings create gases, such as ammonia, which the cows have to breathe. It irritates their lungs and causes them a physical suffering that they cannot escape from.

Cows are naturally vegetarians, their diet consisting of fresh green grass. In the factory farms, however, they are fed a diet of unnatural grains and chemical pellets to fatten them up. They are often given daily low doses of antibiotics to make them grow fatter, faster.

When the cows are fat enough and reach the right age for slaughter, they are stuffed into crates and transported to the slaughter house. When they arrive, they are packed into enclosures where, one by one, they will be killed. The law says that animals must be stunned before they are killed. There are different methods used: cows are usually shot in the head with a small pistol. The bullet does not kill them but knocks them unconscious. The cows are driven one at a time into a roofless, metal box where they are stunned in this way. Often the shot will be made badly or the cow will move, and the bullet is fired into the wrong part of its brain, causing extreme agony. Once unconscious, a chain is tied around the cow's hind leg, and it is hauled into the air where its throat is cut and it's left to bleed to death.

Life in a Factory Farm as a Pig

95% of pigs raised for meat in Britain are factory farmed. Their life is no better than that of a cow. Most of them live only five months before they are slaughtered for sausages, bacon, ham and pork. During this time they live in disease, dirt and over-crowding; being pumped with antibiotics and chemical growth enhancers. Broken legs, abscesses, ruptured stomachs, pneumonia, meningitis, and cuts and lacerations from the metal floor on which they are forced to live, are more than common.

VIVA (Vegetarian International Voice for Animals) investigated many factory farms in the UK, in which footage was taken of the awful conditions in which animals are kept. On one 'farm' in Yorkshire, which supplied major supermarkets, piglets were found in grim, windowless sheds, in which they lived in barren, metal pens, so over-crowded that there was no place to run. The only noise heard was that of their desperate little feet on the metal floor and their high-pitched squeals of fear. The stench was not only of ammonia and faeces but also of dead piglets that had been left to rot in a trailer outside, discoloured and bloated from days of decay. One pig had a broken leg, others were lame, and another had a deformed spine. And this was a farm that supplied major supermarkets.

Pigs are highly intelligent creatures. In these cramped and barren conditions they are driven to despair, sometimes to madness, and start to attack each other by bit-ing the tails of other pigs and damaging their mothers' teats. The industry's answer to this problem is to mutilate the piglets by cutting off their back teeth and tails. Despite routine mutilations being supposedly banned in the UK and Europe, at least 80% of piglets are mutilated in Britain every year, most of them without anaesthetic. VIVA has filmed young piglets being pulled out of their pens, having their back teeth cut off with pliers and their tails cut off with scissors.

Piglets are taken away from their mothers after about three weeks. When the pigs are fat enough, they are transported to the slaughter house. They are put into enclosures where, one at a time, they are stunned and hauled into the air to have their throat slit, right before the eyes of the other pigs who are to have the same destiny. Millions of pigs are conscious when their throats are cut. They are usually electrocuted by something resembling garden shears with headphones attached to the two ends. The headphones are placed on their heads, just in front of their ears, and they are given an electric shock. This only works if the headphones are placed in a specific position on the pig's head and held there for at least seven seconds. Because most workers at slaughter houses are paid per animal slaughtered, and because they have obviously de-sensitised themselves to the fact that they are about to kill a living creature, speed becomes the workers' greatest goal, and the headphones are often placed badly or removed too soon. The pig is then hauled into the air and its throat is slit: often it is still fully conscious. This whole process usually takes between 20 and 30 seconds. Even when the electric stun does work, it only lasts for 20 seconds. The pigs which take more than 20 seconds to be hauled up into the air also die fully conscious.

Sows kept for breeding purposes are artificially inseminated and made to give birth continuously. Sows have strong maternal instincts and would normally spend days building a nest of straw and leaves for their little ones: in the factory farms they give birth in crates with metal floors. The sow's maternal instinct is so strong, however, that she frantically imitates making a nest in her barren cell. The bars on the crate stop the sow from moving around, even from taking a step forwards or backwards or from turning around. Because of this, sows suffer from extreme back and leg aches. Twenty percent of factory farm sows die of stress.

Life in a Factory Farm as a Chicken

Chickens are kept in sheds known as broiler houses. Usually there are up to 40,000 chickens in one shed, each one having a space the size of a computer screen to stand in. The floor is made of concrete and covered with sawdust, yet it is quickly covered with the chickens' excrement, which they are forced to stand in day-in and day-out. This causes them terrible pain from ulcerated feet. The greed for money and for rapid production means that the shed is lit with artificial lighting for 23 ½ hours a day. The chickens are tricked into sleeping for only half an hour and the rest of the time they eat, making them plumper, quicker. The chickens are fat enough for slaughter in only 42 days: half the time it used to take. Because of their unnatural plumpness, chickens often suffer from breaking bones, deformed feet and heart attacks and are in chronic pain for most of their lives. Many die before they are slaughtered.

The process by which chickens and other poultry are slaughtered is terrible and sad: first they have their legs placed in metal shackles. They are then hung upside down and moved along a conveyor belt that will take them through a number of processes before they are actually killed. Many of the birds have broken bones from their treatment in the broiler houses, and this procedure is extremely painful for them. First the chickens are moved to an electric water bath which their heads are dragged through, making them unconscious. Unfortunately some birds raise their heads above the water and remain fully conscious for the next stage, the throat cutting. Often this is done with a standard machine that does not take into account the different size of the birds: the larger birds end up having their breasts slits and the smaller birds, their heads slit. And, as said, many go through this fully conscious. The next stage is to dip the birds into scalding hot water to loosen their feathers. Often the many birds who have had their heads and breasts cut, instead of their throats, escape unnoticed and are dipped into the scalding hot water fully conscious.

Fact Boxes

❖ Almost **900 million** farmed animals are slaughtered for the dinner plate each year in the UK.

❖ Every year in the UK, **1.8 million** electrically stunned pigs regain consciousness before they die from loss of blood.

❖ In Europe, animals in factory farms consume **5 thousand tons** of antibiotics. 1500 of these tons are used to artificially enhance the growth of chickens, pigs, turkeys and calves.

❖ **80%** of British piglets are mutilated every year, most of which without anaesthetics.

❖ Every day in the UK **2.5 million chickens** are slaughtered for meat – that's 30 deaths every second.

❖ In the UK, around **8.4 million birds** a year are conscious when they enter the scalding tank.

❖ **Four-fifths** of broiler chickens have broken bones and deformed feet, legs and other bones.

❖ **20%** of factory farm sows die of stress.

❖ EVERY PERSON WHO BECOMES VEGETARIAN SAVES THE LIFE OF AT LEAST **20 ANIMALS A YEAR.**

Life in a Factory Farm as a Dairy Cow

The majority of dairy cows in the UK graze from April to October- the other six months are spent in small indoor cubicles, often not big enough to lie down in. Some dairy farms in Britain have even adopted the USA's zero-grazing system where cows spend their entire lives indoors.

Dairy cows may have straw bedding, but it is becoming more common to use slatted concrete floors, often resulting in lameness. The cows are milked twice daily by machine, producing 30-50 litres of milk a day, almost 10 times the amount that they would produce naturally. Genetic manipulation and dietary controls are what makes this extraordinary output of milk possible. But all this has a cost: the strain of carrying oversized udders often causes intense lameness, or laminitis; their udders often secrete pus and swell painfully with mastitis; and their bodies consume so much energy for milk production that their muscles fade away.

Like humans, cows produce milk for a reason: to feed their calves. No calves, no milk. About 9 months to a year after having given birth, however, the time when the calf would naturally be weaned, the dairy cow's milk begins to dry up. In order to keep the cycle going, the cow is forcibly impregnated, usually only two or three months after giving birth. For this reason the dairy cow is often referred to as the hardest worked of all farm animals: for seven months out of twelve she has to bear the double burden of pregnancy and lactation. It inevitably takes its toll – in the UK, a quarter of all dairy cows, most under three years old, die due to physical exhaustion. The rest are mostly killed at four to seven years and sold as meat. A cow's normal life expectancy is 21 years.

Calves are taken away from their mothers after only one or two days. This separation is so traumatic for the cow that she can be heard bellowing for days in the hope of being reunited with her calf. Female calves mostly follow in their mothers' footsteps and replace the cows that are killed each year. The first six to eight weeks of the female calf's life is spent in a tiny stall. Artificial insemination begins at 15 months. Male calves can't produce milk, and so, they are either shot or sold to the beef industry. In Britain, around 40% of beef comes from dairy calves.

Fact Boxes

- ❖ A dairy cow is forced to produce up to **50 litres** of milk a day, almost ten times more than she would produce for her calf.

- ❖ **25%** of dairy cows are pregnant when slaughtered.

- ❖ A cow left to graze in the open air has an average life expectancy of **21 years.** Only 25% of intensive farming dairy cows reach the age of seven.

- ❖ In Britain, around **40%** of beef comes from dairy calves.

Life as an Egg-Laying Hen

About 50% of eggs sold in the UK come from hens kept in cages. Until recently, hens were squashed five to a cage slightly bigger than the average microwave oven (each hen with a 550 cm2 space allowance). Since January 2012, conventional cages, by law, have been replaced by new 'enriched' cages. These new cages must provide 750 cm2 of space per hen, as well as limited perching, nesting and scratching facilities. In reality, enriched cages are a small improvement from conventional cages: the extra space requirement amounts to less than a postcard sized extra space per hen, meaning that their movements are still severely restricted and they are still unable to stretch or flap their wings. Only one nest box and very limited perching and dust bathing areas in each cage means that the hens are forced to compete for access to these sites. Dominant hens prevent others from ever accessing these facilities.

Hens are placed in cages at about 18 weeks of age and are not removed until they are about 18 to 24 months old, at which time they are killed due to a decrease in the hens' egg production at this age. Hens in natural conditions will usually live for 7 years.

The wire mesh floors that the birds are forced to stand on are made to slope at 12 degrees. This makes egg collection convenient as all the eggs roll to one side, but it is incredibly uncomfortable for the hens. Of course, the wire mesh floors are an unnatural substitute for the dust and straw that hens require in natural conditions and cut into the birds' feet.

In caged conditions the hens obviously become extremely frustrated, and this frustration is often manifested in aggression towards their cage mates. They peck the feathers and flesh of each other, sometimes even to death (one study of hens in enriched cages found that 1 in 30 birds was pecked to death and eaten by other birds). The solution that farmers have given to this problem is 'beak trimming': the highly sensitive innervated tip of the beak is treated with infrared energy and the tip falls off after a few days. Studies have shown that debeaking causes extreme pain to the birds and can also create problems with eating.

About 5% of eggs sold in the UK are barn eggs. Barn eggs come from hens kept in huge sheds called percheries. The number of birds in each perchery can be in the tens of thousands. Percheries must provide 1100 cm2 of floor space per hen, which still amounts to only about two pieces of A4 paper. Hens kept in percheries never go outdoors and many are still routinely debeaked.

About 45 per cent of the eggs sold in the UK are free-range or organic. Free-range hens are housed in a perchery with a maximum stocking density of 2,500 birds per hectare and have daytime access to outdoor runs. All organic eggs are free-range, although not all free-range eggs are organic. Routine debeaking in organic farming is forbidden. While this may seem a good thing, the problem lies in the fact that beaked birds will attack and peck each other when housed in flocks of over 500 birds. In organic farming, it is permitted to keep hens in groups of up to 2,500 under EU rules.

Whatever the method used for egg production, a common problem that exists across the board is the slaughter of newly born male chicks. Egg-laying chickens are bred to be lean and to eat little. Male chicks are therefore useless for laying eggs and no good for meat. Most are therefore slaughtered shortly after birth. Lawful methods of doing this include maceration, exposure to gas mixtures and dislocation of the neck. It is believed that between 30-40 million male chicks are killed in this way every year in the UK. Another issue that exists, regardless of the method of egg production used, is that all worn-out hens, whether conventionally farmed or organic, are slaughtered when their egg production drops. Their flesh, being of lesser quality than that of chickens bred for their meat, is used in low-quality processed foods, such as soup, pies and baby food.

Look at the Code

The law requires that all eggs are labelled with a code, either on the egg itself or on the packaging, which indicates the method of farming used.

There are currently four types of eggs identified by a code. The first number of the code describes the method of farming.

code **0** Organic

code **1** Free range

code **2** Barn

code **3** Caged

Fact Boxes

❖ Around **50% of hens** in Britain are still caged.

❖ In Britain, most hens are killed at **72 weeks** - a fraction of their natural lifespan. All because they start to lay fewer eggs.

❖ Egg-laying hens lay an average of **314 eggs per year** – nearly one per day. In the wild hens would only lay 20 eggs in a whole year.

❖ In Britain, up to **40 million male chicks** are killed every year at just a day or two old because they don't lay eggs and are too 'skinny' for meat.

Websites containing information on intensive farming and action you can take to help abolish them are:

www.viva.org.uk ● www.themeatrix.com ● www.euroveg.eu

APPENDICE IX

Extraordinary Encounters

Stories of Women Who Lived Without Food

The following two stories are excerpted from Yogananda's Autobiography of a
Yogi. *Yogananda relates his meetings with Therese Neumann and Giri Bala, both
of whom lived without food. Therese Neumann, a Catholic mystic who lived in
Konnersreuth, Bavaria, was born in 1898. From 1923 onwards, Therese completely abstained from food and drink, except for the daily swallowing of one small
consecrated wafer. In 1926, the stigmata, or sacred wounds of Christ, appeared
on Therese's head, breast, hands, and feet and every Friday thereafter, she passed
through the Passion of Christ, suffering in her own body the suffering of Christ's
crucifixion. Giri Bala, an unknown Hindu saint from the small village of Biur in
the Bankara District, in India, learned to live without food and drink from the
age of twelve. When Yogananda met her she was sixty eight. She is the only woman
in the world who is known to have lived without food or drink for over fifty years.*

Therese Neumann,
the Catholic Stigmatist

[...] I followed Dr. Wurz upstairs to the sitting room. Therese entered immediately, radiating an aura of peace and joy. She wore a black gown and spotless
white head dress. Although her age was thirty-seven at this time, she seemed much
younger, possessing indeed a childlike freshness and charm. Healthy, well-formed,
rosy-cheeked, and cheerful, this is the saint that does not eat!

Therese greeted me with a very gentle handshaking. We both beamed in silent
communion, each knowing the other to be a lover of God.

Dr. Wurz kindly offered to serve as interpreter. As we seated ourselves, I noticed that Therese was glancing at me with I curiosity; evidently Hindus had been
rare in Bavaria.

"Don't you eat anything?" I wanted to hear the answer from her own lips.

"No, except a consecrated rice-flour wafer, once every morning at six o'clock."

"How large is the wafer?"

"It is paper-thin, the size of a small coin." She added, "I take it for sacramental
reasons; if it is unconsecrated, I am unable to swallow it."

"Certainly you could not have lived on that, for twelve whole years?"

"I live by God's light." How simple her reply, how Einsteinian!

"I see you realize that energy flows to your body from the ether, sun, and air."

A swift smile broke over her face. "I am so happy to know you understand how I live."

"Your sacred life is a daily demonstration of the truth uttered by Christ: '*Man shall not live by bread alone, but by every word that proceedeth out of the mouth of God.*'*"

Again she showed joy at my explanation. "It is indeed so. One of the reasons I am here on earth today is to prove that man can live by God's invisible light, and not by food only."

"Can you teach others how to live without food?"

She appeared a trifle shocked. "I cannot do that; God does not wish it!"

[...]

Professor Wurz related some of his experiences with the saint.

"Several of us, including Therese, often travel for days on sight-seeing trips throughout Germany," he told me. "It is a striking contrast–while we have three meals a day, Therese eats nothing. She remains as fresh as a rose, untouched by the fatigue which the trips cause us. As we grow hungry and hunt for wayside inns, she laughs merrily."

[...]

From a conversation the next day with two of Therese's brothers, very kind and amiable, we learned that the saint sleeps only one or two hours at night. In spite of the many wounds in her body, she is active and full of energy. She loves birds, looks after an aquarium of fish, and works often in her garden. Her correspondence is large; Catholic devotees write to her for prayers and healing blessings. Many seekers have been cured through her of serious diseases.

Giri Bala, The Woman Yogi
Who *Never* Eats

Soon a short figure came into view in the doorway–Giri Bala! [...] Spirituality enfolded her like her gently shining veil. She *pronamed* before me in the customary gesture of greeting from a householder to a monk. Her simple charm and quiet smile gave us a welcome beyond that of honeyed oratory; forgotten was our difficult, dusty trip.

The little saint seated herself cross-legged on the verandah. Though bearing the scars of age, she was not emaciated; her olive-colored skin had remained clear and healthy in tone.

* Matthew 4:4. [Yogananda explains that in this case "bread" means "food"; "every word" means Cosmic Energy or Life Energy, and "mouth of God" means the medulla oblongata that is found at the base of the brain, the "door" through which Life Energy enters the body. *Authors note.*]

[...]

"Tell me, Mother, from your own lips – do you live without food?"

"That is true." She was silent for a few moments; her next remark showed that she had been struggling with mental arithmetic. "From the age of twelve years four months down to my present age of sixty-eight–a period of over fifty-six years–I have not eaten food or taken liquids."

"Are you never tempted to eat?"

"If I felt a craving for food, I would have to eat." Simply yet regally she stated this axiomatic truth, one known too well by a world revolving around three meals a day!

"But you do eat something!" My tone held a note of remonstrance.

"Of course!" She smiled in swift understanding.

"Your nourishment derives from the finer energies of the air and sunlight, and from the cosmic power which recharges your body through the medulla oblongata."

"Baba knows." Again she acquiesced, her manner soothing and unemphatic.

"Mother, please tell me about your early life. It holds a deep interest for all of India, and even for our brothers and sisters beyond the seas."

Giri Bala put aside her habitual reserve, relaxing into a conversational mood.

"So be it." Her voice was low and firm. "I was born in these forest regions. My childhood was unremarkable save that I was possessed by an insatiable appetite. I had been betrothed in early years.

"'Child,' my mother often warned me, 'try to control your greed. When the time comes for you to live among strangers in your husband's family, what will they think of you if your days are spent in nothing but eating?'

"The calamity she had foreseen came to pass. I was only twelve when I joined my husband's people in Nawabganj. My mother-in-law shamed me morning, noon, and night about my gluttonous habits. Her scoldings were a blessing in disguise, however; they roused my dormant spiritual tendencies. One morning her ridicule was merciless.

"'I shall soon prove to you,' I said, stung to the quick, 'that I shall never touch food again as long as I live.'

"My mother-in-law laughed in derision. 'So!' she said. 'How can you live without eating, when you cannot live without overeating?'

"This remark was unanswerable! Yet an iron resolution scaffolded my spirit. In a secluded spot I sought my Heavenly Father.

"'Lord,' I prayed incessantly, 'please send me a guru, one who can teach me to live by Thy light and not by food.'

"A divine ecstasy fell over me. Led by a beatific spell, I set out for the Nawabganj *ghat* on the Ganges. [...] The morning sun pierced the waters; I purified myself in the Ganges, as though for a sacred initiation. As I left the river bank, my wet cloth around me, in the broad glare of day my master materialized himself before me!

"'Dear little one,' he said in a voice of loving compassion 'I am the *guru* sent here by God to fulfil your urgent prayer. He was deeply touched by its very unusual nature! From today you shall live by the astral light, your bodily atoms fed from the infinite current.'

Giri Bala fell into silence.

The saint resumed the tale, her gentle voice barely audible.

"The *ghat* was deserted, but my *guru* cast round us an aura of guarding light, that no stray bathers later disturb us. He initiated me into a *kria* technique which frees the body from dependence on the gross food of mortals. The technique includes the use of a certain *mantra* and a breathing exercise more difficult than the average person could perform. No medicine or magic is involved; nothing beyond the *kria*."

[…]

"Mother," I asked, "why don't you teach others the method of living without food?"

My ambitious hopes for the world's starving millions were nipped in the bud.

"No." She shook her head. "I was strictly commanded by my *guru* not to divulge the secret. It is not his wish to tamper with God's drama of creation. The farmers would not thank me if I taught many people to live without eating! The luscious fruit would lie uselessly on the ground. It appears that misery, starvation, and disease are whips of our *karma* which ultimately drive us to seek the true meaning of life."

"Mother," I said slowly, "what is the use of your having been singled out to live without eating?"

"To prove that man is Spirit." Her face lit with wisdom. "To demonstrate that by divine advancement he can gradually learn to live by the Eternal Light and not by food."

The saint sank into a deep meditative state. Her gaze was directed inward; the gentle depths of her eyes became expressionless. She gave a certain sigh, the prelude to the ecstatic breathless trance. For a time she had fled to the questionless realm, the heaven of inner joy.

N.B.: In quoting these two stories, the author in no way means to incite the reader to abstain from food completely, thus encouraging food disorders, such as anorexia and bulimia. Living without food requires the spiritual capacity of a saint, accompanied by specific spiritual techniques that are not apt for the average person. The only intent of the author is to demonstrate that "man does not live by food alone" but also by more subtle energies.

Glossary

Amaranth. A wheat and gluten-free grain (technically a seed but classified as a grain), rich in vitamins, minerals, protein and fibre.

Applied Kinesiology. A form of diagnosis using muscle testing as a primary feedback mechanism to examine how a person's body is functioning.

Asafoetida. A powdered root, used in Indian cooking as a substitute for garlic.

Ashram. An intentional community formed primarily for the spiritual upliftment of its members.

Barley. A versatile grain with a rich nutlike flavour. Its least processed form is called pot or hulled barley; pearled barley is more processed. Can be used in its unrefined, whole form for sprouting.

Basmati Rice. A non-glutinous, fragrant rice, cultivated at the foot of the Himalayan mountains, mainly used in Indian and Arabic cuisine. Commonly used in its refined, white form but also found in its unrefined, whole form. (See "About Indian Cooking" at beginning of "Indian Cuisine" chapter.)

Bhagavad Gita. "The Song of God", a Sanskrit epic, revered as one of the sacred and highly-esteemed scriptures of Hinduism.

Biodynamic. A method of farming, conceived in 1924 by the Austrian philosopher Rudolf Steiner, which takes into account the energetical properties of food.

Bio-energetical Testing. A form of diagnosis based upon an energetic understanding, which identifies the body's stress reactions to various stimuli and domains.

Biotin. Vitamin B7.

Black Mustard Seeds. Small seeds of the mustard plant, used as a spice in many ethnic cuisines.

Bran. The hard outer layer of grains, rich in fibre, omegas, protein, vitamins and minerals.

Buckwheat. A wheat and gluten-free grain (from a technical point of view, buckwheat is not actually a graminaceous plant but, because of its use, is classified as a grain), known to lower the risk of high cholesterol and high blood pressure.

Bulgur. A whole-wheat product, made by either steaming and drying, or sprouting and drying, whole-wheat kernels, which are then cracked. Comes in fine, medium or coarse grains.

Cardamom. An aromatic spice with an intense, pungent, sweet flavour, used in Indian curries, rice and pulse dishes, as well as sweets and drinks. Also used as a medicinal herb and digestive aid. Comes as either the whole pod or already ground.

Carob Powder. A high-protein, low-fat, nutritious powder made from carob tree pods, most commonly known as a caffeine-free and theobrombine-free cocoa substitute.

Channa Dhal. Split chickpeas, used in Indian cooking to make a curried soup-like dish, usually served with every meal.

Chutney. An Indian sauce with an intense flavour, combining the tastes of hot, sweet and sour. Eaten with popadoms (large, deep fried crisps), pakoras (deep-fried vegetable fritters) or rice. (See recipes in "Indian Cuisine" chapter.)

Coriander. A native Asian plant, used for both its dried seeds and fresh leaves in Middle-Eastern, Asian, Latin-American and African cuisines. The seeds can be found both whole and ground and have a lemony citrus flavour when crushed; the leaves have a taste similar to parsley but with citrus-like overtones.

Cumin. A spice used in Middle Eastern, Indian, Cuban and Northern Mexican cuisines. Seeds come both whole and ground. Also good for stimulating the digestive system.

Demerara sugar. An unrefined cane sugar with large, golden-brown crystals.

Dhal. A curried soup-like dish, made with split legumes. (See "About Indian Cooking" at beginning of "Indian Cuisine" chapter.)

Dill. A plant with aromatic, fernlike leaves that are used both fresh and dry (dill weed) in cooking. Fresh dill is preferred, as dried dill weed loses its flavour rapidly.

DNA. Deoxyribonucleic acid, the hereditary material in humans and almost all other organisms. Central to the synthesis of proteins.

Durum flour. A high-protein and glutinous flour made from hard wheat, traditionally used to make pasta.

Fenugreek. A plant used for both its leaves and seeds, commonly used in Indian cooking. The seeds act as a digestive aid and increase milk production in nursing mothers. Seeds can also be sprouted. (See "Sprouts" in "Basic Recipes" chapter.)

Folate. Vitamin B9 (in solution).

Folic Acid. Vitamin B9.

Garam Masala. A blend of Indian spices (cardamom, cinnamon, cloves and cumin), commonly used in Indian cooking.

Genetic modification (GM). Direct manipulation of an organism's genes through techniques such as molecular cloning, in order to alter its structure and characteristics.

Ghee. Clarified butter, commonly used in Indian cooking and ayurvedic medicine, considered a healthy alternative to butter. Because ghee does not contain milk proteins it is often tolerated by people with lacto-intolerances. (See recipe in "Basic Recipes" chapter.)

Guru. Spiritual teacher, or guide (from the Sanskrit root gur, to raise, to uplift).

Hatha yoga. A branch of yoga comprising of physical postures or asanas, designed to render the body fit for meditation.

Hydrogenation. A chemical process for converting liquid oils into semi-solid or solid substances at room temperature. During this process, mono- and polyunsaturated fatty acids become converted into trans fats, known to be harmful to heart health.

Kamut. An ancient relative of modern durum wheat. Unlike wheat, kamut has remained 'untouched' by modern plant breeding programs and is therefore superior in taste and nutrition to wheat. Although kamut contains gluten, most people with gluten allergies have found that they are able to tolerate it.

Kombu. A seaweed from the genus Laminaria widely eaten in East Asia.

Life Force. Prana, Life Energy. (See chapter: "Life Force Be With You!")

Malt. A natural sweetener made by low-temperature enzymatic reactions in sprouted cereal grains (barley malt, barley/corn malt and rice syrup). Compared to other sweeteners, malt has a higher content of complex carbohydrates.

Mantra. A sacred word, or a combination of sacred words, that carry a specific spiritual vibration.

Maple syrup. A natural sweetener from the sap of the maple tree, produced in North America. Choose Grade A maple syrup.

Millet. A wheat and gluten-free nutritious grain. When choosing millet, look for a bright, golden colour with no aroma: the pale versions of millet, more commonly found, have little flavour.

Miso. A fermented soyabean paste originating in Japan, commonly recommended as a B12 source for vegans.

Mung Dhal. Split soyabeans, used in Indian cooking to make a curried soup-like dish, usually served with every meal.

Niacin. Vitamin B3.

Nutritional Yeast. A healthy nutritional supplement, also used as a condiment. Available in flakes or as a yellow powder.

Osmosis. The passage of water from a region of high water concentration through a semi-permeable membrane to a region of low water concentration.

Paneer. Indian cottage cheese. (See recipe in "Basic Recipes" chapter.)

Pro-vitamin. A substance that can be converted into a vitamin by animal tissues.

Prana. Life Energy, life force. (See chapter: "Life Force Be With You!")

Quinoa. A wheat and gluten-free nutritious grain (from a technical point of view, quinoa is not actually a graminaceous plant but, because of its use, is classified as a grain) considered the 'Mother of all Grains' by the Incas of South America.

Rajas. The 'activating' quality of the universe. (See chapter: "Spiritualising Your Diet".)

RDA. Recommended Dietary Allowance: The daily amount of vitamins, minerals etc to be consumed, as recommended by the F.D.A.

Riboflavin. Vitamin B2.

RNA. Ribonucleic acid, a close cousin of deoxyribonucleic acid or DNA. Central to the synthesis of proteins.

Rye. A grain native to Southwest Asia but fast becoming popular in Northern European countries. Most commonly used in combination with other grain flours to make bread.

Sanskrit. The classical language of Indian and the liturgical language of Hinduism, Buddhism and Jainism, also one of the 22 official languages of India. The name Sanskrit means "refined", "consecrated" and "sanctified".

Sattwas. The 'elevating' quality of the universe. (See chapter: "Spiritualising Your Diet".)

Selenium. A mineral with antioxidant properties.

Spelt. An ancient and distant cousin of modern wheat. Unlike wheat, modern spelt has maintained many of its original characteristics and remains highly nutritious and full of flavour. Although spelt contains gluten, most people with gluten allergies have found that they are able to tolerate it.

Swami. A Hindu title added to one's name to signify that one follows the path of renunciation in the pursuit of learning and mastery of yoga. Sanskrit roots mean "He who knows and is master of himself", "owner of oneself" or "free from the senses".

Tahini. A paste of ground sesame seeds used in Middle Eastern cooking. Can be made with either unhulled or hulled sesame seeds. The unhulled version is a good source of calcium.

Tamas. The 'darkening' quality of the universe. (See chapter: "Spiritualising Your Diet".)

Tandoori Masala. A blend of Indian spices commonly used in Indian cooking. The specific spices vary somewhat from region to region but typically include garam masala, garlic, ginger, cumin and cayenne pepper.

Thiamine. Vitamin B1.

Turbinado sugar. An unrefined cane sugar with large, light-brown crystals.

Turmeric. A deep yellow-orange coloured spice, best known as one of the primary ingredients in curry powder.

Vegan. Used to describe people who refrain from eating any kind of animal products (eggs, dairy, honey etc).

Wok. A large Chinese frying pan, specifically designed for stir-frying. Although modern woks are available in many different materials, the best are made from cast iron and carbon steel.

Yogi. A Sanskrit term for a male practitioner of any of the various paths of Yoga. The term for females is yogini.

Bibliography

Books

Bavicchi, Dario; Mantellini, Roberta. *I germogli della salute*. Bavicchi S.p.a., 2002

Berkson, Burton; Challem, Jack; Smith, Melissa Diane. *Syndrome X: The Complete Nutritional Program to Prevent and Reverse Insulin Resistance*. John Wiley & Sons, 2000

Brown, Dr. Susan E.; Trivieri, Larry Jr. T*he Acid Alkaline Balance Food Guide*. Square One Publishers, 2006

Capano, Giuseppe. *215 ricette per l'estate*. Cairo Editore, 2005

Food for Life (org.). *Cibo per la Pace*. Coop. C.D.B. Ragusa, 2005

Ehret, Professor Arnold. *Muculess Diet Healing System*. Ehret Literature Publishing Co., 1953

Ehret, Professor Arnold. *Rational Fasting*. Ehret Literature Publishing Co., 1926

Ferriera, Peter; Hendel, Barbara. *Acqua e sale*. INA Verlag AG, 2003

Gala D.R.; Gala, Dhiren; Gala, Sanjay. *Juice-Diet for Perfect Health*. Navneet Publications (India) Limited

Gala D.R.; Gala, Dhiren; Gala, Sanjay. *Nature Cure for Common Diseases*. Navneet Publications (India) Limited

Gala D.R.; Gala, Dhiren; Gala, Sanjay. *Panacea on the Earth: Wheat Grass Juice*. Navneet Publications (India) Limited

Kretzman, Mary. *Divine Will Healing*. From the Original Teachings of Paramhansa Yogananda. International Book Number, 2000

Kriyananda, Swami. *The Essence of the Bhagavad Gita*. Ananda Sangha Publications, 2006

Kriyananda, Swami. *Raja Yoga*. Crystal Clarity Publishers, 2002

Kulvinskas, Viktoras, M.S. *Love Your Body*. Omango d'Press, 1972

Mangani, Valeria; Panfili, Adolfo; *La dieta pH*. Tecniche Nuove, 1997

McKeith, Gillian. *You Are What You Eat*. Michael Joseph, an imprint of Penguin Books Ltd, 2004

Meyerowitz, Steve. *Food Combining and Digestion*. Sproutman Publications, 2002

Parham, Barbara. *What's Wrong with Eating Meat?*. Ananda Marga Publications, 1979

Satvic, Gerard T. *Know Thyself: The Gateway to Physical, Mental and Spiritual Health: Satya Sai Baba's Messages in His Own Words*. G. C. Ter Morshuizen, 1995

Swami Sri Yukteswar Giri. *The Holy Science*. Self-Realization Fellowship, 1972

Vasey, Christopher. *The Acid-Alkaline Diet for Optimum Health*. Healing Arts Press, 2006

Vyas Bharti; Le Quesne. *The pH Balance Diet*. Ulysses Press, 2007

Walker's, Dr. Norman W. *Colon Health*. Norwalk Press, 1979

Yogananda, Paramhansa. *How to Achieve Glowing Health and Vitality*. Ananda Sangha Publications, 2011

Articles

Steinfeld, Henning; Gerber, Pierre; Wassenaar, Tom; Castel, Vincent; Rosales, Mauricio; De Haan, Cees. "Livestock's Long Shadow. Environmental Issues and Options". Food and Agricultural Organization of the United Nations, Rome, 2006

Yogananda, Paramhansa. Various articles. East-West Magazine, 1926-1933

Yogananda, Paramhansa. "Meat Eating Versus Vegetarianism". Inner Culture, April and May 1935

Yogananda, Paramhansa. "Mystic Meaning of Resurrection". Inner Culture, April 1934

Yogananda, Swami. "Amazing Health Recipes for Healing and Prolonging Life". New Super Cosmic Science Course. Yogoda Satsanga Society, 1934

Yogananda, Swami. "Outline Notes on Spiritual Food". Advanced Course on Practical Metaphysics. Yogoda Satsanga Society, 1926

Yogananda, Paramhansa. "Praeceptum n. 1-130". Praecepta Lessons, Vol. 1-5. Yogoda Satsanga Society, 1934-1935

Yogananda, Paramhansa. "Questions and Answers: Diet and Disposition". Inner Culture, February 1940

Yogananda, Paramhansa. "Questions and Answers: What Is Perfect Diet?". Inner Culture, October 1940

Yogananda, Swami. "The Divine Magnetic Diet". Super-Advanced Course n. 1. Yogoda Satsanga Society,1930

Yogananda, Paramhansa. "The Second Coming of Christ: The Sabbath". Inner Culture, January 1935

Internet Sites

Carroll, Will. The Health Benefits of Fasting / Serendip's Exchange. Serendip, 1994-2009. Last consulted 4th May 2009. Available at http://serendip.brynmawr.edu/biology/b103/f02/web1/wcarroll.html

Earthsave. Healthy People, Healthy Planet. Earthsave. Last consulted 28th December 2013. Available at www.earthsave.org/environment.htm

Food Additives and Ingredients Association FAIA – Facts about Additives and Ingredients in Food. Food Additives and Ingredients Association FAIA. Last consulted 9th January 2014. Available at www.faia.org.uk/organic.php

Food Additives and Their Associated Health Risks. Food Democracy, 2008. Last consulted 9th January 2014. Available at http://fooddemocracy.wordpress.com/2008/06/08/food-additives-and-their-associated-health-risks

Food Additives ~ Food Safety. Centre for Science in the Public Interest. Last consulted 9th January 2014. Available at http://www.cspinet.org/reports/chemcuisine.htm

Food Seasons. Eat the Seasons, 2004-2012. Last consulted 9th April 2014. Available at http://eattheseasons.co.uk/

Kulvinskas, Viktoras. Application of Food Combining – Chlorophyll and Hemoglobin. Raw Food Explained, 2008. Last consulted 9th January 2014. Available at www.rawfoodexplained.com/application-of-food-combining-principles/chlorophyll-and-hemoglobin.html

LAV. LAV. Last consulted 9th January 2014. Available at http://www.lav.it

Moock, Colin. The Meatrix Films. Sustainable Table, 2003, 2006. Last consulted 9th January 2014. Available at http://www.themeatrix.com

Research Points to Nutritional Benefits from Organic Food. Third World Network, 2007. Last consulted 9th January 2014. Available at www.twnside.org.sg/title2/susagri/susagri018.htm

Saraswati, Swami Satyamurti, Dott., M.Sc., Ph.D. Prana You Can Eat. Sivananda Math. Last consulted 9th January 2014. Available at www.yogamag.net/archives/1977/ldec77/prana.shtml

Seasonality Table. GoodFood. BBC Worldwide Ltd. Last consulted 9th April 2014. Available at http://www.bbcgoodfood.com/seasonal-calendar/all

Shayne, Vic, PhD. Questions About Vegetarian Diets: How Can I Get Enough Protein? The Protein Myth. PCRM Physicians I for Responsible Medicine. Last consulted 9th January 2014. Available at www.pcrm.org/health/veginfo/protein.html

Starr Hull, Janet. Food Additives to Avoid. Doctor Janet Starr Hull, 2002. Last consulted 9th January 2014. Available at http://www.sweetpoison.com/food-additives-to-avoid.html

Substances that Destroy Nutrients. Innvista. Last consulted 9th January 2014. Available at http://www.innvista.com/health/anatomy/destroys.htm

The Issues, Learn about Sustainable Food, Problems with Factory Farming. Sustainable Table, 2003-2007. Last consulted 9th January 2014. Available at http://www.sustainabletable.org/issues

The World's Healthiest Foods. The George Mateljan Foundation, 2001-2009. Last consulted 9th January 2014. Available at http://www.whfoods.com/foodstoc.php

Viva! – Vegetarians International Voice for Animals. Viva! Last consulted 9th January 2014. Available at http://www.viva.org.uk

About Ananda

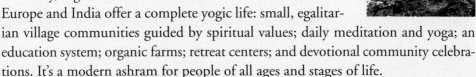

Ananda is a worldwide movement of people living the change they want to see in the world. Founded in 1969 by Swami Kriyananda and guided by the spiritual teachings of Paramhansa Yogananda, best-selling author of *Autobiography of a Yogi*, Ananda will celebrate its 50th anniversary in 2019.

Today, eight Ananda communities in North America, Europe and India offer a complete yogic life: small, egalitarian village communities guided by spiritual values; daily meditation and yoga; an education system; organic farms; retreat centers; and devotional community celebrations. It's a modern ashram for people of all ages and stages of life.

Ananda communities bring to life Paramhansa Yogananda's dream of establishing "world brotherhood communities" in many nations. His teachings emphasise direct inner experience of God, which he called "Self-realisation". Yogananda's teachings are non-sectarian and offer practical solutions to the challenges of modern life.

The Ananda community near Assisi, Italy provides a world-renowned guest retreat where thousands of visitors annually visit for renewal or instruction in many aspects of meditation, yoga and the spiritual life. The Assisi retreat and community also serves Ananda meditation groups throughout Europe.

If you would like more information about Ananda Assisi you can visit our community website www.anandacommunity.it, or our retreat website www.ananda.it. For more information about Ananda worldwide, visit www.ananda.org.

Ananda UK is a holistic yoga centre based in Reigate in Surrey, serving the community with courses, yoga workshops and healing therapies designed for perfect peace of mind. **Preparation for Kriya Yoga** is taught here, as well as Teacher Training and Meditation courses. For children we offer weekly yoga and Akido classes. The centre offers five retreats a year to India, Italy and in the UK. Just thirty-five minutes from central London by train – into Reigate and Redhill – and twenty minutes by car from Gatwick airport, the centre is situated near beautiful Surrey hills, shops and markets. We would love to meet you! For more information please visit us at www.yogaananda.co.uk or write to us at info@yogaananda.co.uk.

About Paramhansa Yogananda

Paramhansa Yogananda (1893-1952) was the first yoga master of India to take up permanent residence in the West. Yogananda arrived in America in 1920 and travelled throughout the United States on what he called his "spiritual campaigns". His enthusiastic audiences filled the largest halls in America. Hundreds of thousands came to see the yogi from India. Yogananda continued to lecture and write up until his passing in 1952.

Yogananda's initial impact was truly impressive. But his lasting impact has been even greater. Yogananda's *Autobiography of a Yogi*, first published in 1946, helped launch a spiritual revolution in the West. His message was non-sectarian and universal. Yogananda's teacher sent him to the West with the admonition, "The West is high in material attainments but lacking in spiritual understanding. It is God's will that you play a role in teaching mankind the value of balancing the material with an inner, spiritual life."

What Yogananda taught in the West was not religion but practical spirituality. The techniques he taught are useful in all fields of human activity. They are based on methods of Self-awareness and Self-discovery which have been used by spiritual seekers for millennia. These practices include techniques for increasing the flow of vital energy into the body, for harmonising body and mind with soul and spirit and for entering higher states of spiritual awareness, which he called "superconsciousness."

About Swami Kriyananda

Swami Kriyananda (J. Donald Walters) was a direct disciple of Paramhansa Yogananda and the founder of Ananda Sangha, a worldwide organisation committed to the dissemination of Yogananda's teachings. In 1968, he founded *Ananda World Brotherhood Village*, the first spiritual cooperative community based on Yogananda's vision of "world brotherhood colonies," dedicated to spreading the spirit of friendship, service, and community around the globe. Ananda is recognised as one of the most successful intentional communities in the world. Over 1,000 people now reside in Ananda communities in North America, India, and Italy.

Born in Romania by American parents, Swami Kriyananda was a spiritual teacher, author, composer and one of the leading representatives of Yoga in the West. Kriyananda became a disciple of Paramhansa Yogananda in 1948 and was one of the last remaining direct disciples. He recounted his own spiritual search and the years of training with Yogananda in his autobiography, *The New Path*, which is widely considered the sequel to Yogananda's autobiography. His story and experience of the guru-disciple relationship are also depicted in the new film, *The Answer.*

Kriyananda spread Yogananda's teachings of Self-realisation all over the world, demonstrating how to apply them in every sphere of existence. He wrote more than 140 books on a wide range of subjects both practical and spiritual, emphasising the need to live wisely by one's own experience of life and not by abstract theories or dogmas.

Kriyananda also composed over 400 works of what he called Inner Quest music. He had a rare gift for soul-stirring melody, and his harmonies express in music the teachings of world brotherhood. "If you want to know me," he would say, "listen to my music." He wrote hundreds of uplifting choral pieces: "painless philosophy," he called them. Many of his later albums are instrumental works, some of which include brief affirmations or visualisations. His books and music, all available from Crystal Clarity Publishers, have sold over 3 million copies worldwide, and have been translated into over 25 languages.

Kriyananda also established *Education for Life* schools for children, which offer character development, strong academics, and development of moral strength. The school curriculum is ecumenical; students of all religious backgrounds may attend. There are schools in America (Portland, Seattle, Palo Alto, Nevada City), Italy, Slovenia and India. Many other schools are adopting the curriculum and ideals of *Education for Life.*

Swami Kriyananda left his body in 2013 in the Ananda Assisi community. His light and message continue to inspire truth-seeking souls all around the globe.

About the Author

Mahiya, by now well known in Italy, is an inspired advocate of the vegan-yogic diet. Originally from England, Mahiya moved to the Ananda Community in Assisi, Italy in 2000 at the age of 22. It was in the Ananda Retreat kitchen that Mahiya first learned to cook. Dynamic and creative chefs guided her first steps towards what were to be fifteen years as a chef and manager in one of the most joyful and inspiring kitchens in Italy! Mahiya recounts the fun circumstances that led her to this point in her culinary life in the Introduction of the recipe section. Cooking daily for anywhere between 20 and 300 guests and community members in a spiritually-orientated environment brought Mahiya to the point at which she became an expert in multicultural culinary arts, vegetarianism and veganism, and the yogic diet.

Recently, Mahiya has left the kitchen to dedicate herself to several new roles that have been entrusted to her. Despite having many new responsibilities, Mahiya continues to pursue her passion of spreading the vegan-yogic diet in Italy, and now throughout the English-speaking world. She is writing new books, giving classes and teaching more cookery courses than ever!

About the Photographer

Andrea first arrived from California for a weekend visit at Ananda Assisi in 2002 and, to her surprise, 12 years later she was still there. Andrea writes: "In my early days at Ananda Assisi, the digital image mania had not quite taken off yet, but I had a background in photography and so I ended up being practically the only photographer for many years. Sometimes I would wander around with my camera wondering about how I could capture and really show the joy and spirit of this community beyond the typical pictures of yoga and meditation needed. When Mahiya began talking about the Ananda Cookbook project, I instantly knew it could also become the perfect way to show the joy of daily life in the community. For me, it was always so much more than just about the wisdom and insight of right eating and recipes (in themselves totally important!) and every photo became a true community effort of love and laughter. Hardly anyone escaped participation in one of our food photo stagings!"

You can see many of Andrea's photos on the Ananda websites and in the Ananda Edizioni publications, as well as in the book *Swami Kriyananda, A Life in God*.

Acknowledgements

This book has not been a personal project but the result of many giving and loving hands working and creating together to make it what it is. I especially want to thank:

Christina, for your belief in me, your love, support and encouragement; for being the most creative channel in the Ananda kitchen; for teaching me how to cook; for your continuous inspiration; and for all the hours you put into translating and editing the book.

Andrea, for the amazing photos that are beyond words of praise (in my small opinion!) I would not have been happy with anyone else.

Shivani, for spending so much time with me at the beginning of the project and for helping me to improve my writing skills.

Tejindra, for your expansive vision and creativity, for without you, this book would not exist.

Sahaja, for refining the book to a professional level that I could never have imagined possible; for your inspiring dedication to service; and for your ever-constant calmness and patience with me, even when I presented you with numerous last-minute changes.

Dad, for transforming my Italianised-English into 'proper' English; for not loosing [sic] patience with me as I continued to misspell "tomorrow" and "practise" throughout my adult years; for your time and precision; for unconditional support in everything I have ever done.

Steph, for your selflessness and support; for your more-than-precise eye; for doing everything you do with a level of dedication, love and professionalism that is inspiring.

Arudra, my amazing husband, for your support, help, clarity and vision, and of course for your "sacrifice" of tasting my kitchen experiments (you poor thing!).

Mantrini, for your caring and non-invasive approach to editing; and for bringing balance into the way in which I express things.

Maitreyi, Nandini, Andrea and all those at Ananda Edizioni, for your enthusiasm about the book, even before you read it (!), and for all the work you did to manifest the book from computer to paper!

Lata, and all those who supported the needs of the kitchen so that I could have time out to write and make recipes.

All those, who contributed a story, even though you didn't have much time.

The whole Ananda community, for all your words of enthusiasm, your encouragement and your belief in me.

And last, but most importantly…

Paramhansa Yogananda, my beloved Guru, for flawlessly guiding every step of my life; for giving me the opportunities I need to be able to grow; and for being my strength and inspiration. *Jai Guru Paramhansa Yoganandaji!*

Yogaland proposes these further explorations

AUTOBIOGRAPHY OF A YOGI, *Original First Edition of 1946*
Paramhansa Yogananda

One of the most beloved spiritual classics of the last 70 years, this original version retains the spirit and vibration of the great Indian Master Paramhansa Yogananda in all its unadulteratied strength and immediacy. An extraordinary book which has given inspiration, hope and illumination to truth-seekers of every spiritual path, and helped launch the spiritual revolution of the West. This edition contains:

- The original, unedited text, as written by Yogananda himself, free from posthumous changes introduced by others.
- An appendix containing the final chapter, written five years after this edition was first published, presented free from all changes made after Yogananda's death.
- An all-new foreword and afterword, written by Swami Kriyananda, one of Yogananda's best-known direct disciples.

CONVERSATIONS WITH YOGANANDA
Stories, Sayings, and Wisdom of Paramhansa Yogananda
Swami Kriyananda

This is an unparalleled firsthand account of Paramhansa Yogananda and his teachings, written by one of his closest students, Swami Kriyananda, who was often present when Yogananda spoke privately with other close disciples. In these situations, Kriyananda recorded the words and guidance of Yogananda, preserving for the ages wisdom that would otherwise have been lost, and giving us an intimate glimpse of life with Yogananda never before shared by any other student. These *Conversations* include not only Yogananda's words as he first spoke them, but also the added insight of an intimate disciple who has spent more than 50 years reflecting on and practicing the teachings of Yogananda.

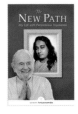

THE NEW PATH
My Life with Paramhansa Yogananda
Swami Kriyananda

The New Path tells the story of a young American's spiritual quest, his discovery of the powerful classic, *Autobiography of a Yogi*, and his subsequent meeting with-and acceptance as a disciple by-the book's author, the great spiritual teacher and yoga master, Paramhansa Yogananda. Swami Kriyananda is an extraordinary narrator: He recreates the vibrancy of his guru's presence, remembers Yogananda's words with perfect clarity, and communicates to the reader the depth of their meaning. Through Kriyananda's eyes and words, you'll be transported into Yogananda's immediate presence as you learn the highest yogic teachings. A marvelous sequel to Paramhansa Yogananda's own *Autobiography*!

MEDITATION FOR STARTERS
Includes CD with instruction, visualization, and music
Swami Kriyananda

Have you wanted to learn to meditate... or tried "sitting in the silence" only to find your mind wandering, wanting to jump up after only a few minutes? This little book with companion CD provides everything you need to begin a steady meditation practice, filled with easy-to-follow instructions, beautiful guided visualisations, and answers to important questions such as what meditation is (and isn't), how to relax, and how to focus the mind. Follow Swami Kriyananda's calm voice as he carries your mind and spirit into a place of inner peace and joy.

THE ESSENCE OF ENLIGHTENMENT
Vedanta, the Science of Consciousness
James Swartz

The Vision of Non duality. This complete guide to enlightenment presents the wisdom of the ancient science of self-inquiry, the time honoured teachings of the East that have been passed down from Guru to Student for millennia, the essence of oneness is common to the esoteric path of many traditions, unfolded here in a clear un secular way, this book will attract all earnest truth seekers.

In an accessible style, James Swartz's new book covers topics such as values and the enlightened person, *dharma* and the essence of enlightenment, and the relationship between consciousness, the individual, and the total.

THE YOGA OF THE THREE ENERGIES
James Swartz

Understanding the Gunas in the the Yogic Science of Energy Management is a sophisticated set of simple principles that allows anyone to eliminate negative emotions and transform the mind into a powerful tool capable of scaling the sacred heights of self realization.

Did you ever wonder why you are either (1) tired, fuzzy-minded, lazy, depressed and confused, (2) stressed, frustrated, disturbed, scattered, restless and unfocused or (3) happy for no reason, blissful, still, focused, dynamic and creative? This book shows you the answer and provides the means to match the energies to your goals.

KRIYA YOGA
A Manual to Inner Freedom
Jayadev Jaerschky

This book presents the many facets of *Kriya Yoga* in a complete and accessible way for the first time: from its history to its philosophy, to the subtleties of the practice to how to prepare for initiation. It is an invaluable text for all those who wish to learn or to deepen their understanding of this ancient science, kept secret for so long. And not only that,it is a treasure trove of practical tools and techniques for all who wish to delve into the wonderful adventure of the inner journey!

This book offers you a chance to board the airplane of *Kriya Yoga* and fly straight to the eternal beauty of your own Self. Never before has the ancient liberating science of *Kriya Yoga*, long kept secret throughout the course of history, been presented so completely, deeply and yet accessibly.

Heavenly Father,

Receive this food.
Make it holy.

Let no impurity
of greed defile it.

The food comes from Thee.
It is to build Thy temple.

Spiritualise it.
Spirit to Spirit goes.

We are the petals of Thy manifestation,
but Thou art the Flower,
its life, beauty, and loveliness.

Permeate our souls with the
fragrance of Thy presence.